*i*Research
Series editor G G Chowdhury

Cultural Heritage Information
Access and management

D0872489

iResearch Series

Series Editor: G. G. Chowdhury, Professor of Information Science and Head of the Department of Mathematics and Information Sciences at Northumbria University in Newcastle, UK.

This peer-reviewed monograph series supports the vision of the iSchools and creates authoritative sources of information for research and scholarly activities in Information Science. Each book in the series focuses on a specific aspect or emerging topic of information studies, provides a state-of-the-art review of research in the chosen field and addresses the issues, challenges and progress of research and practice.

Editorial board

iResearch
Series editor G G Chowdhury

Cultural Heritage Information
Access and management

Edited by
Ian Ruthven and G. G. Chowdhury

facet publishing

Published by Facet Publishing,
www.facetpublishing.co.uk

Facet Publishing is wholly owned by CILIP: the Chartered Institute of
Library and Information Professionals.

British Library Cataloguing in Publication Data
A catalogue record for this book is available from the British Library.

ISBN 978-1-85604-930-6

First published 2015

Text printed on FSC accredited material.

Typeset from editors' files by Facet Publishing Production in
12/15 pt Garamond and Frutiger.
Printed and made in Great Britain by CPI Group (UK) Ltd,
Croydon, CR0 4YY.

Every purchase of a Facet book helps to fund CILIP's
advocacy, awareness and accreditation programmes
for information professionals.

Contents

List of figures and tables vii

Contributors ix

Preface xv
    Gobinda Chowdhury and Ian Ruthven

1 Managing digital cultural heritage information 1
    Gobinda Chowdhury and Ian Ruthven

2 Digital humanities and digital cultural heritage (alt-history and future
   directions)...13
    Chris Alen Sula

3 Management of cultural heritage information: policies and practices........37
    Gobinda Chowdhury

4 Cultural heritage information: artefacts and digitization technologies......63
    Melissa Terras

5 Metadata in cultural contexts – from manga to digital archives in a
   linked open data environment 89
    Shigeo Sugimoto, Mitsuharu Nagamori, Tetsuya Mihara and Tsunagu
       Honma

6 Managing cultural heritage: information systems architecture.................113
    Lighton Phiri and Hussein Suleman

7 Cultural heritage information: users and usability......................135
    Sudatta Chowdhury

8 A framework for classifying and comparing interactions in cultural
   heritage information systems 153
    Juliane Stiller and Vivien Petras

9 Semantic access and exploration in cultural heritage digital libraries.......177
   Ali Shiri

10 Supporting exploration and use of digital cultural heritage materials:
   the PATHS perspective 197
   Paul Clough, Paula Goodale, Mark Hall and Mark Stevenson

11 Cultural heritage information services: sustainability issues 221
   Gobinda Chowdhury

Index 247

List of figures and tables

Figures

Figure 5.1 Conceptual model of content publishing flow 93

Figure 5.2 FRBR Group 1, 2 and 3 entities...93

Figure 5.3 Layered view of metadata schema components............................96

Figure 5.4 Overall structure of metadata framework for manga...................99

Figure 5.5 Metadata and meta-metadata..106

Figure 6.1 High-level architecture of a typical digital library system...........114

Figure 6.2 Repository object organization..125

Figure 6.3 Simple repository container object component structure...........126

Figure 6.4 Simple repository content object component structure...............127

Figure 6.5 Screenshot showing a sample page from the 'Posts and trading' story in the Lucy Lloyd !Kun notebooks...........................128

Figure 6.6 Screenshot showing the Die Mond South plant fossil from the Eastern Cederberg rock art site..129

Figure 8.1 Simplified model of an ideal information system.........................156

Figure 8.2 Second dimension of the framework in relation to different access modes..162

Figure 8.3 The framework visualized in a radar graph 165

Figure 8.4 Percentage of systems among aggregators that provide interactions per class and degree...167

Figure 8.5 Radar graph of Europeana and all aggregators in comparison...171

Figure 10.1 The PATHS conceptual model that identifies the activities of users as they create and consume paths 202

Figure 10.2 Landing page for the PATHS system 208

Figure 10.3 Different ways of navigating the PATHS hierarchy......................209

Figure 10.4 The map-based visualization allows users to inspect the contents of the entire collection...209

Figure 10.5   The PATHS user interface when viewing an artefact from the collection 211

Figure 10.6   An example of a user-generated path showing branching to divide the content into themes or sections 212

Figure 11.1   A model of sustainability of digital information systems and services 225

Tables

Table 6.1   Persistent object storage design decision 123

Table 6.2   Repository metadata storage design decision 123

Table 6.3   Repository object naming scheme design decision 124

Table 6.4   Repository object storage structure design decision 124

Table 6.5   Repository component structural composition 125

Table 6.6   The Bleek and Lloyd collection profile 128

Table 6.7   SARU archaeological database collection profile 129

Table 8.1   Classes of interactions with descriptions of the interaction patterns 160

Table 8.2   Degrees of interactions and their descriptions with regard to the meta-classes 163

Table 8.3   Sample of aggregators, their originating country and number of objects 166

Table 9.1   Information search task support in cultural heritage digital library interfaces 190

Table 10.1   Summary of user needs and the associated system and interface requirements in relation to the PATHS conceptual model and existing models of exploration, creativity and information use 204

Contributors

Gobinda Chowdhury is a Professor of Information Science and Head of the Department of Mathematics and Information Sciences at Northumbria University in Newcastle. He researches in the area of information access and digital libraries, with special reference to how people interact with digital information systems. His current research focuses on the social and environmental sustainability of digital information systems and services.

Sudatta Chowdhury is an independent researcher in information seeking and retrieval. Her PhD research was on human information behaviour, with particular reference to uncertainty in information seeking and retrieval. Her research developed a model of uncertainty and its relation to information seeking and retrieval. Her recent research includes journalists' information seeking behaviour; needs and expectations in an evolving online information marketplace; challenges associated with online information seeking and retrieval in an academic environment; serendipitous information; uncertainty due to information overload; challenges involved in information seeking and retrieval; and information behaviour and information literacy skills of students from an international perspective. Her research emphasizes why and how people search for information, what challenges are involved in this, and how to overcome those challenges. She has carried out a wide range of empirical studies on information users and usability in the digital age.

Paul Clough is Professor in Information Retrieval in the Information School at the University of Sheffield. Prior to joining the University he worked in the telecommunications industry. His research addresses various aspects of data management, text reuse and information retrieval, involving collaborations with external organizations such as Ordnance Survey, the UK Press Association, the UK National Archives and OCLC Inc. Paul is head of the Information Retrieval research group at Sheffield and coordinator for a new Masters programme in Data Science. He has published over 100 peer-reviewed articles, including a co-authored Springer book on multilingual information retrieval.

Paula Goodale is a researcher and PhD student in the Information School at the University of Sheffield, and worked on the PATHS project on user requirements, interface design and user evaluation. Her research interests include information access, human information interaction and information use, particularly in digital cultural heritage contexts. In 2013 she was on the organizing committee for the SUEDL workshop (Supporting Users' Exploration of Digital Libraries), and chaired the session at Theory and Practice of Digital Libraries (TPDL). During her earlier career, she was a senior lecturer in e-business, and has also held senior commercial roles in business development, marketing and consultancy for several e-business and e-publishing organizations.

Mark Hall is a Lecturer in Web Development and Information Retrieval in the Department of Computing at Edge Hill University. He has previously worked as a researcher at the UK National Archives and Sheffield University on a number of EU-funded projects. His research focus is on understanding and supporting the user in the exploration of large digital archives. Other interests include usability evaluation methods, natural language processing, and geographic information retrieval.

Tsunagu Honma is a PhD student at the Graduate School of Library, Information and Media Studies at the University of Tsukuba. He has been involved in the studies on metadata schema interoperability and infrastructure to make metadata schema shareable and reusable on the web. His recent research is on technology to extract metadata schema from metadata instances to enhance metadata schema sharing, which is crucial for Linked Open Data.

Tetsuya Mihara is a PhD student at the Graduate School of Library, Information and Media Studies at the University of Tsukuba. He is also currently working as a freelance producer of Manga. His research includes development of the metadata for manga in the digital and networked information environment, and technologies to improve the production efficiency and searching of manga. He is interested in the use of Linked Open Data to link manga with many aspects of other resources.

Mitsuharu Nagamori is an Assistant Professor at the Faculty of Library, Information and Media Science at the University of Tsukuba. His primary research interest is in the area of metadata schema and the semantic web; developing technologies to help find suitable metadata terms and to help design an application profile in accordance with the requirements of a particular application.

Vivien Petras holds a PhD in Information Management and Systems from the University of California, Berkeley and has been a Professor of Information Retrieval at Humboldt-Universität zu Berlin since 2009. She has been involved with the European Union-funded digital library, museum and archive Europeana since 2007. Other projects research translation facilities and evaluation methodologies in cultural heritage information systems. Her research interests lie in the area of information organization to ensure interoperability and (multilingual) information retrieval and evaluation.

Lighton Phiri is a doctoral student in the Department of Computer Science at the University of Cape Town. His doctoral research is rooted in the Technology Enhanced Learning area, where he is exploring classroom orchestration. He is currently based in the ICT for Development Centre, and occasionally works within the Digital Libraries Laboratory. He received his BSc degree from the University of Zambia in 2007 and his MSc degree from the University of Cape Town in 2013, both in Computer Science. His current research interests are in cultural heritage, digital libraries, educational technology and ICT4D.

Ian Ruthven is a Professor of Information Seeking and Retrieval in the Department of Computer and Information Sciences at the University of Strathclyde. He researches in the area of information seeking and retrieval; understanding how and why people search for information and how electronic systems might help them search more successfully. This brings in a wide range of research including theoretical research on the design and modelling of information access systems, empirical research on interfaces and user interaction, and research on the methodology of evaluating information access systems. His recent research has included interface design research to help children search for information, information seeking studies on information poverty within marginalized groups, studies on how people use online information to create a sense of happiness, and research into digitally mediated access for cultural heritage material.

Ali Shiri is a Professor in the School of Library and Information Studies at the University of Alberta, Edmonton. He teaches in the areas of digital libraries and digital information organization and retrieval. His research areas include user interaction with digital information, digital libraries, search user interfaces, social media and big data. He has recently completed a project on the development and user-centred evaluation of multilingual thesaurus-enhanced visual interfaces for the UNESCO digital library. His recent book entitled *Powering Search: the role of thesauri in new information environments* addresses the importance of thesauri in developing semantically rich search user interfaces for digital information repositories. His current federally funded research project focuses on the development of a digital library infrastructure to address information needs in Canada's northern regions.

Mark Stevenson is a Senior Lecturer in the Department of Computer Science at Sheffield University. Before taking up his current position he worked for Reuters Ltd and British Telecom. His main interest is in natural language processing, an area in which he has published over 100 papers. He co-ordinated the EU-funded PATHS project which developed exploratory search systems for cultural heritage collections by applying natural language processing techniques. Other interests include word sense disambiguation, lexical semantics, information extraction and information retrieval. He is also Assistant Director of the Advanced Computing Research Centre, with responsibility for transferring technologies from academia to industry.

Juliane Stiller is a researcher at the Berlin School of Library and Information Science at Humboldt-Universität zu Berlin, where she works in the EU-funded project Europeana Version 3 on the evaluation of multilingual features. She is also working as a research scholar at the Max Planck Institute for the History of Science in Berlin, where she studies researchers' needs in virtual research environments. She obtained a doctoral degree in information science at Humboldt-Universität zu Berlin, evaluating interactions in cultural heritage digital libraries. Her research centres around the evaluation of digital libraries and purposeful interactions for digitized cultural heritage material.

Shigeo Sugimoto is a professor in the Faculty of Library, Information and Media Science at the University of Tsukuba. His work is in the research communities of metadata, digital preservation and digital libraries. He has been actively working to promote collaboration among information schools, in particular those in the Asia-Pacific region.

Chris Alen Sula is an Assistant Professor and Coordinator of Digital Humanities in the School of Information and Library Science at the Pratt Institute, New York. He teaches graduate courses in digital humanities, information visualization, critical theory, and community building and engagement. His research applies visualization and network science to humanities datasets, especially those chronicling the history of philosophy. He has also published articles that explore the use of citation network analysis in the humanities; the connection between digital humanities, libraries, and cultural heritage institutions; and ethical and activist uses of visualization.

Hussein Suleman is an Associate Professor in Computer Science at the University of Cape Town. His research is situated within the ICT for

Development Centre and the Digital Libraries Laboratory. He obtained his undergraduate degrees and MSc at the then University of Durban-Westville, and in 2002 completed his PhD at Virginia Tech, USA, in the area of component-based digital libraries. He actively advocates for Open Access in South Africa, and works closely with the Networked Digital Library of Theses and Dissertations (NDLTD), which promotes and supports the adoption of electronic theses and dissertations and digital libraries worldwide. He currently manages the South African ETD portal as well as the international ETD Union Archive. He actively collaborates with the Centre for Curating the Archive at UCT, developing software tools for preservation, dissemination and discovery for the Bleek and Lloyd Archive and related collections. His main research interests are in digital libraries, ICT4D, information retrieval, cultural heritage preservation, internet technology and high performance computing.

Melissa Terras is Director of University College London's Centre for Digital Humanities and Professor of Digital Humanities in UCL's Department of Information Studies. With a background in classical art history, English literature, and computing science, her doctorate (Engineering, University of Oxford) examined how to use advanced information engineering technologies to interpret and read Roman texts. Publications include *Image to Interpretation: intelligent systems to aid historians in the reading of the Vindolanda Texts* (Oxford University Press, 2006) and *Digital Images for the Information Professional* (Ashgate Publishing, 2008), and she has co-edited various texts such as *Digital Humanities in Practice* (Facet Publishing, 2012) and *Defining Digital Humanities: a reader* (Ashgate Publishing, 2013). She is currently serving on the Board of Curators of the University of Oxford Libraries, and the Board of the National Library of Scotland. Her research focuses on the use of computational techniques to enable research in the arts and humanities that would otherwise be impossible. You can generally find her on Twitter @melissaterras.

Preface

Memory institutions have long been engaged in managing cultural heritage information resources. However, access to, and use of, such resources have been limited, and in many cases restricted, because of the nature and quality of the resources themselves and the associated conservation issues. This scenario has changed over the past two decades due the advent and proliferation of internet technologies which have opened up new opportunities for the creation of digital copies of cultural heritage information resources that could be accessed from anywhere in the world without causing any physical damage to the resources resulting from everyday usage. Massive digitization of cultural heritage information resources over the past few years has given rise to a number of digital cultural heritage information services created at the national level, such as the American Memory in the USA (memory.loc.gov), and at the international level, such as the Europeana Digital Library (www.europeana.eu). It also facilitated better access to cultural heritage information due to the adoption of advanced interactive information retrieval techniques by cultural heritage digital libraries.

While the internet and the processes of digitization, indexing and retrieval activities offered new opportunities for providing better and wider access to cultural heritage information, they also posed several new challenges. Some of these challenges are associated with the resources, tools and technologies used for digitization, while others are related to access and use. Cultural heritage information resources can range from manuscripts to text and images, audio and video, and are often a combination of many of these forms; these multiple forms can pose specific challenges for metadata and indexing that are the key to providing access to digitized resources. Users of cultural heritage information can also have specific characteristics that need to be considered in order to design the most effective digital information systems that will facilitate interactive and contextual access to information. Since digitization of cultural heritage information is quite resource-intensive, such activities need to be governed by policies and guidelines. Some heritage information resources may be sensitive to specific communities and cultures, and similarly some cultural heritage resources may have commercial potential. Access to such resources therefore needs to be governed by appropriate policies and practices, and a number of policies and guidelines are also associated with the creation, access and management of cultural heritage information resources. Overall, a number of challenges are associated with the design, development and management of cultural heritage information systems and services. This book addresses some of these issues and challenges.

Contributed by 18 researchers from around the world, this book provides a snapshot of current research and development as well as outlining the various challenges and trends of research in relation to the creation, access and management of digital cultural heritage information systems and services. In Chapter 1, the editors provide a general introduction to the topic and the book. In Chapter 2, Sula discusses issues surrounding the current state and future possibilities of analogue versus digital cultural information services. In Chapter 3, Chowdhury discusses various policy issues associated with different aspects of cultural heritage information systems and services, ranging from digitization to access and use. In Chapter 4, Terras discusses the development, issues and challenges associated with digitization of cultural heritage information resources of different kinds. In Chapter 5, Sugimoto, Nagamori, Mihara and Honma discuss the role of metadata in cultural heritage information, by making special reference to Japanese graphic novels or comics called Manga. In Chapter 6, Phiri and Suleman discuss the design and architecture of cultural heritage digital libraries with special reference to the challenges facing such service providers in developing countries. In Chapter 7, Chowdhury discusses the user characteristics and usability challenges of digital cultural heritage digital libraries and information services. In

Chapter 8, Stiller and Petras propose a framework for analysing and comparing user interactions in cultural heritage information services such as the Europeana digital library. In Chapter 9, Shiri critically analyses how semantic access is supported in some selected cultural heritage digital libraries and information services. Referring to a research project under the EU FP7 programme, in Chapter 10 Clough, Goodale, Hall and Stevenson discuss techniques for supporting information access to digital cultural heritage collections, especially recommendations and visualizations. Pointing out that all of the activities associated with the design, development and management of digital cultural heritage information services have a number of sustainability challenges, in Chapter 11 Chowdhury discusses the economic, social and environmental sustainability issues of cultural heritage information.

The book has been published as the first title in Facet Publishing's newly introduced iResearch series, which aims to produce research monographs in contemporary themes that are relevant for the students, academics, researchers and practitioners of information science as envisioned by the iSchools around the world (ischools.org). We are thankful to the members of the advisory board of the iResearch series for their support and expert advice. We are especially thankful to Helen Carley, the Publishing Director, and her team at Facet for bearing with us throughout the process, from the conception of the idea to the publication of the book. Finally we would like to thank all our contributors for their submissions, as well as their co-operation throughout the editorial process.

Gobinda Chowdhury and Ian Ruthven

Managing digital cultural heritage information

Gobinda Chowdhury
Northumbria University, UK

Ian Ruthven
University of Strathclyde, UK

Introduction

Heritage is our legacy from the past, what we live with today, and what we pass on to future generations (UNESCO, 2008). Cultural heritage is commonly divided into two categories (Cane and Conagham, 2009):

1   Tangible cultural heritage that are material, and can be (a) movable objects, such as paintings, antiquities or artefacts and (b) immovable objects such as buildings, monuments or archaeological sites; and
2   Intangible cultural heritage that cannot be touched but which can be felt through other sensory organs – for example, can be seen, as in the case of a dance or performance of a play or ritual, or can be heard, as in the case of music, stories, etc.

A new form of cultural heritage is born when the tangible or intangible heritage objects are digitized; and this is commonly referred to as digital cultural heritage or cultural heritage information resources (Lor and Britz, 2012). Cultural heritage information resources may include a wide variety of content, objects and artefacts. According to the European Commission, Europe's cultural memory includes print (books, journals and newspapers), photographs, museum objects, archival documents, sound and audio visual materials, monuments and archaeological sites (European Commission, 2011).

Cultural heritage in the parlance of the World Intellectual Property Organization may be either intangible, tangible or, most usually, combinations of the two – an example of such a 'mixed expression of folklore' would be a woven rug (a tangible expression) that expresses elements of a traditional story (an intangible expression) (WIPO, n.d.).

Cultural heritage content may come in many different forms, such as:

- verbal expressions, such as folk tales, folk poetry and riddles, signs, words, symbols and indications
- musical expressions, such as folk songs and instrumental music
- expressions by actions, such as folk dances, plays and artistic forms or rituals, whether or not reduced to a material form
- tangible expressions, such as:
  — productions of folk art, in particular, drawings, paintings, carvings, sculptures, pottery, terracotta, mosaic, woodwork, metalware, jewellery, basket weaving, needlework, textiles, carpets, costumes
  — crafts
  — musical instruments
  — architectural forms.

WIPO, n.d.

A number of publications covering different aspects of digital cultural heritage have appeared over the past decade or so (Cameron and Kenderdine, 2007; Cane and Conagham, 2009; Feather, 2006; Lor and Britz, 2012), and they cover a wide range of themes such as:

- broader social, cultural and political issues, e.g., digital cultural heritage as a political concept and practice; the reshaping of social, cultural, and political power in relation to cultural organizations made possible through communication technologies; the representation and interpretation issues of cultural heritage as digital objects; issues of mobility and interactivity both for digital objects and for consumers of digital heritage; the relations between communities and heritage institutions as mediated through technologies

- technical and technological issues that cover a wide range of disciplines and communities of practice such as cognitive science, artificial intelligence, visual art history and theory, cultural communication and learning theory, social research, information management, indigenous knowledge, cultural studies, communications, history, anthropology, museum studies, film studies, and so on.

Digital cultural heritage information: access and management challenges

Rapid progress in ICT, web and mobile technologies have significantly boosted research and development activities aimed at the creation and management of digital cultural heritage resources. Numerous digital libraries and information services on cultural heritage information are now available. The Library of Congress's American Memory collection is one of the earliest and largest digital libraries of cultural heritage information.

Originating from a pilot project of the Library of Congress that began in 1990, the American Memory digital library was launched in 1994. It is a digital record of American history and creativity comprising written and spoken words, sound recordings, still and moving images, prints, maps, and sheet music that document the American experience.[1] Europeana is another example of a large open-access digital library of cultural heritage information. As stated on its website, 'Europeana is a single access point to millions of books, paintings, films, museum objects and archival records that have been digitized throughout Europe'.[2]

Numerous other cultural heritage information services have appeared over the past few years through various national libraries, museums, archives and government organizations, for example:

- The Oral History Collection of the British Library[3]
- The Australian Heritage Database[4]
- The Australian Institute of Aboriginal and Torres Strait Islander Studies' collections on indigenous culture and heritage[5]
- The DigitalNZ[6] Service from the National Library of New Zealand
- TELDAP[7] from Digital Taiwan.

In order to support digitization activities, researchers also began to develop a variety of novel technologies and tools for digitization of specific types of cultural heritage objects. For example, Papadakis et al. (2011) discuss a portable spectral imaging system for digitizing special types of cultural heritage objects, including paintings, encrusted stonework and ceramics. Many such new technologies, tools and standards for digitization of different kinds of digital objects and artefacts have been presented in the literature and used in cultural heritage information projects.

Access to cultural heritage information involves a number of challenges for several reasons, such as these:

- The sources of cultural heritage information may include a variety of objects, ranging from stone carvings to palm leaves, manuscripts, texts, photographs, paintings, audio – spoken words in oral history, sound from various objects such as musical instruments, music – and video of still as well as moving objects. Each of these objects may require different metadata, indexing, retrieval and filtering techniques.
- The users of cultural heritage information may vary from very expert and professional users in a specific domain like history, archaeology or music to schoolchildren and novice users. Each of these user categories may have different information needs and information-seeking behaviour that need to be considered while designing user-centred information access systems.

Many novel tools and techniques have been developed over the past few years to facilitate access to cultural heritage information. For example, Pattuelli (2011) discusses the user-centred design of an ontology for access to cultural heritage information. The temporal and spatial dimension and the context of information are extremely important in the retrieval as well as the preservation of cultural heritage information (Chowdhury, 2010). Kauppinen et al. (2010) comment that time is an essential concept in cultural heritage applications because temporal concepts such as time intervals are used for the annotation of cultural objects and also for querying datasets containing information about these objects.

Emphasizing the importance of user modelling and personalization – both at the specific user and community level – for cultural heritage information systems, Ardissono, Kuflik and Petrelli (2012) review the evolution of personalization techniques in museum websites, virtual collections and mobile guides towards recent extensions of cultural heritage toward the semantic and social web. Oral history has remained an important part of the cultural heritage, and many audio and video collections of such cultural heritage information are now available. Specific language processing and information retrieval challenge are associated with building oral history collections. Psutka et al. (2011), for example, employed novel speech recognition and information retrieval techniques to improve access to the Czech language part of a large video archive containing recorded testimonies of Holocaust survivors.

There are also the long-term access and sustainability issues of cultural heritage information. A significant amount of research resources and efforts have been expended over the past decade on digital preservation, many of which focus specifically on cultural heritage information (see, for example, the EU-funded SHAMAN project).[8] Since most of the cultural heritage information services have appeared as an outcome of specific research projects, or have been funded by governments or individual institutions such as national libraries, continuing funding support and thus the economic sustainability of such digital cultural heritage information services will remain a major concern.

Due to the rapid growth in the volume and variety of cultural heritage information, and the rapid growth of user-generated cultural information, cultural heritage information systems will be a growing organism requiring more and more resources to run them in years to come. Furthermore, although there is the 'social good' aspect of cultural heritage information services, it is important to assess how 'good' they are, and more importantly how the success of such services can be measured in specific social and economic contexts. This is essential for the long-term sustainability of cultural heritage information systems and services.

The organic growth of cultural heritage information systems and services also cause concerns in terms of environmental sustainability because of the increasing use of ICT infrastructure and the corresponding energy consumptions. Appropriate measures need to be taken to curb the growing energy consumptions of the ICT equipment and infrastructure in order to make the digital cultural heritage information systems and services more environment-friendly.

While open access to cultural heritage information will increase equity of access, this may be affected by a number of factors, such as the digital divide and information literacy. A recent study noted that 16 million people in Britain do not have basic internet skills. This means that almost one in four, or one in three if only the adult (over-16) population is counted, in Britain lack the basic internet skills to access digital cultural heritage; and the situation in many other countries may not be significantly better. Therefore, digital literacy and information skills have to be improved quite significantly in order to enable the public to make optimum use of digital cultural heritage information systems and services. This is an issue we return to in depth in Chapter 11.

About this book

This book aims to provide an overview of various challenges and contemporary research activities in cultural heritage information, focusing particularly on the cultural heritage content types, their characteristic and digitization challenges; cultural heritage content organization and access issues; users and usability; and various policy and sustainability issues associated with digital cultural heritage information systems and services.

We intend the book to be useful for researchers in information science, specifically in the areas of digital libraries, digital humanities and digital culture. It will also be useful for practitioners and students in these areas who want to know the different research issues and challenges and learn how they have been handled in course of various research projects.

There are 11 chapters in this book, contributed by 18 authors from 6 countries. While this chapter provides a brief overview of the topic of digital cultural heritage information, the other chapters address specific issues and research activities in this topic. The ordering of the chapters moves from scene setting on policies and infrastructures, through considerations of interaction, access and objects, to concrete system implementations. Finally, we look forward to issues around sustainability, in the widest sense, that need to be thought about in order to maximize the availability and longevity of our digital cultural heritage.

In Chapter 2 Sula presents a critical account of the histories of digital heritage, the challenges of defining the concept and the complementarities between digital and non-digital heritage. He then turns to the future and considers possible futures for digital heritage and concrete suggestions for this future.

In Chapter 3, Gobinda Chowdhury discusses various policy issues associated with the digitization and management of cultural heritage information. He argues that management of digital cultural heritage information involves a number of social, legal and policy issues. For example, while there is a general consensus that cultural heritage information should be made available to everyone for social good, there are a number of intellectual property and digital rights management issues. There are also some ownership and cultural sensitivity issues; for example, specific government policies and guidelines have been formulated for handling of cultural heritage information related to specific indigenous communities in countries like Australia and New Zealand. Chapter 3 discusses some of these policies and their implications as well as the provenance and digital rights management issues associated with cultural heritage information.

Terras points out that there is now an expectation that institutions should be undertaking digitization programmes, and best practices in this area are now well documented and understood. In Chapter 4 she scopes out the background to the current digitization environment, giving an overview of the methods and approaches involved. She discusses the current developments, highlighting the use of both two- and three-dimensional digitization methods for the creation of digital surrogates of objects and artefacts, indicating the potential for further development in the sector, whilst drawing attention to current issues faced when digitizing objects and artefacts including cost, sustainability, impact evaluation, and expectation management in the changing information environment. She points out that affordances of previously prohibitively expensive techniques – such as multi-spectral imaging and 3D scanning – are now available at relatively inexpensive rates. However, she raises questions about digital literacy and our understanding of what it means, for both the end-user and information professional, to create digital versions of our cultural inheritance.

Sugimoto, Nagamori, Mihara and Honma point out that metadata plays a key role in finding, accessing, collecting, using, organizing, storing, delivering and preserving cultural heritage information in a networked information environment. In Chapter 5, they discuss various metadata issues for digital resources and archives in the networked information environment in the context of a novel metadata framework development for publishing and management of 'manga', a Japanese term which means graphic novel or comics. They conclude that having an appropriate and interoperable metadata framework does not only facilitate better access and management of cultural heritage information resources, but also helps us add value to those resources through such activities as linking, annotations, etc.

In Chapter 6, Phiri and Suleman discuss the systems architecture that store, preserve and provide access to digital cultural heritage objects. They discuss major design considerations for implementing cultural heritage system architectures and some existing architectural patterns currently in use. They argue that the current digital library systems architectures are not suitable for institutions and researchers in many Third World countries that suffer from poor network infrastructure and access. They propose a simpler architectural design and demonstrate, through two case studies, how such a simple design can facilitate the management of cultural heritage information collections in South Africa.

While Chapters 4–6 focus more on the cultural heritage information objects, metadata and system architecture, Chapters 7–10 focus more on the users, access and usability issues. In Chapter 7, Sudatta Chowdhury discusses various issues and challenges of users and usability studies in digital humanities and digital culture. By drawing several examples from large cultural heritage information services such as the Europeana digital library, she discusses some specific characteristics of users of digital humanities and digital culture and how they influence the design and usability of cultural heritage information systems and services. She also discusses some emerging trends in the context of users and usability studies of cultural heritage information systems and services.

In Chapter 8, Stiller and Petras argue that there are several significant distinct characteristics of user interactions in cultural heritage information services in comparison to conventional information services. They discuss some strategies for cultural institutions to provide users with means for purposeful interactions with digital cultural heritage while maintaining their mandate to offer universal access to curated content. By drawing examples from the European digital library, they provide a framework for evaluating interactions and critically analysing them with regard to serving users and cultural institutions alike. They conclude that for cultural heritage information, it is not only necessary to provide certain features and consequently interactions but it is also important to be aware of their influence on the access modes.

Following on from this in Chapter 9, Shiri provides an overview of knowledge organization systems and metadata standards used in cultural heritage digital libraries. His chapter examines and analyses, using three selected cultural heritage digital libraries as case studies, the ways in which digital libraries have incorporated controlled vocabularies in their search user interfaces and the degree to which this use of semantic access maps to recent research on the information search strategies of cultural heritage information seekers.

In Chapter 10, Clough, Goodale, Hall and Stevenson discuss techniques to support information access to digital cultural heritage collections and, in particular, helping users explore and use the information they contain. They focus on a particular system called 'PATHS' – Personalised Access To cultural Heritage Spaces) project, funded under the European Commission's FP7 programme – which aims to support multiple user groups with varying degrees of domain knowledge through the provision of state-of-the-art functionalities, such as recommendations and visualizations.

The lifecycle of digital cultural heritage information services is resource-intensive in many ways. First, activities associated with digitization and preservation of digitized content are hugely expensive affairs. Second, the growth of digital cultural heritage content vis-à-vis the growth of users and their information need from such services can be quite demanding. Furthermore, as discussed in Chapter 3, there are various social, cultural and legal issues associated with the management of, and access to, cultural heritage information. All these bring to the fore the question of sustainability of cultural heritage information systems and services. Arguing that the sustainability of information systems and services has so far remained a poorly researched area, in Chapter 11, Gobinda Chowdhury discusses the issues and challenges associated with the economic, social and environmental sustainability issues and challenges of cultural heritage information.

Notes

1 http://memory.loc.gov/ammem/index.html.
2 http://pro.europeana.eu/about?utm_source=portalmenu&utm_medium=portal&utm_campaign=Portal%2Bmenu.
3 www.bl.uk/oralhistory.
4 www.environment.gov.au/heritage/ahdb/index.html.
5 www.aiatsis.gov.au.

6 http://digitalnz.org.
7 http://culture.teldap.tw/culture.
8 http://shaman-ip.eu.

References

Ardissono, L., Kuflik, T. and Petrelli, D. (2012) Personalization in Cultural Heritage: the road travelled and the one ahead, *Modeling and User-adapted Interaction*, **22** (1–2), 73–99.

Cameron, F. and Kenderdine, S. (eds) (2007) *Theorizing Digital Cultural Heritage: a critical discourse*, MIT Press.

Cane, P. and Conagham, J. (2009) *The New Oxford Companion to Law*, Oxford University Press.

Chowdhury, G. G. (2010) From Digital Libraries to Digital Preservation Research: the importance of users and context, *Journal of Documentation*, **66** (2), 207–23.

European Commission (2011) *Commission Recommendation of 27 October 2011 on the Digitisation and Online Accessibility of Cultural Material and Digital Preservation*, (2011/711/EU), http://eur-lex.europa.eu/LexUriServ/ LexUriServ.do?uri=OJ:L:2011:283:0039:0045:EN:PDF.

Feather, J. (2006) Managing the Documentary Heritage: issues for the present and future. In Gorman, G. E. and Shep, S. J. (eds), *Preservation Management for Libraries, Archives and Museums*, Facet Publishing, 1–18.

Kauppinen, T., Mantegari, G., Paakkarinen, P., Kuittinen, H., Hyvonen, E. and Bandini, S. (2010) Determining Relevance of Imprecise Temporal Intervals for Cultural Heritage Information Retrieval, *International Journal of Human–Computer Studies*, **68** (9), 549–60.

Lor, P. J. and Britz, J .J. (2012) An Ethical Perspective on Political-Economic Issues in the Long-Term Preservation of Digital Heritage, *Journal of the American Society for Information Science and Technology*, **63** (11), 2153–64.

Papadakis, V., Orphanos, Y., Kogou, S., Melessanaki, K., Pouli, P. and Fotakis, C. (2011) 'IRIS': a novel spectral imaging system for the analysis of cultural heritage objects. In Pezzati, L. and Salimbeni, R. (eds), *Proceedings of SPIE 8084, O3A: Optics for Arts, Architecture, and Archaeology III*, Munich,

23 May 2011, 80840W, DOI: 10.1117/12.889510.

Pattuelli, M. C . (2011) Modeling a Domain Ontology for Cultural Heritage Resources: a user-centered approach, *Journal of the American Society for Information Science and Technology*, **62** (2), 314–42.

Psutka, J., Svec, J., Psutka, J. V., Vanek, J., Prazak, A., Smidl, L. and Ircing, P. (2011) System for Fast Lexical and Phonetic Spoken Term Detection in a Czech Cultural Heritage Archive, *Eurasip Journal on Audio Speech and Music Processing*, Article Number 10, 1-1, DOI: 10.1186/1687-4722-2011-10.

UNESCO (2008) *World Heritage Information Kit*, http://whc.unesco.org/uploads/activities/documents/activity-567-1.pdf, 5.

WIPO (World Intellectual Property Organization) (n.d.). *Intellectual Property and Traditional Cultural Expressions/Folklore*, www.wipo.int/edocs/pubdocs/en/tk/913/wipo_pub_913.pdf.

CHAPTER 2

Digital humanities and digital cultural heritage (alt-history and future directions)

Chris Alen Sula
Pratt Institute, USA

Introduction

Most commentators locate the origin of digital humanities (DH) in humanities computing of the mid-20th century. Dalbello (2011), for example, begins her account in 1946 with Roberto Busa's *Index Thomisticus*, a massive attempt to encode nearly 11 million words of Thomas Aquinas on IBM punch cards. This event (and the narrative that follows) is found throughout the literature, leading some to believe that early DH work 'concentrated, perhaps somewhat narrowly, on text analysis (such as classification systems, mark-up, text encoding, and scholarly editing)' (Presner, 2010, 6). Others seem convinced that DH is *still* only text analysis – and misguided in its approach (Fish, 2012b).

Acceptance rates for the Digital Humanities conference indeed reflect a strong interest in text and language (Weingart, 2013), but most of the projects are rooted in fields other than computational linguistics. The interdisciplinary nature of DH has opened doors to geographers (through GIS), social scientists (through statistics and network analysis), information scientists (through visualization and citation analysis), demographers (through decomposition and event analysis), engineers and architects (through modelling), media studies scholars (through gaming and new media formats), computer scientists (through a great variety of code that supports this work), and more. Alternative histories of DH, grounded in these and other disciplines, remain to be written, and this chapter addresses yet another field: cultural heritage (through source materials) and its relation to DH.

The first section of this chapter is critical, discussing historical accounts in the literature and arguing for alt[ernate-]histories of DH. Scheinfeldt (2014) has recently issued a similar call for recognizing disciplinary diversity in the history of DH.[1] The second part of this chapter is constructive, sketching a history of DH based on cultural heritage institutions, including libraries, archives, and museums (LAMs). The third section is prospective, examining possibilities for overlap between DH and cultural heritage institutions. In some cases, cultural heritage institutions and the humanities face parallel challenges (e.g., threats to funding, an increasing need to demonstrate public relevance), which could be met jointly by both fields. In these instances, cultural heritage institutions and DHers will be aligned in their structures and values, making for flexible, even seamless partnerships. In other cases, however, the movement of DH may invite a fresh examination of traditional missions and practices within cultural heritage and suggest new directions for policy and management.

Toward alt-histories of digital humanities

Hockey begins one of the first histories of DH with a warning about the dangers of writing the narrative of an interdisciplinary – and, I would add, young – field:

> Tracing the history of any interdisciplinary academic area of activity raises a number of basic questions. What should be the scope of the area? Is there overlap with related areas, which has impacted on the development of the activity? What has been the impact on other, perhaps more traditional, disciplines? Does a straightforward chronological account do justice to the development of the activity? Might there be digressions from this, which could lead us into hitherto unexplored avenues?
>
> Hockey, 2004, 1

In the case of DH, these questions are compounded by the field's apparent resistance to definition. Everyone agrees that humanists using computers does not automatically amount to DH work. A computer could be a glorified typewriter; a blog may be a faster, cheaper, more distributable periodical; e-mail is ubiquitous. Genuine DH work involves more thoroughgoing, transformative interactions with computing technology: we find data 'falsifying existing theoretical explanations' (Moretti, 2005, 30), it 'change[s] my understanding of the field' (Siemens et al., 2009), and so on.

Beyond this broad characterization, however, the field seems divided between those who content themselves with the use of new methods, platforms, and tools (Moretti, 2005; Scheinfeldt, 2010a) and those who seek, in addition, critical and humanistic reflections on those methods, platforms, tools, and even technology itself (McCarty, 2005; Berry, 2012; Frabetti, 2012; Fitzpatrick, 2012; Rieder and Röhle, 2012; Svensson, 2012). For the first camp, applying these new methods leads to broader, faster, less biased, more accessible, different, or perhaps unique results as compared to traditional methods of humanistic research, and that's what makes DH exciting. For the second camp, those methods are interesting, but this particular moment of technology as well as the general theoretical rigour of humanities require that DHers take a step further and ask critical questions about the methods and technologies they are using (and why they are using them). Frabetti captures this view well in saying, 'if the digital humanities encompass the study of software, writing and code, then they need to critically investigate the role of digitality in constituting the very concepts of the "humanities" and the human' (2012, 161). Put differently, 'the digital humanities need to engage with the concept of the "digital" at a much deeper level than the instrumental one' (162).

Some authors seem neutral on this debate, endorsing a maximally inclusive view of the field that accepts computational and theoretical work (Davidson, 2008; Kirschenbaum, 2010; Alvarado, 2011; Hayles, 2012; Gold, 2012). This pluralism is reflected in the National Endowment for the Humanities' criteria for Digital Humanities Start-Up Grants, which include both tools and scholarship as potential products:

- research that brings new approaches or documents best practices in the study of the digital humanities;
- planning and developing prototypes of new digital tools for preserving, analyzing, and making accessible digital resources, including libraries' and museums' digital assets;
- scholarship that focuses on the history, criticism, and philosophy of digital culture and its impact on society;
- scholarship or studies that examine the philosophical or practical implications and impact of the use of emerging technologies in specific fields or disciplines of the humanities, or in interdisciplinary collaborations involving several fields or disciplines;
- innovative uses of technology for public programming and education utilizing both traditional and new media; and
- new digital modes of publication that facilitate the dissemination of humanities scholarship in advanced academic as well as informal or formal educational settings at all academic levels

National Endowment for the Humanities (NEH), 2010

These guidelines are significant because they reflect state-of-the-art work in DH and have been used to fund hundreds of projects to date, making them responsible, in no small part, for shaping the field over time. It's worth noting here that those who hold pluralist definitions of the field must accept as genuine both applied work in the field and theoretical work in the field (and perhaps other work), without favouring one camp or the other. Pluralists must accept that applied work holds a place in the DH canon (even if it is not accompanied by theoretical reflection) and that theoretical work also belongs (even if it does not depend epistemically on computation). To put it simply, pluralists must accept applied work just as much as theoretical work, though *good* or *great* work may lie somewhere in between. Also, as I have noted elsewhere (Sula, 2013), pedagogy is often excluded from these lists despite the fact that DHers are at the forefront of new instructional methods, platforms, and tools. In any case, the pluralist account is favoured by many in DH, perhaps because it accords with key values of the field, among them openness and inclusivity (Scheinfeldt, 2010b).

Despite the variety and breadth of definitions of DH, narratives of its history have been surprisingly homogenous. Hockey (2004) and later authors (Svensson, 2009, 2010, 2012; Kirschenbaum, 2010; Dalbello, 2011) ground DH in mid-20th century humanities computing, a view that is all but orthodox in short and anecdotal histories of the field. According to this narrative, DH begins in 1946 with Busa's *Index Tomisticus* – a project based on machine searching and concordance analysis – and proceeds through advances in corpus linguistics to the founding of the journal *Computers and the Humanities* in 1966. These early projects are hindered by storage capacity, hardware costs, and processing limits; progress is slow. Though Svensson (2009) admits that not every article during this time is about text analysis, he notes that the field had narrowed enough by 1986 for *Literary and Linguistic Computing* to supplant *Computers and Humanities* (note the titles) as the premier humanities computing journal. Hockey similarly describes the 1970s and 1980s as a period of 'consolidation' for methods of text analysis. As storage and processing capabilities increased from the late 1970s onward, structured electronic text and multimedia archives dominated the field, followed in the 1990s by internet-enabled hypertexts, digital libraries, and collaborative editing. The overarching theme of this narrative is text, with the plot revolving around corpora of increasing size and susceptibility to machine analysis.

Though this account dominates historical views of the field, it suffers from four separate problems. First, it privileges certain methods, tools, projects, and disciplines at the expense of others in the field. For example, the standard narrative omits early work in 'quantitative history' (also called new economic history, econometric history, and cliometrics), which applied statistics to familiar historical questions, such as the causes of the American Civil War. Though many examples of this work were controversial (Conrad and Meyer, 1958; Fogel, 1964, 1966; Woodman et al., 1972), its methods would almost certainly count as DH in the present day. Yet it falls outside the narrow focus on text that is put forward in the standard narrative and receives no mention. The same may be true of related work in other areas of the humanities. Moreover, the link between DH and specific departments is so pervasive that Kirschenbaum (2010) develops an entire article around the conjoint question: 'What is digital humanities and what's it doing in English departments?' His answer depends (unsurprisingly) on historical connections between texts, computing, and composition – all the trappings of humanities computing – as well as interest in editorial processes, hypertext and cultural studies (2010, 60). Other disciplines have received short shrift in the literature, and the *Blackwell Companion to Digital Humanities* (Schreibman, Siemens and Unsworth, 2004) – now almost 10 years old – remains one of the few sources that systematically describes DH work in archaeology, art history, classics, history, lexicography, music, multimedia studies, performing arts and philosophy and religion. Much important DH work takes place in English departments and much more involves text analysis. But limiting the history of DH to a single, (methodologically) exclusionary narrative does little to advance a young and experimental field, especially one that values openness.

Second, most histories of DH fail to chart an actual, historical course from humanities computing, with its singular focus on text, to present DH work in all its variety. Any work that falls outside of text analysis must be treated (narratively) as anomalous, revolutionary, even freak, or ignored altogether. Indeed, the existing histories balk when it comes to describing 'big tent' DH work of the 21st century. Dalbello, for example, includes social learning, tagging, digital persona, self-broadcasting, public/ audiences, materialism, new media *Bildung*, social software sites, scalable networks, reimagining the archive, cultural heritage, and digital libraries – all, arguably, text-based approaches – in her description of recent work (Dalbello, 2011, 487). Even this long list leaves out current work with statistics, GIS, social network analysis, visualization, modelling, and more. Svensson, aware of this work, is forced to note some incongruence between the 'disciplinary boundaries and epistemic culture' of humanities computing and digital humanities. He attributes these differences to humanities computing's (1) interest in technology as a tool, as opposed to DH's occasional interest in technology as an object of study; (2) methodological unity, as opposed to diversity within DH; (3) focus on text, as opposed to the 'visual turn' or multimodal interests of DH; and

(4) exclusion of data types other than text: image, number, and sound counting among the objects of DH studies (Svensson, 2009, 43–56). Despite these apparently huge differences – or rather *because* of them – Svensson concludes that humanities computing has, after all, acquired a vast new scope and that any apparent tensions are simple garden-variety disputes within the academy over disciplinary boundaries.[2] The differences between the two seem much greater, and a successful history should at least be able to describe a clear transition between them.

Third, the standard history precludes historicizing and contextualizing DH work that falls outside text analysis, and it obscures connections to other fields, including the social and applied sciences. When a new project appears using network analysis, for example, there is nothing in the so-called history of DH to relate the project to, no chain of past projects to link it with, no sense of understanding about how this project applies network analysis in better (or worse) ways. One worries that this may lead to a lack of attention to method in all its complexity (and especially its historical development) and, consequently, to poor applications of that method. The social science techniques that DH often borrows do have long and important histories – just not in the humanities – and restricting the history of DH to text analysis does little to encourage interest in these accounts and a better understanding of methodology.

Fourth and finally, the standard history has rarely been given explicit defence; it is assumed and applied rather than documented. Svensson chooses humanities computing for his account because of its 'rich heritage, historical and current accomplishments, the sheer number of people involved, and the apparent discursive transition to "digital humanities"' (Svensson, 2009, 8). Unfortunately, none of these marks out any essential historical connection between the two. Biology, for example, has a rich heritage, historical and current accomplishments, and plenty of people involved, yet none of these make it an appropriate field in which to ground DH. Moreover, young fields often attach themselves to some forerunner as a way of establishing credibility, especially when that forerunner is relatively unknown and unable or unlikely to put up much resistance. Conversely, waning fields attempt to rebrand themselves, to appear new and different and attract followers to their cause, especially younger scholars or those unaware of the past. In neither case is there *necessarily* a true genealogy between the two fields. DH may indeed be descended from humanities computing (or other fields), but in the absence of empirical data about the fields (e.g., citation studies, topic analysis), it is hard to adjudicate between competing historical accounts.

So what are the alternatives? Davidson (2008) gives a helpful introduction to DH through a distinction between Web 1.0 and Web 2.0. Her account is more metaphorical than historical and covers a decade or two, at best. Evans and Rees (2012) describe DH in broad, inter-disciplinary terms, but their historical discussion focuses on the shift from traditional humanities to digital humanities, with little specific attention to the history of DH. McPherson (2009) prefers a distinction between computing humanities, blogging humanities, and multimodal humanities – all covered by the DH umbrella – but does not attempt a history of these tracts. Burdick et al. (2012, 8–9, 123) avoid characterizing the field solely in terms of text analysis, but their account is too brief to compare to the fuller treatments discussed here. Manovich's (2012) approach to DH might inspire an interesting and unorthodox history of DH, but to my knowledge, he has not written one yet.[3]

Those interested in the history of DH – or, better yet, the multiple histories of DH – would do well to attend to the various methods, platforms, and tools that animate current DH work and to investigate the origins of those. An alt-history model of DH would trace the genealogy of each method, platform, or tool that is currently part of DH, noting milestones and humanists engaged with this work. Ball (2013), for instance, has drawn attention to long-standing interest in computers and technology within writing studies. Scheinfeldt (2014) has pointed to the historical importance of oral history in DH. Such accounts need not be mutually exclusive but can instead function as overlapping and complementary, together treating the history of the field in the broadest possible sense. Many of these alt-histories would involve social and applied sciences (e.g., statistics, geography, sociology, demography, information science, engineering, architecture, computer science), with the list expanding over time and across new and innovative projects.

The following section sketches one of these alt-histories: the long-standing connection between (digital) humanities and cultural heritage. This alt-history begins with user studies of the mid-20th century, tracing its way through massive digitization efforts at the turn of the century toward present-day DH work.[4] A full treatment of this history is beyond the scope of this chapter. Instead, I give a sense of the overall theme, highlights, and content of such a history, leaving it to others to fill in the details.

Cultural heritage and the humanities

For nearly three decades, the user-centred approach made popular by Dervin and Nilan (1986) has guided policy, practice, and professional training in cultural heritage. In their seminal article, they call for a shift away from systems understandings of information, which they characterize as objective, mechanistic, and universal, and toward conceptions of users and uses of information that are more subjective, constructionist, and situated (12–16). This paradigm plays a central role in the history of cultural heritage and (digital) humanities, and some have argued it extends back even further in the literature.

Bates (2004) argues that this user-centred approach can be traced back to studies of scholarly communication in the 1950s and 1960s, which, to varying degrees, took stock of individual scholars' information-seeking behaviours. Talja and Hartel (2007) review this claim at length, finding that Dervin and Nilan were seemingly unaware of this literature – otherwise they would not have levelled the charges they did. But Talja and Hartel also find that early studies reflect a surprising sensitivity to the 'context of library-oriented, site-specific, and service-oriented research.' Similarly, Case (2006, 6) maintains that this literature was not about information seeking behaviours *per se* but rather the artefacts and venues of information seeking. In any case, such early studies are relevant to the present discussion both because they inform present-day cultural heritage work and because they concern academics and their use of information.

Stone (1982, 294–5) gives a comprehensive review of these studies about humanities scholars and their work, some of which remains relevant today. Her description of this literature can be summarized in four points. First, humanists tend to work alone and are reluctant to defer to others for their information needs, possibly because they lack staff, distrust others, have trouble communicating their needs, or see searching as an integral part of the research process. As Wiberley and Jones (1989, 639) later put it, 'While scientists spend much of their time with collaborators working with laboratory equipment and social scientists spend much time with coinvestigators planning and executing field work, surveys, and data analysis, humanists spend most of their time alone, reading'. Whether or not humanists still work alone is an open question. Linmans (2009), for example, reports that journal publications in the humanities between 1980 and 2007 averaged a flat 1.06 authors per article, though this figure varies by field and collaboration is often discussed as a central value of DH.

Second, Stone (1982, 295) reports that humanists rely on shelf-browsing (i.e., discovery of adjacent items organized by author, subject, or some other heuristic) for 'serendipitous interaction' with research materials. Shelf-browsing is principally a feature of physical collections, in which items are placed together to meet space constraints, with collocation being an added benefit. Svenonius (2000, 18–20) laments the loss of this 'navigation' feature in newer, digital collections, and calls on information professionals to restore this function in their systems.

Third, humanists use a variety of research methods and materials. Some prefer to work from chronologies, others from critical or philosophical stances. Some begin with hypotheses and seek out data for confirmation; others compare various sources before making judgements. These sources are even more heterogeneous. Stone again (1982, 296): 'These materials include primary sources such as original scores, works of art, texts, manuscripts, recordings, original literary works, technical records, site records, maps, and so on. The need for all editions of texts, drafts, galley and page proofs is expressed, and for works of criticism, interpretation, and opinion. The list is almost endless'. Secondary sources, including bibliographies, indexes and guides, abstracts, and databases, are also discussed, though Stone concludes that 'the picture of the use of, need for, availability and acceptability of secondary serves is piecemeal and poorly researched' (297). Wiberley and Jones (1989, 643) also stress the importance of geographic and genealogical research, in which humanists visit local, regional, or national repositories to discover rare materials unavailable elsewhere. These myriad needs, in addition to shelf-browsing, make stock and remote storage difficult, though this problem disappears where digital collections are concerned.

Finally, Stone reviews research on humanists' use of technology – at that time limited to basic computers and word processors. While some humanists are found to embrace this technology, much of the field regards it with scepticism. In particular, two sources (Reagor and Brown, 1978; Raben and Burton, 1981) lead Stone (1982, 300) to note: 'It is suggested . . . that it may be a part of the humanistic tradition to be anti-machine and those scholars who combine training in computing technology with a more traditional academic training are sometimes viewed with suspicion and apprehension by their colleagues'. The surrounding context shows that Stone has *Computers and the Humanities* in mind in discussing this work, and some commentators retain this sceptical stance toward DHers' use of technology (Fish, 2011, 2012a, 2012b; Marche, 2012).

The overarching narrative found in early studies (1950s–1980s) is that of the lone humanist poring over documents for insights to be shared later, publicly through conferences, journals, and letters. Present, though rarely acknowledged, are libraries, archives, and museums: the institutions that furnish humanists with primary source materials and the information resources for locating them. With the exception of Stieg (1981, 551), who examines historians' use of manuscripts and materials held in archives, most researchers fail to discuss venues beyond academic and, occasionally, public libraries. Even academic libraries are discussed only instrumentally as sites where books, bibliographies, and other resources reside. By the 1990s and the rise of more digital collections, that narrative begins to change, especially for non-text materials.

Bates, Wilde and Siegfried (1993), for example, examine humanists' use of search terms on the Getty online searching project during the late 1980s and early 1990s. Black (1995) gives an extensive overview of the rich film collections available in archives across the USA, noting their lack of use because of problems with organization and access. Auffret and Prié (1999) advance a method for managing audiovisual materials that involves full indexing, a necessary search feature for humanities scholars.

More recent studies have put direct emphasis on cultural heritage institutions and (digital) humanities (Warwick et al., 2008; Tahir, Mahmood and Shafique, 2010). In particular, Sinn (2012) examines the impact of digital archives on historical research, finding that use of collections has increased considerably over the past few years. She is particularly critical of the notions of 'increased access' and 'impact,' partially because they are vague and partially because they do not always reflect quality and relevance of digital resources. As a remedy, Sinn suggests citations as the gold standard of use for digital materials – a point that will surely gain importance as discussion about evaluation techniques gain momentum.

In the case of libraries, the discussion of (digital) humanities has been even more extensive. Showers (2012), for example, highlights five areas of overlap between DH and libraries: managing data, 'embedded' librarianship, digitization and curation, digital preservation, and discover and dissemination. Ramsay goes further in linking DH to one of the oldest functions of the library, namely knowledge organization:

> Of all scholarly pursuits, Digital Humanities most clearly represents the spirit that animated the ancient foundations at Alexandria, Pergamum, and Memphis, the great monastic libraries of the Middle Ages, and even the first research libraries of the German Enlightenment. It is obsessed with varieties of representation, the organization of knowledge, the technology of communication and dissemination, and the production of useful tools for scholarly inquiry.
>
> Ramsay, 2010

Additional discussions of libraries and DH are found in articles from a January 2003 special issue of the *Journal of Library Administration*, together with responses, in *Make It New? A dh+lib Mini-Series* (Dh+ lib, 2013). In a later post, Muñoz (2013) is critical of the lack of historical perspective in many of these articles, which draw a bright line between 'traditional library service' and newer forms of DH work. In the same spirit as this article, he notes that, 'The appeal to "traditional library service" as a unitary concept blunts the generative potential of alternative proposals like Nowviskie's, mine, and others . . . through a suspect history that collapses into claims about identity.'

Though the history of cultural heritage and DH given here is far from complete, I have pointed to a long-standing interest in humanists within the cultural heritage community. Since the 1950s, there have been clear attempts to understand humanists' information needs and information seeking behaviours. Though cultural heritage institutions were somewhat invisible in the early literature, more recent work has explicitly addressed the role of libraries, archives, and museums by considering the potential for digital collections and their impact on scholarship. Much work remains, and it is important to remember that DHers, with their particular interest in computation and technology, may be a special (but growing) subset of users within the humanities at large.

With that in mind, I turn now to future directions for digital humanities and cultural heritage work. To inform this discussion, I begin by presenting core values of DH developed in the literature, values that have broad appeal and are likely to be resilient to changes in particular approaches or technologies over time. By attending to these aspects of the culture of DH, cultural heritage institutions can engage in mutually beneficial relationships with DHers and their work.

Future directions for digital humanities and cultural heritage

In discussing the definition of DH, Spiro (2012, 17) argues that the community needs 'a keener sense of what it stands for and what is at stake in its work'. Her initial attempt to define these values outlines five areas in which DHers aspire to succeed:

- *Openness.* DHers have a commitment to the open exchange of ideas, the development of open content and software, and transparency in their practices and procedures. They are avid supporters of the open access and open source movements, advocating the democratization of knowledge and the empowerment of others through freely accessible resources. This commitment extends to teaching as well, with many calling for open educational resources, such as tools, syllabi, and even course evaluations. As Spiro puts it, 'Rather than cheapening knowledge by making it free, embracing openness recognizes the importance of the humanities to society' (25).
- *Collaboration.* DHers rely on many collaborators in the course of their work, especially given its technological and methodological complexity. These collaborations span various disciplines (e.g., humanities, social sciences, computer science, libraries) and levels (e.g., faculty, graduate students, technologists, librarians). Rather than treating these contributions as instrumental or outsourced labour, DHers attempt to have mutually respectful and beneficial exchange with their collaborators, with all parties receiving appropriate credit for their contributions.
- *Collegiality and connectedness.* Given their dependence on collaborators, DHers strive to be inclusive of others, recognizing the different skills and interests they have to contribute. This ethos is reflected in a variety of informalities of the field – question-and-answer boards, skillshares, unconferences – in which participants meet in horizontal spaces to learn from each other, regardless of skill level. When parts of the field have been criticized for setting up divisions and fiefdoms, they have generally responded quickly to make things broader and more inclusive.
- *Diversity.* DHers are interested in a diversity of methods, questions, and views, and the field shows impressive demographics in professional status, nationalities, ages, disciplines, and gender (though not always race – and, I would add, class). However, the field does not always address more structural questions of these categories (Fiormonte, 2012; Liu, 2012; McPherson, 2012; Whitson,

2012), and it may reproduce those structures if it does not give greater attention to them. This again underscores the truly social view of the humanities among DHers.

- *Experimentation.* DH work involves novel applications of technologies to questions in the humanities. As such, it requires a strong sense of play, the ability to take risks and to make meaningful errors. While certain products may be anticipated, the process of DH may involve unforeseen turns and unexpected results, some positive and some negative. Accordingly, much of the field's infrastructure is modelled on labs, places of continuous scholarly activity where stable support allows for risk-taking and innovation.

Though Spiro acknowledges that this list may be incomplete, it is still a good place to ground a discussion of the future of DH with respect to cultural heritage.

To this account, I would add only that discussions of DH have also taken place against the broader backdrop of a 'crisis in the humanities' (Sibley 2013) and the 'university in ruin' (Mowitt, 2012; Adamson, 2012; Sitze, 2012). The past few decades have seen drastic cuts in funding and support for universities, especially public universities, and for the humanities in particular. Many programmes have been consolidated into smaller units; some departments have been shuttered completely. Humanists are called upon increasingly to quantify and measure the impact of their work, not only for external grants but also for the pleasure of accreditors, politicians, and taxpayers. The same could be said of cultural heritage institutions, so the recommendations that follow are an attempt to advocate for both groups through joint endeavours.

First, cultural heritage institutions should do everything they can to digitize materials as quickly as possible. These efforts make collections available to a much broader range of users, in line with many of the values discussed above. They may be able to identify and prioritize local resources that are unique (Anderson, 2013) or they may want to attend to the needs of their immediate users, recognizing that this might be a smaller base than potential online users. By providing digital collections, cultural heritage institutions offer DHers the raw, large-scale data needed to conduct their work. In cases where humanists have their own materials they wish to digitize, cultural heritage institutions would do well to seek out new partnerships, sharing resources (and credit) for these new collections and helping to disseminate them to a wider audience.

Beyond simply digitizing materials, cultural heritage institutions must give full access to DHers to use and mine those collections, along the lines of an API (application programming interface) model. APIs allow users to make structured calls for data and, in some cases, to send updates back to a centralized data warehouse. This allows DHers to access large amounts of information in a simple, efficient manner – something that, say, a web-based gallery display would make tedious or perhaps impossible, practically speaking. By opening their collections in this way, cultural heritage institutions give full meaning to the term 'access' and they facilitate a wide range of uses of their material. (They may still charge reproduction rights if necessary, but a general pay-per-view model for their content only makes it impossible for many users to access their materials, defeating the very purpose of digitizing their collections.)

In addition to making their collections accessible, cultural heritage institutions can also facilitate the process of citing those materials by providing suggestions with each item or collection in a variety of popular citation styles. Citation manuals have sometimes lagged behind digital resources in providing clear guidance on how to cite these resources. Making citation easier will ensure that more collections are cited, increasing the visibility and impact measures for those collections.

Relatedly, cultural heritage institutions can work with DHers to involve the public on a wide range of projects and activities. A simple example is crowdsourcing, which leverages a large body of interested users to digitize, transcribe, organize or otherwise process materials. Many DH projects have relied on this technique to accomplish their work, and the communities associated with cultural heritage institutions may be quite large, allowing for new possibilities that DHers could not accomplish on their own. In addition, cultural heritage institutions have a long history of public programming, which can prove useful for DHers looking to make a public impact with their scholarship. Consultation with these institutions at any point in a project cycle can make a huge difference in planning and help advance the role of the humanities in a democratic society. By working together on projects that have a visible, public impact, DHers and cultural heritage professionals can offer a joint response to many of the austerity measures imposed on their respective institutions.

Conclusion

Humanists have complex motives for their scholarship. Some topics receive attention because humanists believe them to be worthy, independent of external factors such as the availability of source materials, trends in scholarship, funding, etc. Some topics receive attention simply because they *can* be studied: the primary source material exists, appropriate analytical methods are available, etc. Cultural heritage institutions play a major role in determining these extrinsic factors, particularly by making materials openly accessible in digital formats. In some cases, this may reflect a dramatic shift from older, gatekeeper models at particular institutions. By attending to the central values of DH, cultural heritage institutions may be able to bring their practices in line with a more open, connected, and diverse world.

Notes

1 At the time this chapter was first submitted (13 September 2013), the field seemed to lack any calls for alternative histories. I am pleased to see a shift in this direction and hope the charge is taken up by others.

2 At some points, Svensson (2012) appears open to pluralist histories of DH, discussing its epistemic traditions (plural) and describing the field as 'no tent', 'meeting place', and 'trading zone' (Galison, 1997). More often, he holds fast to the standard account.

3 It is curious to note that most of these authors come from an American background, while most of those discussed earlier come from a European background. This may point to regional differences in the way that the

history of DH is construed, and if so, it would be interesting to see how other areas of the globe line up on this issue.

4   One could also investigate the role of LAMs in particular early DH projects and draw larger conclusions from these cases. This could be an interesting part of ongoing work creating an oral history of DH (Nyhan and Welsh, 2013). I think this case-based approach would still need to account for the literature discussed here.

References

Adamson, M. (2012) Response to John Mowitt's 'Humanities and the University in Ruin', *Lateral*, **1**, http://lateral.culturalstudiesassociation.org/issue1/content/adamson.html.

Alvarado, R. (2011) The Digital Humanities Situation, *The Transducer*, http://transducer.ontoligent.com/?p=717.

Anderson, R. (2013) Can't Buy Us Love: the declining importance of library books and the rising importance of special collections, *Issue Briefs, Ithaka S+R*, www.sr.ithaka.org/blog-individual/cant-buy-us-love-rick-anderson-kicks-new-ithaka-sr-issue-briefs-series.

Auffret, G. and Prié, Y. (1999) Managing Full-indexed Audiovisual Documents: a new perspective for the humanities, *Computers and the Humanities*, **33** (4), 1 December, 319–44, DOI: 10.1023/A:1002477204396.

Ball, C. (2013) Digital Publishing in the Tradition of Making Within Writing Studies, *Digital Humanities 2013 conference*, Lincoln, Nebraska, http://prezi.com/8hrhbrqfw4fs/digital-publishing-in-the-tradition-of-making-within-writing-studies.

Bates, M. J. (2004) Information Science at the University of California at Berkeley in the 1960s: a memoir of student days, *Library Trends*, **52** (4), 683–701.

Bates, M. J, Wilde, D. N. and Siegfried, S. (1993) An Analysis of Search Terminology Used by Humanities Scholars: the Getty Online Searching Project Report Number 1, *The Library Quarterly*, **63** (1), 1–39.

Berry, D. M. (2012) Introduction: understanding the digital humanities. In Berry, D. M. (ed.), *Understanding the Digital Humanities*, New York, NY,

Palgrave Macmillan, 1–18.

Black, G. (1995) Film History and Film Archives, *Literature Film Quarterly*, **23** (2), 102–109.

Burdick, A., Drucker, J., Lunenfeld, P., Presner, T. and Schnapp, J. (2012) *Digital_Humanities*. Cambridge, MA, MIT Press.

Case, D. O. (2006) Information Seeking. In Cronin, B. (ed.), *Annual Review of Information Science and Technology*, **41**, Medford, NJ, Information Today, 293–326.

Conrad, A. H. and Meyer, J. R. (1958) The Economics of Slavery in the Ante Bellum South, *The Journal of Political Economy*, **66** (2), April, 95–130.

Dalbello, M. (2011) A Genealogy of Digital Humanities, *Journal of Documentation*, **67** (3), 26 April, 480–506, DOI: 10.1108/00220411111124550.

Davidson, C. N. (2008) Humanities 2.0: promise, perils, predictions, *PMLA*, **123** (3), May, 707–17, DOI: 10.1632/pmla.2008.123.3.707.

Dervin, B. and Nilan, M. (1986) Information Needs and Uses. In Williams, M. E. (ed.), *Annual Review of Information Science and Technology*, **21**, White Plains, NY, Knowledge Industry Publications, Inc., 3–33.

Dh+ lib (2013) *Make It New? A Dh+lib Mini-Series*, Pressbooks.com, http://zachcoble.com/dhlib/Make-It-New-A-dhlib-Mini-Series.pdf.

Evans, L. and Rees, S. (2012) An Interpretation of Digital Humanities. In Berry, D. M. (ed.), *Understanding the Digital Humanities*, New York, NY, Palgrave Macmillan, 21–41.

Fiormonte, D. (2012) Towards a Cultural Critique of the Digital Humanities, *Historical Social Research*, **37** (3), 59–76.

Fish, S. (2011) The Old Order Changeth, *The New York Times*, 26 December, http://opinionator.blogs.nytimes.com/2011/12/26/the-old-order-changeth.

Fish, S. (2012a) The Digital Humanities and the Transcending of Mortality, *The New York Times*, 9 January, http://opinionator.blogs.nytimes.com/2012/01/09/the-digital-humanities-and-the-transcending-of-mortality.

Fish, S. (2012b) Mind Your P's and B's: the digital humanities and interpretation, *New York Times*, 23 January, http://opinionator.blogs.nytimes.com/2012/01/23/mind-your-ps-and-bs-the-digital-humanities-and-interpretation.

Fitzpatrick, K. (2012) The Humanities, Done Digitally. In Gold, M. K. (ed.), *Debates in the Digital Humanities*, University of Minnesota Press, 12–15, http://dhdebates.gc.cuny.edu/debates/text/30.

Fogel, R. W. (1964) *Railroads and American Economic Growth: essays in econometric*, Johns Hopkins University Press.

Fogel, R. W. (1966) The New Economic History. I. Its findings and methods, *The Economic History Review*, **19** (3), 642, DOI: 10.2307/2593168.

Frabetti, F. (2012) Have the Humanities Always Been Digital? For an understanding of the 'digital humanities' in the context of originary technicity. In Berry, D. M. (ed.), *Understanding the Digital Humanities*, New York, NY, Palgrave Macmillan, 161–171.

Galison, P. (1997) *Image and Logic: a material culture of microphysics*, Chicago, University of Chicago Press.

Gold, M. K. (2012) The Digital Humanities Moment. In Gold, M. K. (ed.), *Debates in the Digital Humanities*, University of Minnesota Press, ix–xvi.

Hayles, N. K. (2012) How We Think: transforming power and digital technologies. In Berry, D. M. (ed.), *Understanding the Digital Humanities*, New York, NY, Palgrave Macmillan, 42–66.

Hockey, S. (2004) The History of Humanities Computing. In *A Companion to Digital Humanities*, Oxford, Blackwell, 1–19, http://onlinelibrary.wiley.com/doi/10.1002/9780470999875.ch1/summary.

Kirschenbaum, M. G. (2010) What Is Digital Humanities and What's It Doing in English Departments?, *ADE Bulletin*, **150**, 55–61.

Linmans, A. J. M. (2009) Why with Bibliometrics the Humanities Does Not Need to be the Weakest Link: indicators for research evaluation based on citations, library holdings, and productivity measures, *Scientometrics*, **83** (2), August, 337–54, DOI: 10.1007/s11192-009-0088-9.

Liu, A. (2012) Where is Cultural Criticism in the Digital Humanities? In Gold, M. K. (ed.), *Debates in the Digital Humanities*, University of Minnesota Press, 490–509, http://dhdebates.gc.cuny.edu/debates/text/20.

McCarty, W. (2005) *Humanities Computing*, Basingstoke and New York, NY, Palgrave Macmillan.

McPherson, T. (2009) Introduction: media studies and the digital humanities, *Cinema Journal*, **48** (2), 119–23, DOI: 10.1353/cj.0.0077.

McPherson, T. (2012) Why Are the Digital Humanities so White? or Thinking the Histories of Race and Computation. In Gold, M. K. (ed.), *Debates in the Digital Humanities*, University of Minnesota Press, 139–60, http://dhdebates.gc.cuny.edu/debates/text/29.

Manovich, L. (2012) How to Compare One Million Images? In Berry, D. M. (ed.), *Understanding the Digital Humanities*, New York, NY, Palgrave Macmillan, 249–78.

Marche, S. (2012) Literature is Not Data: against digital humanities, *Los Angeles Review of Books*, 28 October, http://lareviewofbooks.org/essay/literature-is-not-data-against-digital-humanities.

Moretti, F. (2005) *Graphs, Maps, Trees: abstract models for a literary history*, Brooklyn, NY, Verso.

Mowitt, J. (2012) The Humanities and the University in Ruin, *Lateral*, **1**, http://lateral.culturalstudiesassociation.org/issue1/content/mowitt.html.

Muñoz, T. (2013) In Service? A further provocation on digital humanities research in libraries, *dh+lib*, http://acrl.ala.org/dh/2013/06/19/in-service-a-further-provocation-on-digital-humanities-research-in-libraries.

National Endowment for the Humanities (NEH) (2010) *Digital Humanities Start-Up Grants*, 6 August, www.neh.gov/grants/guidelines/digitalhumanitiesstartup.html.

Nyhan, J. and Welsh, A. (2013) Uncovering the 'Hidden Histories' of Computing in the Humanities 1949–1980: findings and reflections on the pilot project, paper presented at the Digital Humanities conference, University of Nebraska–Lincoln, 16–19 July 2013, http://dh2013.unl.edu/abstracts/ab-200.html.

Presner, T. (2010) *Digital Humanities 2.0: a report on knowledge*, http://cnx.org/content/m34246/1.6.

Raben, J. and Burton, S. K. (1981) Information Systems and Services in the Arts and Humanities, *Annual Review of Information Science and Technology*, **16**, 247–66.

Ramsay, S. (2010) Care of the Soul, Lecture 8 October, Emory University, http://stephenramsay.us/text/2010/10/08/care-of-the-soul/.

Reagor, S. and Brown, W. S. (1978) The Application of Advanced Technology to Scholarly Communication in the Humanities, *Computers and the*

Humanities, **12** (3), 1 September 1, 237–46, DOI: 10.1007/BF02400084.

Rieder, B. and Röhle, T. (2012) Digital Methods: five challenges. In Berry, D. M. (ed.), *Understanding the Digital Humanities*, New York, NY, Palgrave Macmillan, 67–84.

Scheinfeldt, T. (2010a) Where's the Beef? Does digital humanities have to answer questions?, *Found History*, www.foundhistory.org/2010/05/12/ wheres-the-beef-does-digital-humanities-have-to-answer-questions.

Scheinfeldt, T. (2010b) Why Digital Humanities Is 'Nice', *Found History*, www.foundhistory.org/2010/05/26/.

Scheinfeldt, T. (2014) The Dividends of Difference: recognizing digital humanities' diverse family tree/s, *Found History*, www.foundhistory.org/2014/04/07/the-dividends-of-difference-recognizing-digital-humanities-diverse-family-trees.

Schreibman, S., Siemens, R. and Unsworth, J. (2004) *Companion to Digital Humanities*, Blackwell Companions to Literature and Culture, Oxford, Blackwell Publishing Professional, www.digitalhumanities.org/companion.

Showers, B. (2012) Does the Library Have a Role to Play in the Digital Humanities?, *JISC Digital Infrastructure Team*, http://infteam.jiscinvolve.org/wp/2012/02/23/does-the-library-have-a-role-to-play-in-the-digital-humanities.

Sibley, D. (2013) A Crisis in the Humanities?, *The Edge of the American West, The Chronicle of Higher Education*, 10 June, http://chronicle.com/blognetwork/ edgeofthewest/2013/06/10/the-humanities-crisis.

Siemens, R., Leitch, C., Blake, A., Armstrong, K. and Willinsky, J. (2009) 'It May Change My Understanding of the Field': understanding reading tools for scholars and professional readers, *Digital Humanities Quarterly*, **3** (4), www.digitalhumanities.org/dhq/vol/3/4/000075/000075.html.

Sinn, D. (2012) Impact of Digital Archival Collections on Historical Research, *Journal of the American Society for Information Science and Technology*, **63** (8), 1521–37, DOI: 10.1002/asi.22650.

Sitze, A. (2012) Response to John Mowitt's 'Humanities and the University in Ruin', *Lateral*, **1**, http://lateral.culturalstudiesassociation.org/issue1/ content/sitze.html.

Spiro, L. (2012) 'This Is Why We Fight': defining the values of the digital humanities. In Gold, M. K. (ed.), *Debates in the Digital Humanities*, University of Minnesota Press, 16–35, http://dhdebates.gc.cuny.edu/debates/text/13.

Stieg, M. F. (1981) Information Needs of Historians, *College & Research Libraries News*, **42**, November, 549–60.

Stone, S. (1982) Humanities Scholars: information needs and uses, *Journal of Documentation*, **38** (4), 31 December, 292–313, DOI: 10.1108/eb026734.

Sula, C. A. (2013) Digital Humanities and Libraries: a conceptual model, *Journal of Library Administration*, **53** (1), 10–26, DOI: 10.1080/01930826.2013.756680.

Svenonius, E. (2000) *The Intellectual Foundation of Information Organization*, MIT Press.

Svensson, P. (2009) Humanities Computing as Digital Humanities, *Digital Humanities Quarterly*, **3** (3), www.digitalhumanities.org/dhq/vol/3/3/000065/000065.html.

Svensson, P. (2010) The Landscape of Digital Humanities, *Digital Humanities Quarterly*, **4** (1), www.digitalhumanities.org/dhq/vol/4/1/000080/000080.html.

Svensson, P. (2012) Beyond the Big Tent. In Gold, M. K. (ed.), *Debates in the Digital Humanities*, University of Minnesota Press, 36–49, http://dhdebates.gc.cuny.edu/debates/text/22.

Tahir, M., Mahmood, K. and Shafique, F. (2010) Use of Electronic Information Resources and Facilities by Humanities Scholars, *The Electronic Library*, **28** (1), 16 February, 122–36, DOI: 10.1108/02640471011023423.

Talja, S. and Hartel, J. (2007) Revisiting the User-centred Turn in Information Science Research: an intellectual history perspective, *Information Research*, **12** (4), http://informationr.net/ir/12-4/colis/colis04.html#der06.

Warwick, C., Terras, M., Galina. I., Huntington, P. and Pappa, N. (2008) Library and Information Resources and Users of Digital Resources in the Humanities, *Program: Electronic Library and Information Systems*, **42** (1), 15 February, 5–27, DOI: 10.1108/00330330810851555.

Weingart, S. (2013) Acceptances to Digital Humanities 2013 (part 1), *The Scottbot Irregular*, www.scottbot.net/HIAL/?p=35242.

Whitson, R. (2012) *Does DH Really Need to Be Transformed? My reflections on #mla12*, www.rogerwhitson.net/?p=1358.

Wiberley, Jr., S. E. and Jones, W. G. (1989) Patterns of Information Seeking in the Humanities, *College & Research Libraries News*, **50** (6), 638–45.

Woodman, H. D., Fogel, R. W., Engerman, S. L., Parker, W. N., Davis, L. E. and North, D. C. (1972) Economic History and Economic Theory: the new economic history in America, *Journal of Interdisciplinary History*, **3** (2), 323, DOI: 10.2307/202334.

CHAPTER 3

Management of cultural heritage information: policies and practices

Gobinda Chowdhury

Northumbria University, UK

Introduction

As discussed in Chapter 1, managing digital cultural heritage information involves a number of challenges ranging from digitization of objects and artefacts to various knowledge organization and access issues that include metadata, indexing and retrieval; various user and social challenges such as information seeking and retrieval in the context of various community, culture, language, etc.; accessibility to ICT and internet, including digital divide and social exclusion; intellectual property and digital rights management issues; and so on.

Digitization – the process of converting analogue cultural heritage content into its digital form – is a resource-intensive activity and a successful digitization programme should be governed by a number of policy decisions. Since cultural heritage may include a wide variety of two- and three-dimensional objects in different forms, shapes and sizes with different specific characteristics and attributes, digitizing them in the most appropriate form poses a number of challenges. Terras (2012) argues that although mass digitization of cultural heritage objects began only a decade ago, small-scale initiatives in creating digital images of information objects in library and information institutions can be traced back to the early

1980s. However, she notes that massive digitization programmes began within the last decade with the introduction of major externally funded initiatives, such as the European eContentplus programme (European Commission, 2014) and the Jisc Content Digitization programme (Jisc, 2013). In order to support digitization activities a variety of best-practice guidelines have been produced over the past decade by experts (see, for example, Hughes, 2004; Anderson and Maxwell, 2004; Puglia and Rhodes, 2007) as well as institutions (see, for example, various guidelines that appeared under The Federal Agencies Digitization Guidelines Initiative (FADGI, 2014), the British Library Digitisation Strategy (British Library, 2014) and the Jisc Digitization Workflow Guidelines (Abu-Zayed, 2009). This chapter discusses some of these policies and guidelines for digitization that form the foundation of digital libraries of cultural heritage information.

Managing digital cultural heritage information also involves a number of social, legal and policy issues. There is a general consensus that cultural heritage information should be made available to everyone for social good. However, there are a number of intellectual property and digital rights management issues. Tsolis et al. (2011) discuss the complex copyright and digital rights management issues and challenges associated with digital cultural heritage information. There are also some ownership and cultural sensitivity issues. For example, specific government policies and guidelines have been formulated for handling – both for the information professionals as well as the potential users – of cultural heritage information related to specific indigenous communities in countries like Australia and New Zealand. This chapter discusses some of these policies and their implications. It also discusses the provenance and digital rights management issues associated with cultural heritage information.

Cultural heritage information resources

As discussed in Chapter 1, cultural heritage information resources may include a wide variety of content, objects and artefacts, including books, journals and newspapers, photographs, museum objects, archival documents, sound and audiovisual material, and monuments and archaeological sites. Most of these information resources are available in analogue form and hence digitization is the first step in building a digital library or information services of cultural heritage information. A variety of tools, techniques and standards are used for digitization of cultural heritage information some of which have been discussed by Terras in this book (in Chapter 4), and elsewhere (Terras, 2012). However, such digitization activities are very resource-intensive activities. Furthermore, in order to make the digital resources suitable for easy access and management, a number of policies and guidelines have been formulated. Some such policies and guidelines are discussed in the following sections, not to provide an exhaustive review, but to point out some salient features of such policies.

Digitization policies and guidelines

Digitization is a complex process with many crucial dependencies between different stakeholders, and therefore using a holistic lifecycle approach for digitization initiatives is needed to develop sustainable and successful digitization projects (Beagrie, n.d.). Clearly articulated intentions could be a good starting point for a digitization and digital preservation programme, and it should be an ongoing process requiring proactive management and periodic review (Webb, Pearson and Koerbin, 2013).

The US Library of Congress guidelines suggest that a digitization programme should be guided by the following basic questions:

- What is the purpose of the digitizing project?
- Who will be the users of the digital surrogates?
- How will the digital surrogates be presented?
- What will be the effect on the original collection item of making the digital surrogate?
- How will the digital files be accessed and stored?

Library of Congress, 2014b

However, since information services and their resources are primarily directed for meeting the needs of the present generation of users, projects for digitization of content keeping in view the interests of the future generations may not be a priority for many cultural institutions and funding bodies. The Blue Ribbon Task Force (BRTF) Report (2010) notes that the interests of future users are poorly represented in selecting materials to preserve. It also points out that libraries, archives, museums, professional organizations and others can play important roles in identifying the demand of their stakeholders and this can feed into the decisions for preservation. The report recommends that sustainable approaches to managing digital information assets for suitable access by the current and future generations require the mobilization of human, technical, and financial resources across a spectrum of stakeholders.

Focusing on the cost of massive digitization and digital preservation programmes, the BRTF Report (2010) provides the following specific guidelines:

- Articulate compelling value proposition, e.g., who will be using the digital information, for what purpose and what will be the benefits of such use, etc.
- Provide clear incentives to preserve in the public interest. This can be achieved by
  — building appropriate policy mechanisms such as financial incentives and other benefits to private owners who preserve digital materials for the benefit of the public
  — mandates to preserve when appropriate
  — revision of the prevalent copyright laws to enable preservation of privately owned materials in the interest of the public.
- Define roles and responsibilities among stakeholders in order to clearly identify the activities and the associated workflow throughout the digital lifecycle.

Although the various issues and the associated guidelines, discussed above, have been specifically meant for digital preservation programmes, they can guide any digitization programmes that aim to convert analogue content to their digital form for better, wider and easier access for present and future generations.

The US Federal Agencies Digitization Guidelines Initiative was formed in 2007 as a group of federal agencies engaged in defining common guidelines, methods and practices to digitize historical content in a sustainable manner. It operates as two specialized working groups: the *Federal Agencies Still Image Digitization Working Group*, which focuses on image content such as books, manuscripts, maps, and photographic prints and negatives; and (2) the *Federal Agencies Audio-Visual Working Group*, focusing on sound, video, and motion picture film. All the activities of these working groups are guided by a common philosophical framework, mentioned below, that can form the basis of any mass digitization initiative (FADGI, 2014):

- Digitization guidelines should be based on clearly articulated objectives describing the expected uses of the digitized content.
- Digitization methodologies and requirements should be based on recognized approved standards or empirical data to the extent possible.
- All digitization related activities must be prioritized by project forecasts and a robust guideline.
- All digitization efforts should be conducted in a transparent manner so that other agencies can undertake such activities with a clear understanding of what needs to be done, why and how.
- Digitization activities should engage all the stakeholders, and hence all the participating members should actively seek input from public, governmental and academic institutions, as well as corporate entities and trade organizations.

Public-private partnership and collaborations at different stages of digitization have been identified as the primary means to meet the demands for huge resources required for mass digitization projects. However, when private partners are involved, specific mechanisms should be built to support their interests, which may be different from those of the public sector funders. A Jisc (2010) report points out that there is a particular risk of 'free riding' with digital materials because the cost of digitization may be borne by one organization but the benefits may accrue to many. Therefore 'effective governance mechanisms are needed to aggregate the collective interest into an effective preservation strategy that ensures that the effort and cost of preservation are appropriately apportioned' (Jisc, 2010).

The need for collaborations and the supporting mechanisms for digitization and preservation of cultural heritage information have been highlighted in several EC directives and guidelines. The *Digital Agenda for Europe* initiative (European Commission, 2014) points out that online accessibility of Europe's cultural heritage requires the right conditions for proceeding with digitization, online accessibility and the preservation of cultural content; and this requires close collaboration between EU member states and cultural institutions, and also between these cultural institutions and other stakeholders. The Council of the European Union in its 'Conclusions on the digitization and online accessibility of cultural material and digital preservation', of 20 April 2012, invites the European member states to:

- Consolidate their strategies and targets for the digitisation of cultural material;
- Consolidate the organisation and provision of funding for digitisation, promoting public-private partnerships;
- Improve the framework conditions for the online accessibility and use of cultural material;
- Contribute to the further development of Europeana, the Europeana Digital Library and
- To ensure long-term digital preservation.

Council of the European Union, 2012, 5

What to digitize and why?

The digitization policy of the National Library of Australia (National Library of Australia, 2014a) provides the following guidelines for selection of content for digitization that are based on certain specific attributes of content, for example:

- content of cultural and/or historical significance
- content with certain uniqueness and/or rarity of the material
- content in high demand
- content at risk because of its physical condition
- content at risk because of impending format obsolescence, such as sound and audiovisual recordings.

The European Commission's Recommendations also provide similar guidelines for selection of cultural heritage objects in the context of the Europeana digital library (Europa, 2011):

- content that are the most beautiful, historic or highly regarded items
- content that users most often want to consult or view
- content that are hidden treasures, for example little-known items that could be enormously attractive to users once digitized
- items that are too fragile for uses to consult, or to be displayed.

In addition to these generic guidelines, some specific guidelines have also been provided by different agencies. For example, the digitization policy of the National Library of Australia (2014a) recommends that only those items should be digitized for which copyright status is suitable for digitization or the appropriate permission to digitize has been obtained. The European Commission recommendations on the digitization of cultural heritage information in Europe suggests that appropriate mechanisms should be developed so that (Europa, 2011):

- the same objects from different collections should not be not digitized twice

- related collections are digitized in a shared context.

The European Commission's Recommendations on the digitization of cultural materials (European Commission, 2011) point out the following benefits of the digitization of cultural memory:

1   Digitization is an important means for ensuring greater access to, and use of, cultural material.
2   The online accessibility of cultural material will make it possible for citizens throughout Europe to access and use it for leisure, studies or work.
3   It will give Europe's diverse and multilingual heritage a clear profile on the internet.
4   Digitization of their assets will help Europe's cultural institutions to continue carrying out their mission of giving access to and preserving Europe's culture and heritage in the digital environment.

The digitization strategy of the British Library identifies similar benefits of digitization but they are more clearly stated for better access by the current and future generations (British Library, 2014):

1 Access to content:
   - 'open up access to content in the British Library's collection
   - add value to, and open up previously unimagined areas for research
   - support innovative methods of research
   - facilitate the interpretation of our content by others for new audiences'
   - transform discoverability of our content
   - 'make our content more visible and increase use
   - reveal illegible and hidden text or images and permit non-intrusive testing of materials.'
2 Preservation:
   - 'preserve unique, rare and fragile heritage items by digital reproduction and protect vulnerable documents.'

As discussed, one of the major goals of a digitization programme is to provide easy access to cultural information and knowledge to the general public, or to specific communities of users. These may be classed as the educational and social benefits of digitization. However, there are several immediate and long-term economic benefits of digitization as well. Some of these economic benefits may be realized through the immediate job creation associated with the digitization and related activities, but the longer-term benefits may arise from the commercial use of the digitized information resources, or through the development of a better workforce.

Digital cultural heritage information can contribute to the economy and businesses in a number of ways. It is estimated that creative industries account for 3.3% of GDP and 3% of employment in EU (European Commission, 2011). According to the Department of Media, Culture and Sport, creative industry is the UK's fastest-growing sector, worth £71.4bn a year and making up 5.6% of the workforce (BBC News, 2014). However, it is noted that creative industries are faced with 'a digital transition that is shaking up traditional models, transforming value chains and calling for new business models. Digitizing and providing wider access to cultural resources offers enormous economic opportunities and is an essential condition for the further development of Europe's cultural and creative capacities and of its industrial presence in this field' (European Commission, 2011). Thus it can be expected that with the development of appropriate mechanisms for addressing the digital rights management, digital cultural heritage content can be used for developing learning and educational content, documentaries, tourism applications, games, animations and design tools.

In its report the Comité des Sages highlighted several areas in which digitized cultural content can stimulate economic growth and job creation, including:

- **In the digitisation process itself and the technologies linked to it.** If European companies can develop the most efficient technologies and working methods in this field, they will be the first to benefit from public contracts for digitisation. The process of digitisation is also labour-intensive and will generate new jobs.

- **As raw material for services and products in areas such as tourism, education and new technologies.** The arrival of millions of new digitised cultural works online is likely to spur a wave of innovation and new business models for companies specialised in various stages of the digitisation chain. One example is Arkhopôle, based in the French Aquitaine region. It is a cluster of 125 SMEs who collaborate with cultural institutions and universities. They specialise in the creation and commercialisation of cultural content and try to develop a new market for digital heritage material.

Europa, 2011

However the potential commercial use of cultural heritage information brings forth the issues of digital rights management, and appropriate mechanisms for access and use/re-use of cultural heritage content. In the UK the recently launched Digital Copyright Hub, currently in its test phase (Copyright Hub, 2014), is designed to help people and businesses deal with the digital rights management issues associated with the commercial use of digital cultural heritage content.

A summary of guidelines for managing cultural heritage information

As discussed so far in this chapter, appropriate policies and guidelines have to be formulated and followed for all the activities related to digitization and digital preservation of cultural heritage content, and the resulting digital cultural heritage information services. While the reasons for digitization and selection of cultural heritage materials for digitization can be guided by the principles and guidelines discussed in the previous two sections, a number of other guidelines have been formulated to address some specific issues associated with building digital cultural heritage information services. These are discussed in the following sections.

Managing resources for digitization

The fact that digitization, preservation and provision of information services based on cultural heritage information are extremely resource-intensive activities has been well recognized. For example, it is estimated that the digitization cost of cultural heritage information in Europe could be €100 billion (Europa, 2011). Hence partnership, collaborations and resource-sharing activities have been recommended in many policy guidelines, for example:

- Funding models for all digitization and digital preservation activities should be tailored to the norms and expectations of anticipated users (Jisc, 2010).
- National governments, for example EU member states, should put in place appropriate plans for their investments in digitization (Europa, 2011). However, such investments can also bring in some returns, for example, in the form of new job creation directly through digitization and information service-related activities. The indirect economic benefits may arise through the use of the digitized content by creative industries or for specialist education and research applications, and so on.
- In order to meet the huge resource requirements, the efficient use of digitization capacity and, where possible, the sharing of digitization equipment between cultural institutions and countries should be encouraged (Europa, 2011).
- Public–private partnerships for digitization should be encouraged, and national governments in the EU countries should foster public–private partnerships in order to share the gigantic cost of digitization (Europa, 2011).

However, in order to successfully build public–private partnerships, it is necessary to build appropriate mechanisms so that each stakeholder can achieve their own objectives. For example, wherever public investment is involved, it is expected that the resulting digital content should be available free of cost at the point of use. However, a mechanism may have to be built for recovering costs, or return on investment, where such content is used exclusively for commercial purposes. Similarly, interests of the private partners should also be protected. The EC directive in this regard makes the following recommendations (Europa, 2011):

- Public funding for future digitization should be conditional on the accessibility of the digitized material through Europeana, and existing metadata should be widely and freely available for re-use.
- Preferential use of digitized material by private partners should not exceed seven years.

Access to digitized content

As discussed earlier, the main purpose of any digitization or digital preservation programme is to facilitate access to cultural heritage content. The digitization policy of the Australian National Library clearly states that:

> We aspire to document Australia's cultural, intellectual and social life by collecting, storing and preserving Australian print and digital publishing, personal papers, paintings, photographs, maps and oral histories.
>
> National Library of Australia, 2014b

Similarly, American Memory, a service of the US Library of Congress, has been created to provide:

> free and open access through the Internet to written and spoken words, sound recordings, still and moving images, prints, maps, and sheet music that document the American experience. It is a digital record of American history and creativity. These materials, from the collections of the Library of Congress and other institutions, chronicle historical events, people, places, and ideas that continue to shape America, serving the public as a resource for education and lifelong learning.
>
> Library of Congress, 2014a

The Digital Agenda recommendation of the European Commission (Europa, 2011) clearly states that the Europeana digital library should become the central reference point for Europe's online cultural heritage. It is further recommended that it is necessary to ensure that

> public domain content remains in the public domain once digitized, and the use of intrusive watermarks or other visual protection measures on copies of public domain material as a sign of ownership or provenance should be avoided.
>
> Europa, 2011

However, understanding the user needs in a specific context, for example in the context of cultural heritage information, and building that into the information access systems is a challenging task. The Digital Agenda recommendation of the European Commission (Europa, 2011) points out that access to and use of digitized cultural material in the public domain needs to be improved. The British Library Digitization Strategy outlines some specific activities related to understanding user needs and improving access to information in the following terms:

- We will seek to understand the needs of our users and meet them as resources permit in terms of the collections that we digitise and the means of resource discovery that we provide.
- We will develop, refine and monitor interactions with our digitised collections using a range of tools, and will use the feedback to improve the experience.
- We will continue to investigate the digitisation landscape to ensure that we contribute to a growing corpus of national, European and international digital content.

> British Library, 2014

Over the past few years there have been some useful research and development activities not only at the British Library but by other institutions and experts around the world that are directed towards making cultural digital library and information services more useful. Some of these issues are discussed in Chapters 4 and 9 of this book.

Legal issues

IP (intellectual property) rights such as copyright, patents and trademarks are some of the relevant legal frameworks that are designed to protect the output of human intellectual activities. In summary, they (WIPO, 2003):

- establish economic rights in creations and innovations in order to grant control over their exploitation, particularly commercial exploitation
- provide incentives for further creation and dissemination of the intellectual output of human creativity
- facilitate the lawful and orderly functioning of markets through the avoidance of confusion and deception
- safeguard the integrity and rights of attribution to certain works and creations
- protect undisclosed information from bad faith use or appropriation
- monetize IP assets, generate revenue when used strategically in a market context.

It should be noted that IP rights are not designed to prevent others from using content that is protected, but rather they enable lawful use of content through the licensing of IP assets. In other words, IP rights ensure that the creators of protected content get their due economic benefits and credits, but at the same time create a mechanism for lawful use of the protected content; so in a way it builds a bridge between the creators and consumers of intellectual output.

Prior to the early 1980s, 'cultural property' was invoked largely to denote portable works of art and architectural monuments that embodied the history and identity of particular peoples or nation-states (Brown, 2005). In today's world, ICT, web, social networking and allied technologies provide multiple and unprecedented ways for cultural products to be created, replicated, exchanged and used. The scope of creation and dissemination of cultural heritage information has also expanded due to the emerging web, mobile and social networking technologies.

The World Intellectual Property Organization recommends that the intellectual property management of cultural heritage content should be guided by issues such as (WIPO, 2003):

- the preservation and safeguarding of cultural heritage
- the promotion of cultural diversity
- the respect for cultural rights
- the promotion of creativity and innovation as ingredients of sustainable economic development.

Establishing the ownership and copyright of source content, and digital rights management issues, have remained at the core of digitization, digital preservation and digital information management activities. However, this is a rather complex area and hence appropriate guidelines need to be built and followed. The following specific recommendations of the European Commission make these points quite clear:

- Since intellectual property rights are a key tool to stimulate creativity, Europe's cultural material should be digitised, made available and preserved in full respect of copyright and related rights.
- The conditions for the digitisation and online accessibility of in-copyright material need to be improved to avoid the absence of recent and contemporary material online.
- Get more in-copyright material online, by – for example – creating the legal framework conditions enabling large-scale digitisation and cross-border accessibility of out-of-commerce works.
- For the large-scale digitisation of out-of-commerce works, legislative backing for licensing solutions voluntarily developed by stakeholders may be needed in the Member States, taking into account the need to ensure a cross-border effect.

- Rights information databases connected at European level can bring down transaction costs for rights clearance. Such mechanisms should therefore be encouraged in close cooperation with all stakeholders.

  European Commission, 2011

A survey of the IP-related codes, protocols, policies, practices and standard agreements created by various agencies around the world in relation to the safeguarding of, access to, ownership of, and control over, cultural heritage content is available on the WIPO website (WIPO, 2014).

The Hargreaves Review

Acknowledging the fact that the current IP laws do not adequately support the growth of the digital economy, the UK Prime Minister commissioned a review in 2010 under the chairmanship of Professor Ian Hargreaves. The report, known as the *The Hargreaves Review of Intellectual Property and Growth*, or *Digital Opportunity – a review of Intellectual Property and Growth*, appeared in May 2011. It reviewed the UK IP laws in the context of digital economy and made several recommendations for modifications. It noted that:

- Digital technology is probably the most important and transformative technology of our time. Because digital is fundamentally an information and communication technology (ICT), intellectual property rights lie at its heart. Not only has ICT adoption and use been among the strongest drivers of growth, but it has pushed content and communication technology into new uses, meaning the IP system has become part of people's daily lives.
- Because copyright governs the right to own and use data and information, as well as the output of authors, musicians, photographers and film makers, copyright law is now of primary interest to players across the whole of the knowledge economy, not just those involved in the creative industries. Digital technologies are

based on copying, so copyright becomes their regulator: a role it was never designed to perform.

Hargreaves, 2011, 13, 14

The *Hargreaves Review* made 10 specific recommendations, some with many sub-sections. Of these, a major, and probably the most significant, recommendation was for creation of a Digital Copyright Exchange (DCE). The report recommended that:

> In order to boost UK firms' access to transparent, contestable and global digital markets, the UK should establish a cross sectoral Digital Copyright Exchange.

Hargreaves, 2011, 8

Digital Copyright Hub

In response to the Hargreaves Review, the UK government commissioned a feasibility study that came up with a detailed report and a series of recommendations in July 2012 (Hooper and Lynch, 2012). This report defined a Digital Copyright Exchange (DCE) as 'an automated online web-based computer system that allows licensors to offer their rights and allows licensees/rights users to license them' (Hooper and Lynch, 2012, 8). The feasibility report identified six major functions of DCE that would allow rights users to:

1. Look for different types of content across the range of media types
2. Define and agree what uses they wish to make of the chosen content with the licensors
3. Be quoted a price by the licensor for those uses of the specified content that the system is programmed to offer
4. Pay for the rights online within the normal e-commercial framework
5. Have the content delivered to them in the appropriate format
6. Account back to the licensor as to what content was actually used so that the right creators can be paid their shares.

Hooper and Lynch, 2012, 12

It may be noted that a similar idea had been put forward by Chowdhury and his associates over the past few years (see for example, Chowdhury, 2009; Chowdhury and Fraser, 2011). They called it CSN (Content Service Network), which would have an almost similar set of functions to those of DCE:

> a content service network (CSN) that will be complementary to traditional channels for content, will enable users to choose information from a myriad of information channels and sources, with sufficient levels of granularity, required for their use, and produce a new information package for access and distribution through a variety of media – institutional or personal computers, handheld devices, on-demand print, and so on, within the framework of a new and easy to implement business model.
>
> Chowdhury, 2009, 216

The Hooper and Lynch (2012) report recommended the creation of:

> a not-for-profit, industry-led Copyright Hub based in the UK that links interoperably and scalably to the growing national and international network of private and public sector digital copyright exchanges, rights registries and other copyright-related databases, using agreed cross-sectoral and cross-border data building blocks and standards, based on voluntary, opt-in, non-exclusive and pro-competitive principles.
>
> Hooper and Lynch, 2012, 5

The report further recommended that the Copyright Hub should be easy to navigate, accessible and an authoritative port of call for all, especially SMEs and individual users, but also larger companies who need better and cheaper access to copyright licensing.

It is believed that the digital copyright exchanges and a Copyright Hub will bring a tremendous opportunity for both the content creators and content users in terms of digital content distribution and access, and this will boost the digital economy through better education and research, and through promotion of content-intensive businesses. As mentioned in the

Hargreaves Review, in the subsequent Hooper and Lynch report and also in the studies of Chowdhury and his associates (Chowdhury, 2009; Chowdhury and Fraser, 2011), this will create an online content marketplace where side by side the content from commercial content producers – book and journal publishers, music companies, etc. – small content creators such as individual authors, musicians, photographers, artists, and performers will be able to make their content available online, and the users can choose such content lawfully within the specific terms of access set by the content creators/producers.

The Digital Copyright Hub in the UK (www.copyrighthub.co.uk) went live on 8 July 2013. It links the users to the relevant parts of the websites so that they can find out about the copyright of a content – text, images, music, video and multimedia. It allows the users to learn who owns what rights for a specific content. It also allows the users get permission to use specifically defined types of works for a specific purpose. Over a period of time this can become one of the world's large online content marketplaces, providing a level playing field for all kinds of content creators and producers to do their business lawfully, and giving the users an opportunity to choose and use content easily and lawfully. The work on the Copyright Hub is in progress, and as the site says, phase 2 of the Copyright Hub will include more organizations.

Indigenous cultural heritage information

As discussed earlier, resolving copyright issues is a prerequisite to any digitization programme, and usually negotiations and copyright clearance processes pose one of the major challenges for digitization programmes. However, there is another major challenge where indigenous heritage content is concerned, when a separate level of engagement and negotiation is required. Indigenous cultural heritage content may include photographs, oral histories, films, geographic and genealogical information and flora and fauna (Francis and Liew, 2009). 'What is in the legal "public domain" for one culture can be sacred for another', comment Francis and Liew while studying the gaps, and sometimes conflicts, between the common copyright laws and access policies in the context of indigenous cultural heritage information. The World Intellectual Property Organization (WIPO) recommends that:

> Challenges of multiculturalism and cultural diversity, particularly in societies with both indigenous and immigrant communities, require cultural policies that maintain a balance between the protection and preservation of cultural expressions – traditional or otherwise – and the free exchange of cultural experiences. Mediating between the preservation of cultural heritage and cultural distinctiveness on the one hand, and the nurturing and nourishing of 'living' culture as a source of creativity and development on the other, is another challenge.
>
> WIPO, 2003

Francis and Liew (2009) comment that as a number of cultural heritage institutions 'hold substantial collections of Indigenous cultural knowledge such as the case in Australia, New Zealand, North America, Latin America and northern parts of Europe, it is essential that these institutions build digital collections in consultation with Indigenous communities, putting in place internationally acceptable guidelines, policies and practices'. WIPO (2003) acknowledges that indigenous communities often feel that:

- their cultural expressions and representations are used without authority in disrespectful and inappropriate ways, causing cultural offence and harm
- on many occasions while indigenous communities are unable to acquire IP protection over their cultural heritage and traditional cultures, others from outside the community acquire IP protection for creations and innovations derived from and inspired by their cultural heritage.

Thus two major issues need to be considered in the context of the management of indigenous cultural heritage information. First it is to be ensured that access to, and use of, indigenous heritage information by the wider community is in no way disrespectful of the cultural values of the source community. Second, wider access and use of indigenous cultural heritage resources should not cause the source indigenous community some material harm, either by denying it legitimate economic benefits or by undermining shared understandings essential to its social and cultural health.

Nakata et al. (2008) comment that indigenous customary rules for knowledge access can place clan, moiety, age, gender, initiate status, role and specialization restrictions on access to certain knowledge. They further point out that 'increasingly, the original or descendant Indigenous custodians of knowledge held in collections seek to negotiate the terms of access and use of Indigenous materials through negotiations over forms of representations, attributions and appropriate use of some materials'.

Francis and Liew (2009) observe that the issue for protecting cultural heritage is multilayered and complex, especially where specific legislation exists at the state and national levels, and at an international level such as those from WIPO, the International Labour Organization (ILO) and the United Nations Educational, Scientific and Cultural Organization (UNESCO).

The National Aboriginal and Torres Strait Islander arts policy acknowledges 'the Aboriginal people and Torres Strait Islanders of Australia as the traditional owners and custodians of Australia and its territories' (Australian Government, 2014). There is a major difference between the conventional view, often called the Western world's view, of copyright and ownership of heritage information and that of indigenous communities across the world. Oguamanam (2009) comments that the TRIPS Agreement (the Agreement on Trade-Related Aspects of Intellectual Property Rights) has left the traditional knowledge of indigenous communities vulnerable to misappropriation by outsiders. Only proper consultation with members of the representative indigenous groups can provide a good understanding of the cultural sensitivity of indigenous heritage information, and thus appropriate measures can be taken for managing it. Francis and Liew provide the following examples of such arrangements:

> Some of these groups were placed within the organisation itself such as the State Library of Queensland's *State Library's Indigenous Advisory Committee and the Torres Strait Islander Reference Group*. The Auckland Museum has a *Taumata-a-Iwi* (Māori Advisory group) and a *Maori values team* and the National Library of New Zealand have an independent group *Te Komiti Māori* and also the *Guardians/Kaitiaki of the Alexander Turnbull Library* established under the *National Library of New Zealand (Te Puna Mātauranga o Aotearoa) Act 2003*. These groups play an important part in representing the Indigenous point of view for policy creation and other Indigenous issues at the institutions guiding not only users of the collection, but the management of these artefacts as an evolving and continuing process.
>
> Francis and Liew, 2009

Summary

As discussed in this chapter, building and managing a digital library of cultural heritage information is a resource-intensive process. There is a massive economic cost of digitization, which is estimated to be €100 billion for European cultural heritage material alone. In addition, a significant amount of ongoing cost is associated with the preservation of digital content in order to ensure access by future generations. Consequently digitization and digital preservation activities need to be guided by appropriate policies. As discussed in this chapter, several such guidelines and policies have been developed by various national and international agencies. Such documents provide a number of guidelines, ranging from the selection of materials to their digitization, indexing, management and preservation.

In addition to a number of educational, research and social benefits, cultural heritage information can also play a key role in the digital economy by opening up various opportunities for commercial use of cultural heritage content. However, in order to ensure that this is done lawfully and also to the benefit of the creators of such content, appropriate IP laws and mechanisms should be developed to support their easy use or re-use. Fortunately such policies and mechanisms are being built at the national and international level, for example through the establishment of the Copyright Hub in Britain, or by the mechanisms built within the Europeana digital library for commercial use of cultural heritage content. These issues are discussed in more detail in Chapter 11.

References

Abu-Zayed, A. (2009) *Digitisation Workflow and Guidelines: digitisation processes*, University of Exeter, https://projects.exeter.ac.uk/charter/documents/ DigitisationWorkflowGuidev5.pdf.

Anderson, C. G. and Maxwell, D. C. (2004) *Starting a Digitization Centre*, Chandos Publishing.

Australian Government (2014) *National Aboriginal and Torres Strait Islander Arts Policy*, www.australiacouncil.gov.au/about/policies/national_aboriginal_ and_torres_strait_islander_arts_policy.

BBC News (2014) *UK's Creative Industries Beat Employment Downturn*, 15 January, www.bbc.co.uk/news/entertainment-arts-25742231.

Beagrie, N. (n.d.). *Going Digital: issues in digitisation for public libraries*, Earl: the Consortium of Public Libraries Networking, www.ukoln.ac.uk/public/earl/issuepapers/digitisation.htm.

Blue Ribbon Task Force on Sustainable Digital Preservation and Access (2010) *Final Report*, February, http://brtf.sdsc.edu/publications.html.

British Library (2014) *Digitisation Strategy, 2008–2011*, www.bl.uk/aboutus/stratpolprog/digi/digitisation/digistrategy.

Brown, M. F. (2005) Heritage Trouble: recent work on the protection of intangible cultural property, *International Journal of Cultural Property*, **12**, 40–61, DOI: 10.1017/S0940739105050010.

Chowdhury, G. G. (2009) Towards the Conceptual Model of a Content Service Network. In *Globalizing Academic Libraries Vision 2020*, Proceedings of the International Conference on Academic Libraries, Delhi, 5–8 October, 2009, Delhi Mittal Publications, 215–20.

Chowdhury, G. G. and Fraser, M. (2011) Carbon Footprint of the Knowledge

Industry and Ways to Reduce It, *World Digital Libraries*, **4** (1), 9–18.

Copyright Hub (2014) *Your Gateway to Information About Copyright*, www.copyrighthub.co.uk.

Council of the European Union (2012) *Draft Council Conclusions on the Digitisation and Online Accessibility of Cultural Material and Digital Reservation: adoption of Council conclusions*, Brussels, 20 April, https://ec.europa.eu/digital-agenda/sites/digital-agenda/files/Council%27s%20conclusions_0.pdf.

Europa (2011) *Digital Agenda: recommendation on the digitisation of cultural material and its preservation on line – frequently asked questions*, European Commission, MEMO/11/745 28/10/2011, http://europa.eu/rapid/press-release_MEMO-11-745_en.htm?locale=en.

European Commission (2011) Commission Recommendation of 27 October on the Digitisation and Online Accessibility of Cultural Material and Digital Preservation (2011/711/EU), *Official Journal of the European Union*, http://eur-lex.europa.eu/LexUriServ/LexUriServ.do?uri= OJ:L:2011:283:0039:0045:EN:PDF.

European Commission (2014) *Digital Agenda for Europe: a Europe 2020 initiative. Digitization and digital preservation*, http://ec.europa.eu/digital-agenda/en/digitisation-digital-preservation.

FADGI (2014) *Federal Agencies Digitization Guidelines Initiative*, www.digitizationguidelines.gov.

Francis, K. D. and Liew, C-L. (2009) Digitised Indigenous Knowledge in Cultural Heritage Organisations in Australia and New Zealand: an examination of policy and protocols, *Proceedings of the American Society for Information Science and Technology*, **46** (1), 1–21, https://www.asis.org/Conferences/AM09/open-proceedings/papers/5.html.

Hargreaves, I. (2011) *Digital Opportunity: a review of intellectual property and growth. An independent report*, May, https://www.gov.uk/government/publications/digital-opportunity-review-of-intellectual-property-and-growth.

Hooper, R. and Lynch, R. (2012) *Copyright Works: streamlining copyright licensing for the digital age. An independent report*, July, www.copyrighthub.uk/Documentsdce-report-phase2.pdf.

Hughes, L. (2004) *Digitizing Collections: strategic issues for the information manager*, Facet Publishing.

Jisc (2010) *Sustainable Economics for a Digital Planet: ensuring long term access to digital information*, www.jisc.ac.uk/publications/reports/2010/blueribbontaskforcefinalreport.aspx.

Jisc (2013) *Digitisation and Content*, www.jisc.ac.uk/digitisation.

Library of Congress (2014a) *American Memory: mission and history*, http://memory.loc.gov/ammem/about/index.html.

Library of Congress (2014b) *Collections Care: preservation guidelines for digitizing library materials*, www.loc.gov/preservation/care/scan.html.

Nakata, M., Nakata, V., Gardiner, G., McKeough, J., Byrne, A. and Gibson, J. (2008) Indigenous Digital Collections: an early look at the organisation and culture interface, *Australian Academic & Research Libraries*, **39** (4), 223–36, DOI: 10.1080/00048623.2008.10721360.

National Library of Australia (2014a) *Collection Digitisation Policy*, https://www.nla.gov.au/policy-and-planning/collection-digitisation-policy.

National Library of Australia (2014b) *Strategic Direction 2012–2014*, www.nla.gov.au/corporate-documents/directions.

Oguamanam, C. (2009) Documentation and Digitization of Traditional Knowledge and Intangible Cultural Knowledge: challenges and prospects (2009). In Kono, T. (ed.), *Intangible Cultural Heritage and Intellectual Property: cultural diversity and sustainable development*, Antwerp, Intersentia, 357–83, http://ssrn.com/abstract=2296199.

Puglia, S. and Rhodes, E. (2007) Digital Imaging: how far have we come and what still needs to be done?, *RLG DigiNews*, **11** (1), 15 April, www.rlg.org/en/page.php?Page_ID=21033.

Terras, M. (2012) Digitization and Digital Resources in the Humanities. In Warwick, C., Terras, M. and Nyhan, J. (eds), *Digital Humanities in Practice*, Facet Publishing, 47–70.

Tsolis, D., Sioutas, S., Xenos, M. N. and Styliaras, G. (2011) Copyright and IPR Management for Cultural Heritage Digital Content in Peer-to-peer Networks, *Journal of Cultural Heritage*, **12** (4), 466–75.

Webb, C., Pearson, D. and Koerbin, P. (2013) 'Oh, You Wanted Us to Preserve That?!' Statements of preservation intent for the National Library of Australia's digital collections, *D-Lib Magazine*, **19** (1/2), www.dlib.org/dlib/january13/webb/01webb.print.html.

WIPO (World Intellectual Property Organization) (2003) *Consolidated Analysis of the Legal Protections of Traditional Cultural Expressions/ Expressions of Folklore*, www.wipo.int/export/sites/www/freepublications/en/tk/785/wipo_pub_785.pdf.

WIPO (World Intellectual Property Organization) (2014) *Surveys of Existing Practices, Protocols and Policies*, www.wipo.int/tk/en/resources/surveys.html.

CHAPTER 4

Cultural heritage information: artefacts and digitization technologies

Melissa Terras

University College London, UK

Introduction

Since the 1970s, the gallery, library, archive and museum sector has promoted and encouraged digitization – the conversion of analogue into digital information – to increase access to cultural heritage material through various incarnations of digital media. Indeed, it is now expected by both users and professionals that institutions should be undertaking digitization programmes, and best practices in this area are now well documented and understood. This chapter scopes out the background to the current digitization environment, giving an overview of the methods and approaches involved. It points to current developments, highlighting the use of both two- and three-dimensional capture methods for the creation of digital surrogates of objects and artefacts, indicating the potential for further development in the sector, whilst drawing attention to current issues faced when digitizing objects and artefacts, including cost, sustainability, impact evaluation and expectation management in the changing information environment. The affordances of previously prohibitively expensive techniques – such as multi-spectral imaging and 3D scanning – are now available at relatively inexpensive rates, which also raises questions about digital literacy and our understanding of what it means, for both the end-user and the information professional, to create digital versions of our cultural inheritance.

Digitization of cultural and heritage content

Digitization, 'the conversion of an analog signal or code into a digital signal or code' (Lee, 2002, 3), is now commonplace across the heritage sector, as digital representations of cultural and historical documents, artefacts and images are created, usually for putting into institutional repositories and for featuring on websites, encouraging remote viewing by online users. Digitization may appear to be a recent phenomenon in memory institutes, but the current state of affairs where libraries, archives, museums, galleries and even private individuals are expected to make available their collections in digital form follows a period of experimentation with and appropriation of available digital technologies which dates back almost 40 years (see Terras, 2010, for a fuller account of the history of digitization). The information, culture and heritage sectors were quick to embrace digitization technologies as they became available, primarily to facilitate access to items in collections by providing them in electronic format, firstly with the creation of electronic catalogues in the 1970s, then conversion of printed source material into digital files in the 1980s (Van Horick, 2005). One of the first digitization projects was the Optical Digital Image Storage System (ODISS) launched in 1984 by The National Archives and Records Administration (NARA) in Washington, which aimed to test the utility of digital image and optical disk technologies for the reproduction, storage and retrieval of archival documents (see González 1992, 1998 and NARA, 1991, for an overview).

As network infrastructure grew, and the cost of computational devices fell, users increasingly consumed digitized content (Naughton, 2000), and libraries, archives and museums continued to experiment with the appropriate application of digital technologies within their institutional remit, being keen to embrace digitization which gives potential for 'for learning, teaching, research, scholarship, documentation, and public accountability' (Kenney and Rieger, 2000, 1). In the 1980s, digitization generally focused on specific in-house material such as particular manuscripts, paintings or artefacts, usually targeting resources to digitize rare documents or objects with high scholarly value. A prime example of this is the digitization of the *Beowulf* manuscript in the British Library, with publication of the *Electronic Beowulf* in 1992 (Kiernan, 1981, 1991; Prescott, 1997).

In the 1990s, as the cost of capture and processing equipment fell, and access to resources increased, many organizations moved towards a more large-scale digitization of their holdings, galvanized in part by the availability of funding by national bodies. For example, the UK government's Joint Information Systems Committee (Jisc – a centralized body supported by all four of the higher education funding bodies for Scotland, England, Northern Ireland and Wales) announced a variety of initiatives to encourage the development of electronic libraries (or eLib) related resources, and infrastructure and services to support the use of digital content in higher education. More than £100 million was spent on digitization in this area in the UK by Jisc by the close of the 1990s (Jisc, 2010). An example of an eLib-funded project typical of the scope of digitization carried out at the time is the Internet Library of Early Journals (ILEJ),[1] a joint project by the Universities of Birmingham, Leeds, Manchester and Oxford, which digitized some 200,000 pages of 18th- and 19th-century journals (ILEJ, 1999). At the start of the 1990s, then, 'In the early days of the Web, museums provided some of the best content and some of the most compelling reasons to go on-line' (Peacock, Ellis and Doolan, 2004). Towards the close of the millennium, 'A decade of digitization and documentation for the Web . . . created a rich array of cultural and historical information across the museum, library and archive sectors' (ibid).

Links with commercial information providers, such as Google and Microsoft, and mass digitization of printed content, followed in the 2000s. These industry providers have the resources to digitize everything they possibly can, often in conjunction with world-leading institutions that cannot afford to digitize their holdings in such an all-encompassing manner, and so can avoid the targeted approach of digitization favoured by the funding councils. The belief is that the supporting computational infrastructure is developed enough to search through vast repositories of digitized content (Google Books, 2007). However, such digitization initiatives bring with them very difficult issues regarding copyright, and access, and also raise questions about the potential exploitation of their dominance of ownership of digitized versions of cultural and heritage content (Singel, 2009).

At time of writing, the interest in the adoption of new technologies to forward institutional aims is keenly felt as the costs of digital technology and storage media continue to fall, and processing power – or what we can do with digitized content once it is acquired – continues to advance. Research is ongoing into advanced digitization capture practices, such as the use of multi-spectral imaging (a process that captures image data at specific frequencies across the visible and invisible spectrum) to uncover detail in cultural and heritage objects. An example of this is a project which has collected multi-spectral data on the degradation of an 18th-century parchment by a series of physical and chemical treatments, in order to inform best practice on how to image similarly damaged texts (MacDonald et al., 2013). The affordances of 3D capture and 3D printing are also being explored in the GLAM (Galleries, Libraries, Archives and Museums) sector, such as the E-Curator project,[2] which established the value of 3D models for sharing detailed information about museum objects among curators and conservators (Robson et al., 2012).

Moving beyond capture practices, the use of social media, the relationship of social media to more staid digitization practices and the relationship of institutions to individuals are being investigated as the sector explores these relatively low-cost mechanisms for dissemination of digitized material (Terras, 2011). An example of this is the British Library's Mechanical Curator,[3] which randomly selects artwork from their database and posts it to a Tumblr blog every hour. The logical conclusion of this is the use of social media platforms in conjunction with digitized content to ask online users to help with tasks in the cultural and heritage sectors, through a process known as 'crowdsourcing'. For example, the digitized manuscripts of the philosopher and social reformer Jeremy Bentham

(1748–1842) have been put online via a Wikimedia platform and are being transcribed by volunteer labour in the Transcribe Bentham[4] project (see Causer and Terras, 2014): more than 3 million words of Bentham's writing have now been transcribed, speeding up the costly process of creating machine-readable text from digitized images of manuscript material.

There is also huge interest in the cultural sector for the possibilities that are inherent in 'linked data': the ability to link or merge data with sources that follow other standards, to allow different collections of digitized content to be searched, analysed and visualized (De Boer et al., 2012). An example of this is the British Museum's Research Space,[5] which is developing a range of flexible tools to search across the 2 million objects in the museum's collections, which, in time, will also search across other institution's catalogues, documents, images and records. Research in digitization therefore is still ongoing, as we investigate the possibilities involved in new technologies and platforms in capture, re-use and dissemination of digitized content.

The digitization process

Digitization is dependent on capturing a representation of existing, analogue material (as opposed to 'born-digital' media which was created on a computational system). It is important to establish that the act of digitization is one of translation: the resulting digitized representation of an original analogue object is not a replacement for the object. Computational systems depend on exact numerical strings. The ordinary, or 'real' world, of our senses exists in a continuous flowing stream of signals across time and often space. A document – or even a traditional photograph of a document – exists in analogue, where a varying signal represents a continuous range of values. In order to record, copy, transmit, or analyse such a complex signal using computational methods, it is necessary to translate this into a form which is more simple, predictable and processable. All telecommunication systems work with one underlying principle: the information to be sent is converted into signals which can be transmitted, and reassembled on reception, to be converted into something we can perceive as a fair copy of the original. Digital systems are those which rely on a sequence of discrete numeric values, rather than the unconstrained and continually varying qualities of analogue signals. Numeric values are used in digital systems for processing, display, transmission and input, often sampling values from analogue sources in the process we call 'digitization'. Digital systems rely on the binary numeric system, where all numbers are represented using only two symbols, such as 0 and 1, known as binary digits or 'bits'. Strings of bits can build up a representation of text, image, sound or 3D object, but the more complex the representation, the more bits are required to describe it, and the more complicated the mechanisms are that are required to capture, store, display, process, analyse and convert the information held in the binary data stream.

Providing a digital representation of an analogue object has various advantages: the digital representation can usually be more easily copied, shared, accessed, analysed and processed than the original (provided users have access to computational infrastructure – such as machines, software, networks and subscriptions, which should not always be taken for granted – see Gooding, 2013). The creation of digitized versions of primary historical sources also opens up new potential for research using advanced computational methods, to show different facets, relationships, views or details of the original content. However, it should always be remembered, that although digital representations of historical artefacts can be seductive, they are not the historical artefact itself, as they are only a digital representation limited to what has been captured during the sampling process:

> A digital representation of an artefact is a representation of certain relevant characteristics of the artefact. It is not the original and complete artefact, nor even a metonymy or simulacrum of the complete artefact. It is only a representation of some 'relevant characteristics'.
>
> Arnold, 2008, 127

Digitization technologies

The digitization methods available to the cultural and heritage sector are dependent on those which are commercially available, and affordable: these have changed over the past few years as the costs of digital capture equipment have fallen. For most of the 1980s and 1990s, scanning was the most commonly used way to capture digital versions of historic content, and scanners were often used in conjunction with traditional photography, to capture a photographic representation of an object or text with the resulting slide, photograph, or microfilm being converted to a digital version. Deegan and Tanner (2002, 34) described the range of digitization processes which were commonly used, including scanning of existing image material, microfilming and then scanning the microfilm, photography followed by scanning of the photographic surrogates, rekeying (typing in) of textual content, OCR (optical character recognition) of scanned textual content, encoding textual content to create a marked-up digital resource and advanced imaging techniques for large format or specialist items. In the last few years, as the costs of digital camera equipment have fallen, it is increasingly common to use digital cameras (specifically, digital SLRs which have high-quality lenses but a 'digital back') to capture digital 2D and 3D images of cultural and heritage objects, without digitizing existing surrogate material (such as scanning existing photographs):

> The introduction of digital camera backs as a means of digitization has superseded the previous methods which were flatbed and drum scanners. Both of these scanning methods are now obsolete and the standard for high-quality digitization nowadays is the use of professional digital camera backs in medium and large format made by companies such as Mamiya Leaf and Phase One. The accuracy and quality of the optical lens system used by these cameras is essential in minimising distortion. This method of capture . . . is also far quicker than the traditional scanning method as well as producing a higher quality image. This is due to the increase in size of the image sensor, commonly a CCD (charge-coupled device) chip in digital camera backs as well as the difference of the image sensor being static

rather than having to pane across underneath the slide in a flatbed scanner
. . . One of the advantages when using digital camera back duplication
setups is the greater control over the light source, which is a lightbox
consisting of a photographic flash with a uniform colour temperature . . .
Since the launch of professional digital back cameras, there has been little
development in scanning technology.

Weidner, 2013

Nowadays, digital SLR cameras are the most commonly used technology
for taking still images of cultural and heritage content: even the market
leading 'book scanners' commonly used in mass digitization projects, such
as the Atiz Book Drive Pro,[6] are actually composed of digital cameras
mounted over a cradle. Images of text can be converted into electronic
text through ever-advancing improvements in OCR technology, or by
keying in (which is often outsourced to developing countries). Sound and
moving images can also be digitized, by converting video and audio into
digital formats, and a range of technologies exist to aid in their conversion.
(For up-to-date, accessible introductions to a range of digitization
technologies for a variety of media, the Jisc Digital Media service
maintains a wealth of online material on this topic – see www.
Jiscdigitalmedia.ac.uk/creating). Moving away from purely two-
dimensional representations of artefacts, 3D scanning technologies are
now being explored for used in the cultural and heritage sectors as the
technology becomes more affordable (Robson et al., 2012). 3D capture is
also allied with 3D printing of the resulting models, and the sector is
investigating how 3D printing technology can be gainfully used. There is
also great interest in using and broadcasting the content from digitization
via social media channels, such as Twitter, Facebook, Tumblr and Flickr,
providing institutions with a relatively easy way to increase public
engagement with digitized content, with projects building crowdsourcing
platforms which ask for the general public's help in categorizing, analysing,
cataloguing, reading and transcribing digitized material. Capture of
digitized content can therefore lead to a variety of useful outcomes for an
institution.

It should also be noted that whilst the digitization process creates core content for digital resources, it is a time-consuming and costly task. Additional infrastructure is also required in order to deliver digitized material in a useful manner (such as a database or content management system, a website front end, some kind of explanatory apparatus or additional teaching materials, the resources to engage frequently with online visitors and to update content and, in the case of crowdsourcing, helping recruit and retain volunteers). Project management, and records creation and cataloguing of each digital item, are often more time-consuming than the creation of digital surrogates themselves (Boughida et al., 2011). A digitization project should thus be seen as a range of activities which result in digital representations of historical source material being captured, catalogued, stored and made accessible to target users, potentially for a range of uses and in a variety of guises: it is not just simply about the act of scanning or taking photographs of artefacts and objects.

Digitization guidelines

Producing digital versions of holdings through digitization has become an industry in itself, and there has been much effort devoted to producing guides to best practice for undertaking the digitization of library and archive material to provide a framework in which those who wish to undertake digitization of primary source materials can operate. The issue is that there are now over 40 different guidelines for undertaking digitization in existence, and each of those

> is a complex, multifaceted production. Each represents a synthesis of experience, drawn in part from earlier versions of a given guideline and in part from secondary literature, workshops and conference presentations (and other forms of hearsay), and the specific experience of consultants and other experts who develop a specific guideline.
>
> Conway, 2009, 10

Care should therefore be taken as to which guidelines are followed and used for advice, and part of project planning is to decide the protocols, benchmarks and procedures that a digitization project will use within a specific institutional context. Jisc Digital Media[7] is a good first port of call for up-to-date digitization advice, but other commonly consulted and respected guidelines include the *Library of Congress Technical Standards for Digital Conversion of Text and Graphic Materials* (Library of Congress, 2006) and the US National Archives *Technical Guidelines for Digitizing Archival Materials for Electronic Access: creation of production master files – raster images* (Puglia, Reed and Rhodes, 2004). However, available digitization technology has changed considerably since the most commonly used guidelines were written, and best practice in newer techniques, such as the use of 3D scanning in the cultural and heritage industry, is still being established (Robson et al., 2012).

Digitization in libraries, archives and museums

Anything visual that is accessible to photography can be digitized, and the range of digitized material in the cultural and heritage sector is as broad as the range of material held in libraries, archives, museums, archaeological sites and private collections, including (but not limited to) printed books, printed journals, manuscripts, maps, photographs, photographic transparencies, music manuscripts, woodcuts, line drawings, paintings, archaeological site plans, archaeological finds, blueprints and architectural illustrations or plans, medical illustrations, documents, correspondence, newspapers, papyri, sculpture, clothing, artefacts, *objets d'art*, furniture, buildings, archaeological sites and ephemera of any nature.

There are many reasons why a programme of digitization of cultural and heritage material may take place, and there are a variety of potential advantages, which are summarized by Deegan and Tanner:

> immediate access to high-demand and frequently used items; easier access to individual components within items (e.g. articles within journals); rapid access to materials held remotely; the ability to reinstate out of print

materials; the potential to display materials that are in inaccessible formats, for instance, large volumes, or maps; 'virtual reunifaction' – allowing dispersed collections to be brought together; the ability to enhance digital images in terms of size, sharpness, colour contrast, noise reduction, etc.; the potential to conserve fragile/precious objects while presenting surrogates in more accessible forms; the potential for integration into teaching materials; enhanced searchability, including full text; integration of digital media (images, sounds, video, etc.); the ability to satisfy requests for surrogates (photocopies, photographic prints, slides, etc.); reducing the burden of cost of delivery; the potential for presenting a critical mass of materials.

Deegan and Tanner, 2002, 32–3

In addition to this, there is further potential for raising revenue from the licensing of digitized content, raising the profile of institutions, and increased public engagement and knowledge transfer opportunities (Terras, 2012). However, there are also good reasons *not* to digitize content: Hughes (2004, 50–2), summarizes issues which cause problems in digitization projects, including unresolved copyright issues, lack of adequate funding, lack of institutional support, technical drawbacks, the potential for digitization to damage or compromise fragile or rare original materials, and issues which arise when digitization is used instead of adequate conservation techniques or instead of robust cataloguing systems. It is worth stressing that digitization is a costly and time-consuming endeavour, and projects are expensive to deliver, manage and sustain (Denbo, Haskins and Robey, 2008): not everything is worth digitizing, once things are digitized the resulting representations have to be maintained and looked after, and therefore strategic choices need to be made as to where resources are best employed.

Digitization in institutional contexts

The potential inherent in digitization is dependent on a variety of factors, including, but not limited to: the nature of the primary source content; the approach of the project; the technology available, appropriated and used; and the aims of the institution. The potential and nature of digitization therefore varies greatly from programme to programme and project to project, even within institutions. Looking at recent digitization initiatives in the author's home institution – University College London – alone, can give some indication as to the different scope and remit of digitization initiatives.

Digitization projects can revolve around one object and what it means for a particular community: for example, a project based at UCL and the British Museum[8] digitized a 12-metre-long plank-built war canoe from the Melanesian Southwest Pacific, dating from 1910. 3D laser scanning, paired with anthropological research, delivered a holistic virtual reconstruction, multimedia interactive delivery and a 3D printed colour replica of a detail of the boat for digital repatriation to the source community (Hess et al., 2009). This project was therefore a research project as well as one to create content: from the ethnographic point of view, the team were exploring how digitization technologies could work with museums and communities to build links around a particular object which now physically resides in a museum on the other side of the world to the community who revere it. From a technical point of view, the team were researching how best to utilize 3D scanning within this context. There is therefore still opportunity for digitization to be a fruitful research topic: as new technologies develop their potential and affordances for the cultural sector should be investigated.

In a larger project at UCL, digitization can be seen to be used to build up an illustrated catalogue of a particular collection. UCL Art Museum[9] holds over 10,000 paintings, drawings, prints and sculptures dating from the 1490s to the present day, including an important collection of 16th-century German drawings and Old Master prints by Dürer, Rembrandt and Van Dyck, later watercolour material by J. M. W. Turner, Thomas Rowlandson and Joseph Wright of Derby and a unique archive of works by staff and students from the Slade School of Fine Art, one of the leading art schools in the world, based at UCL. A digitization project based in the UCL Art Museum is gradually cataloguing and digitizing prints to create a definitive online catalogue of the art museum's holdings[10] over a number of years, dependent on a variety of relatively small internal and external sources of funding. The online database is a work in progress as records are checked and updated, and images of digitized content are added, as they are created, and at time of writing includes around 80% of the collection. This online resource allows those interested in the contents of the UCL Art Museum to understand the scope of their holdings, and to find and refer to works in the collection more easily. The eventual addition of digital images of the art to its associated record will mean that users can access this catalogue online prior to visiting the Museum and requesting the artwork in question. Digitization, in this project, is then primarily used to assist access and record-keeping, as well as to promote the content of the UCL Art Museum, and to assist both casual browsers and researchers in understanding the scale of its holdings. The digitization is being undertaken in-house as funding allows, with the resulting catalogue being hosted on UCL's own library servers, as part of an institution-wide activity to catalogue and make accessible the collections of various museums within UCL. The museum also links closely into UCL's teaching programme: with work placement students from the Master's degree in Digital Humanities aiding in the project, and suggesting and implementing new ways in which the image-based content can be used. It has been noted, using UCL museums as a case study, that university libraries and museums can provide an ideal platform to experiment with different modes of digital delivery of cultural and heritage content (Nelson and MacDonald, 2012).

At the other end of the scale of digitization, the mass creation of digital records of a range of collections can be achieved to foster access to anyone in the internet-wide community who may wish to use them, collaborating in larger, federated digitization efforts. Another project at UCL, Europeana Travel,[11] digitized 'over a million resources including maps, manuscripts, photos, films, books and postcards on the themes of travel, tourism, trade routes and exploration' to 'enable public access to previously unpublished travel memories' (UCL Library Services, 2009). This is part of the European Commission's eContentplus Programme,[12] a centrally managed programme which is digitizing material from cultural heritage institutions to feed into the Europeana[13] portal that links to tens of millions of digital resources from over 2000 museums, archives, libraries and audiovisual collections from all over Europe. Digitization in this project has a different set of aims than the previous projects, is undertaken at industrial scale, and is driven also by policy and strategy from beyond the home institution. This has an impact on project planning, and the range of standards and technologies used, to ensure that resulting outputs can be used in conjunction with those of the other Europeana partners.

The act of digitization – creating a digital version of the primary source material – may be technically similar in all three of these projects, but the purview, scope, output and infrastructure surrounding both projects from the same institution differs greatly depending on the project aims, objectives and purpose.

The current digitization cultural environment

Given the range and scope of activity in creating digitized content in the cultural and heritage sectors, it has been difficult to follow and fully comprehend how digitization is now being used and appropriated in galleries, libraries, museums and archives, and 'statistical data on Europe's digital heritage is tentative and scattered at best' (Enumerate, 2013). To counteract this issue the European Commission funded a project called Enumerate[14] under its ICT Policy Support Programme. The Enumerate project runs for three years from February 2011 and aims to 'create a reliable baseline of statistical data about digitization, digital preservation and online access to cultural heritage in Europe' (Enumerate, 2013). In 2012, Enumerate published its *Survey Report on Digitization in European Cultural Heritage Institutions* (Stroeker and Vogels, 2012), which gave a snapshot of current digitization activity in the sector, gathering responses from 2000 institutions (including many national libraries and archives) across 29 European countries. The survey ascertained the state of digitization within each organization, whilst also asking about expenditure, access to digital collections and the institutional digital preservation strategy.

Of the institutions which responded, 83% were participating in digitization activities in 2011, and 100% of national libraries have a digital collection. Only about 20% of the materials which are deemed to be important enough to be digitized currently are: art museums have the highest percentage of digitized content, averaging at 42% of their holdings, whilst national libraries only have 4% of their content digitized, although they have a target to get 62% of their collections digitized within time. Photographs are the most digitized object type – 66% of respondents have digitized them, with 46% of institutions digitizing archival records, 35% digitizing drawings, 32% digitizing posters, 31% digitizing postcards, 29% digitizing rare books, 29% digitizing paintings and less than a quarter of institutions digitizing non-rare books, newspapers, serials, sheet music, microfilms and video and audio recordings. The least digitized formats were 3D objects (7%) and whole monuments and sites (8%), showing that there are still issues in dealing with the organizational complexities, and temporal and financial investment needed to capture these.

Of the respondents, 34% of institutions have their own written digitization strategy, and almost one-third (half in the case of national libraries) are included in a national digitization strategy; 31% of institutions have some kind of policy for the use of their digital collections, and 23% of institutions have a written digital preservation strategy; 85% of institutions say that they use web statistics to measure the use of their digital collections, yet only 42% of them say that they actively monitor use. These statistics indicate that there is much more to be done to ensure that digitization is a planned, targeted activity where the ramifications of the investment of limited resources are understood.

The Enumerate project reveals that digitization is resource-intensive: the national libraries have on average 15 staff involved in the digitization process, whilst other types of institutions have a team of around 5.5 staff (in total, 3.3% of all staff in cultural heritage institutions are working on digitization). The costs of digitization are in the range of €20,000 to

€40,000 per full-time member of staff, unless the project involves audiovisual digitization, when the costs rise to €103,000 per full-time member of staff. The use of volunteers is common, being mostly used at archives and records offices. Funding for digitization is sourced from internal budgets in 87% of the institutions, although 40% mention some form of public grant or subsidy, 5% say they raised finances via private investment and 4% indicate that they had some commercial sponsorship.

It can be seen, then, that digitization is now a core activity across the heritage sector, although there is a significant way to go until all the content that institutions deem worthy and necessary of digitization is captured, and that this will require much further financial investment and support from the sector, over a long period of time, to reach the goals they have set themselves in delivering digitized cultural and heritage material. It should also be considered that the more accessible digitized content that there is, the more useful existing content will be, as rich connections can be made across collections, encouraging excellence in research, learning and teaching.

Impact and expectation

Although there has been significant investment in digitization in the cultural and heritage sectors for decades, it can be difficult to prove the value of this activity. This is increasingly necessary in an economic climate where 'impact' of publicly funded activity is measured and evaluated: 'The global economic decline that began in 2007 has led to serious cuts in funding for almost all humanities and cultural heritage initiatives, including the development of, and support for, digital collections' (Hughes, 2011, 2). Yet it is difficult to establish value: 'Digital resources are valuable to different audiences for different reasons, and some value may not be realized immediately . . . Value is subjective, changes over time and has different meanings that are contingent on external factors' (Hughes, 2011, 5–7). In response to this issue, Tanner suggests that there are five different modes of value in digitized resources, in order to provide an impact assessment of the often intangible benefits of digitization. There is Option Value to digitized resources: when people enjoy the digitized content, and produce some form of output, such as research output by academics. There is Prestige Value, where people derive utility from knowing that a digitized resource is cherished by individuals both inside and outside of their community. There is Education Value, where people are aware that their digitized resources contribute to their own or other's education, training and knowledge. There is Existence Value, where people benefit from knowing that a resource exists, even if they do not use it themselves. And finally, there is Bequest Value, where people derive satisfaction from the fact their communities will be able to access these resources in the future (Tanner and Deegan, 2011, 34). Tanner's modes of value are an extremely useful taxonomy for those attempting to frame discussion of the potential – or known – impact of their digitization project, to show the benefits that it could possibly have to a range of users, and perhaps persuade funding sources of the necessity for digitization. An alternative means of assessing impact is provided by TIDSR (Toolkit for the Impact of Digitized Scholarly Resources),[15] funded by the JISC e-Content Impact and Embedding Programme, which provides a framework of both qualitative (interviews, focus groups) and quantitative (log analysis) methods for assessing the use of a digital resource. At a time of rapid development and creation of digitized resources, we are only now being able to frame discussions about the use and usefulness of them: 'The value, impact and use of collections take time to evolve and to be understood, and this needs to be reconciled in a world of responsive, short-term funding opportunities' (Hughes, 2011, 10).

The current lack of external funding for the creating of digitized material can be juxtaposed with issues of user expectations regarding digitized content. With ongoing changes in networked technologies, including the emergence of ever-connected smartphones in the digital environment, the number of potential users of digitized cultural and heritage content has increased enormously. Expectations have been raised that all content is available digitally (even though, as we have seen above, only a small fraction of institutional holdings are currently available in digital format). Expectations and needs of potential user groups differ, and it can be difficult for heritage organizations to be agile enough to respond to a rapidly changing information environment, and the needs of users who learn their digital behaviour mostly through engaging with well resourced commercial websites:

> Digital tools have worked their way into every aspect of our lives. Even those people with high levels of digital fluency take for granted the increased levels of speed, access and mobility that as little as three years ago were hard to imagine. For many, the possibilities still feel a little bit sci-fi-esque, but as William Gibson observed so insightfully in 2003, 'the future is already here – it's just not evenly distributed'. This is as true for the cultural sector as anyone, with many organizations struggling to embrace the new reality of audience behaviour, let alone go boldly into a future of big data, the semantic web and seamless participation.
>
> Finnis, quoted in Malde et al., 2013, 2

A report recently published by Culture24, a not-for-profit cultural organization which supports arts and heritage venues in reaching online audiences, suggests that institutions should look at the range of digital material they are creating and the way it is delivered, and should encourage: the measurement of value (both what the institution and their users value, before exploring how these can be enhanced through digital channels); regular reporting and analysis of what works for the institution and what doesn't; a focus on user behaviour and demand, moving away from the institutional supply-driven model of digital content; understanding the changing behaviours of audiences; being honest about the effort and time it takes for digital activities to be carried out; understanding web, mobile and social behaviours; and conducting experiments in the way content is created, communicated and delivered (Malde et al., 2013, 5–6). This will, then, affect the digitization policy and strategy of an organization: 'The starting point should . . . be the mission of the organization and the needs of the target audience. You need to know what you want to achieve and who it is for' (Malde et al., 2013, 4). Perhaps the biggest change in digitization in recent years is this necessary move towards understanding user needs and communities, rather than creating 'scan and dump' or 'build it and they will come' digitization projects (Warwick et al., 2008).

Although, as we have seen in the Enumerate survey earlier, only one-third of major cultural and heritage institutions across Europe have considered their digitization activities in enough detail to have such a policy.

Digital literacy and digitized content

It is also worth returning, here, to the issue of representation in digitization, in the light of increased user expectation and regular use of digital media. As people turn to the digital as a convenient means to view and access a wide variety of digitized cultural and heritage content, we have to ask: do they understand the processes which created it, and what they are looking at for evidence, or sources of information? The persuasive nature of digital visualization and display can mean we do not stop to question the very nature of digitized content:

> its labor of production has been concealed and therefore bears less evidence of authorship, provenance, originality, and other commonly accepted characteristics attributed to physical objects. For these reasons the digital object's materiality is not well understood.
>
> Cameron, 2007, 70

Understanding digitization is then a particular extension of digital literacy:

> the confident and critical use of Information Society Technology (IST) for work, leisure and communication. It is underpinned by basic skills in ICT: the use of computers to retrieve, assess, store, produce, present and exchange information, and to communicate and participate in collaborative networks via the Internet.
>
> Digital Literacy, 2006

This is combined with information literacy:

> knowing when and why you need information, where to find it, and how to evaluate, use and communicate it in an ethical manner.

CILIP, 2013

Those creating digital material, and particularly digitized cultural and heritage content, have an obligation to their users to explain the nature of the resources they are publishing, and fully documenting and describing them (something which seldom happens). Indeed, there may be a further obligation to inform the user community about issues of representation so they fully understand the material that they are accessing: this particularly comes into play when dealing with advanced representations of material, such as 3D scans, or multi-spectral images, where it is difficult to understand the relationship of the primary historical source to its digital representation. If institutions, and by extension, their users, do not understand the digitization process, can our interpretation of digitized material ever be robust? This is an issue that the sector needs to explore with greater awareness.

Conclusion

This chapter has provided an overview of the current digitization environment in the cultural and heritage sectors. After a period of adoption and experimentation we are now at a juncture where institutions are expected to provide digital versions of their holdings, although there is much work to be done to create digital representations of all that is deemed to be digitization-worthy. Digitization has been shown to be a complex and costly process, in which the translation of analogue content into a digital form is only a small part: much is dependent on the institutional framework, resources and aims in which the digitization project operates, rather than merely considering technical issues about capture and storage. Best practice in newer areas of digitization, such as 3D capture and printing, or the use of multi-spectral imaging, is still being investigated, and it will continue to be the case that as new technologies emerge their affordances should be explored for the particular use requirements of the cultural and heritage sectors. In addition to technical aspects, there are pressing issues regarding the use and usage of digitized resources, and how we can show that the digitization process adds value to the user experience, and to society at large. We are only just beginning to understand how institutions can best respond to a rapidly changing information environment, and evolving user expectations – which may not be combined with the same advances in digital literacy within our use communities.

Throughout this chapter, the importance of understanding institutional contexts and aims has been shown to be paramount when planning, or considering undertaking, a digitization project. Organizations must now take a more holistic view of the digital environment in which they operate, to understand their users, their resources, and the ever-growing potential inherent in the creation of digitized versions of historical and culturally important content. A wealth of digitized heritage material has now been created, with many more digital treasures to follow in the forthcoming decade. Attempting to understand the possibilities this delivers across the sector, to a wide range of users, is now part of the role of every individual digitization project, as we look to a future where further advancements in digital capture, access, search, analysis and dissemination will affect how users interact with, perceive and understand their cultural inheritance.

Notes

1 www.bodley.ox.ac.uk/ilej.
2 https://www.ucl.ac.uk/museums/petrie/research/research-projects/3dpetrie/3d_projects/3d-projects-past/e-curator.
3 http://mechanicalcurator.tumblr.com.
4 www.ucl.ac.uk/transcribe-bentham.
5 www.researchspace.org.
6 http://pro.atiz.com.
7 www.Jiscdigitalmedia.ac.uk.
8 www.mhm.ucl.ac.uk/mhm-research/western-solomon-islands-war-canoe.php.
9 www.ucl.ac.uk/museums/uclart.
10 http://artcat.museums.ucl.ac.uk.

11 www.ucl.ac.uk/ls/europeanatravel.
12 http://ec.europa.eu/information_society/apps/projects.index.cfm?menu =secondary&prog_id=ECP.
13 www.europeana.eu/portal.
14 www.enumerate.eu.
15 http://microsites.oii.ox.ac.uk/tidsr.

References

Arnold, D. (2008) Digital Artefacts. Possibilities and Purpose. In Greengrass, M. and Hughes, L. (eds), *The Virtual Representation of the Past*, Farnham, Ashgate Publishing, 159–70.

De Boer, V., Wielemaker, J., Van Gent, J., Hildebrand, M., Isaac, A., Van Ossenbruggen, J. and Schreiber, G. (2012) Supporting Linked Data Production for Cultural Heritage Institutes: the Amsterdam Museum case study. In *The Semantic Web: research and applications, lecture notes in computer science*, Vol. 7295, 733–47.

Boughida, K., Whittaker, L., Colet, M. and Chudnov, D. (2011) *Cost Forecasting Model for New Digitization Projects*, Coalition for Networked Infrastructure Conference, 13 December 2011, www.cni.org/wp-content/uploads/ 2011/12/cni_cost_boughida.pdf.

Cameron, F. (2007) Beyond the Cult of the Replicant: museums and historical digital objects – traditional concerns, new discourses. In Cameron, F. and Kenderdine, S. (eds), *Theorizing Digital Cultural Heritage: a critical discourse*, Cambridge, MA, MIT Press, 49–76.

Causer, T. and Terras, M. (2014) Crowdsourcing Bentham: beyond the traditional boundaries of academic history, *International Journal of Humanities and Arts Computing*, **8** (1), 46–64.

CILIP (2013) *Information Literacy: definition*, CILIP, the Chartered Institute of Library and Information Professionals, www.cilip.org.uk/get-involved/ advocacy/learning/information-literacy/pages/definition.aspx.

Conway, P. (2009) Building Meaning in Digitized Photographs, *Journal of the Chicago Colloquium on Digital Humanities and Computer Science*, **1** (1), https://letterpress.uchicago.edu/index.php/jdhcs/article/view/12.

Deegan, M. and Tanner, S. (2002) *Digital Futures: strategies for the information age*, Digital Futures Series, London, Library Association Publishing.

Denbo, S., Haskins, H. and Robey, D. (2008) *Sustainability of Digital Outputs from AHRC Resource Enhancement Projects*, Arts and Humanities Research Council (AHRC), www.ahrcict.rdg.ac.uk/activities/review/sustainability08.pdf.

Digital Literacy (2006) *What is Digital Literacy?*, http://eur-lex.europa.eu/LexUriServ.do?uri=OJ:L:2006:394:0010:0018:en:PDF.

Enumerate (2013) *About Enumerate*, www.enumerate.eu.

González, P. (1992) The Digital Processing of Images in Archive and Libraries, Large Scale International Projects. In Thaller, M. (ed.), *Images and Manuscripts in Historical Computing, Proceedings of a workshop at International University Institute, Firenze, November 15th 1991*, Göttingen, Max Planck Institute, 97–120.

González, P. (1998) *Computerization of the Archivo General de Indias: strategies and results*, Council on Library and Information Resources, Pub. 76, www.clir.org/pubs/reports/gonzalez/contents.html.

Gooding, P. (2013) The Digitized Divide: mapping access to subscription based digitized resources. Digital Humanities conference, University of Nebraska–Lincoln, 16–19 July, http://dh2013.unl.edu/abstracts/ab-260.html.

Google Books (2007) *Google Books History*, http://books.google.com/googlebooks/about/history.html.

Hess, M., Robson, S., Were, G., Simon Millar F., Hviding E. and Berg C. A. (2009) Niabara – the Western Solomon Islands War Canoe at the British Museum. 3D documentation, virtual reconstruction and digital repatriation. In *Proceedings of the 15th International Conference on Virtual Systems and Multimedia VSMM 2009. 'Vision or Reality? Computer Technology and Science in Art, Cultural Heritage, Entertainment and Education'*, Vienna, 9–12 September 2009.

Van Horik, R. (2005) *Permanent Pixels: building blocks for the longevity of digital surrogates of historical photographs*, The Hague, DANS Studies in Digital Archiving.

Hughes, L. (2004) *Digitizing Collections: strategic issues for the information manager*, London, Facet Publishing.

Hughes, L. (2011) Introduction: the value, use and impact of digital collections. In Hughes, L. (ed.), *Evaluating and Measuring the Value, Use and Impact of Digital Collections*, London, Facet Publishing, 1–10.

ILEJ (1999) *What is ILEJ?*, Internet Library of Early Journals, www.bodley.ox.ac.uk/ilej.

Jisc (2010) *Electronic Libraries Programme (eLib)*, www.Jisc.ac.uk/whatwedo/programmes/elib.aspx.

Kenney, A. R. and Rieger, O. Y. (2000) *Moving Theory into Practice: digital imaging for libraries and archives*, Mountain View, CA, Research Libraries Group.

Kiernan, K. S. (1981) *'Beowulf' and the 'Beowulf' Manuscript*, New Brunswick, NJ, Rutgers University Press.

Kiernan, K. S. (1991) Digital Image Processing and the *Beowulf* manuscript, *Literary and Linguistic Computing*, **6** (1), 20–7 .

Lee, S. (2002) *Digital Imaging: a practical handbook*, London, Facet Publishing.

Library of Congress (2006) *Library of Congress Technical Standards for Digital Conversion of Text and Graphic Materials*, http://memory.loc.gov/ammem/about/techIn.html.

MacDonald, L., Giacometti, A., Campagnolo, A., Robson, S., Weyrich T., Terras, M. and Gibson, A. (2013) Multispectral Imaging of Degraded Parchment. In *Computational Color Imaging, Lecture Notes in Computer Science*, vol. 7786, 143–57.

Malde, S., Finnis, J., Kennedy, A., Ridge, M., Villaespesa, E. and Chan, S. (2013) *Let's Get Real 2: a journey towards understanding and measuring digital engagement*, report from the second Culture24 Action Research Project, Culture 24, http://weareculture24.org.uk/projects/action-research.

NARA (1991) *Digital Imaging and Optical Media Storage Systems: guidelines for state and local government agencies*, Washington DC, National Archives and Records Administration and National Association of Government Archives and Records Administrators.

Naughton, J. (2000) *A Brief History of the Future: origins of the internet*, London, Phoenix Press.

Nelson, T. and MacDonald, S. (2012) A Space for Innovation and Experimentation: university museums as test beds for new digital technologies. In Jandl, S. S. and Gold, M.S. (eds), *A Handbook of Academic*

Museums: beyond exhibitions and education, Edinburgh, Museums Etc, 418–44.

Peacock, D., Ellis, D. and Doolan, J. (2004) Searching For Meaning: not just records. In Bearman, D. and Trant, J. (eds), *Museums and the Web 2004 Conference: proceedings*, Toronto, Archives & Museum Informatics, www.archimuse.com/mw2004/papers/peacock/peacock.html.

Puglia, S., Reed, J. and Rhodes, E. (2004) *Technical Guidelines for Digitizing Archival Materials for Electronic Access: creation of production master files – raster images*, Washington, DC, National Archives and Records Administration, www.archives.gov/preservation/technical/guidelines.pdf.

Prescott, A. (1997) The Electronic Beowulf and Digital Restoration, *Literary and Linguistic Computing*, **12**, 185–95.

Robson, S., MacDonald, S., Were, G. and Hess, M. (2012) 3D Recording and Museums. In Warwick, C., Terras, M. and Nyhan, C. (eds), *Digital Humanities in Practice*, London, Facet Publishing, 91–115.

Singel, R. (2009) Critics: Google book deal a monopoly, privacy debacle, *Wired*, 2 June, www.wired.com/business/2009/06/google_books.

Stroeker, N. and Vogels, R. (2012) *Survey Report on Digitization in European Cultural Heritage Institutions 2012*, Enumerate Project, www.enumerate.eu/en/surveys/core_survey_1/.

Tanner, S. and Deegan, M. (2011) *Inspiring Research, Inspiring Scholarship: the value and benefits of digitized resources for learning, teaching, research and enjoyment*, Jisc Digitization Programme Report, www.kdcs.kcl.ac.uk/fileadmin/documents/Inspiring_Research_Inspiring_Scholarship_SimonTanner.12page_2011.pdf.

Terras, M. (2010) The Rise of Digitization: an overview. In Rikowski, R. (ed.), *Digital Libraries*, Rotterdam, Sense Publishers, 3–20.

Terras, M. (2011) The Digital Wunderkammer: Flickr as a platform for amateur cultural and heritage content, *Library Trends*, Special Issue: Involving Users in the Co-Construction of Digital Knowledge in Libraries, Archives, and Museums, ed. Marty, P. and Kazmer, M., **59** (4), 686–706.

Terras, M. (2012) Digitization and Digital Resources in the Humanities. In Warwick, C., Terras, M. and Nyhan, C. (eds), *Digital Humanities in Practice*, London, Facet Publishing, 47–70.

UCL Library Services (2009) *Europeana Travel*,

www.ucl.ac.uk/ls/europeanatravel.

Warwick, C., Terras, M., Huntington, P. and Pappa, N. (2008) If You Build It Will They Come? The LAIRAH Study: quantifying the use of online resources in the arts and humanities through statistical analysis of user log data, *Literary and Linguistic Computing*, **23** (1), 85–102.

Weidner, T. (2013) *Dying Technologies: the end of 35 mm slide transparencies*, Tate Research Projects, www.tate.org.uk/about/projects/dying-technologies-end-35-mm-slide-transparencies/digitisation.

CHAPTER 5

Metadata in cultural contexts – from manga to digital archives in a linked open data environment

Shigeo Sugimoto, Mitsuharu Nagamori,
Tetsuya Mihara and Tsunagu Honma
University of Tsukuba, Japan

Introduction

We have experienced drastic changes in our information and knowledge infrastructure over the past few decades. As consumers of information resources, we find and access the resources from the internet. As producers of information resources, we create information resources in digital formats and provide access to them through the internet. Libraries, museums and archives, which we refer to as memory institutions, have been keenly working to provide better accessibility to their holdings using the internet and world wide web. In this chapter, we discuss metadata issues for digital archives of cultural resources.

Metadata, meaning 'data about data', play an important role in finding, accessing, collecting, using, organizing, storing, delivering and preserving resources in our networked information environment. Catalogue data of holdings at libraries and museums are typical metadata. Memory institutions and their communities have been key players in building metadata standards. The fundamental changes in our information environment for the past few decades caused by the rapid growth of the internet and mobile devices have drastically increased the importance of metadata at memory institutions. Moreover, connecting cultural resources on the internet through metadata is crucial to improving the usability of the resources across communities.

Memory institutions and publishers have been keenly working to enrich their services for the networked information society. This includes activities such as converting cultural resources, which may be tangible or intangible, into digital objects, and collecting 'born-digital' resources such as electronic books, journals, governmental records and digital audio and visual images. Various types of metadata are created for those resources, such as bibliographic information, rights management information, technology and structural features, and preservation information. Metadata created for digital resources and used in the networked information environment have significantly different features from those for conventional non-digital resources; metadata may be embedded in the body of a digital resource, metadata may be a first-class object as well as a primary resource, and metadata may be linked to each other in order to produce a richer environment for users to access the resources over the internet.

Digital archives, which are collections of digital resources built and maintained for the long term, are an important service for memory institutions. Digital archives have to provide users with access to the archived resources and keep the resources safe over time. Those users of digital archives may have diverse demands, and there is a wide variety of digital resources to be collected in digital archives, e.g., documents, digital photos and motion pictures, audio, databases, games, and so forth. This means that the requirements of metadata for digital archives are complex.

In this chapter, resources such as books, paintings and music performances are sometimes called 'primary resources' in order to explicitly distinguish them from metadata. In other words, metadata are a secondary resource created from a primary resource. Meta-metadata, which are defined as data (or metadata) about metadata, is a crucial concept for the interoperability of metadata. Typical meta-metadata are a metadata schema which defines representations of metadata, structural constraints of metadata and semantics of terms used in metadata. Crucial meta-metadata are descriptions of metadata, such as functional requirements, and guidelines to create and use metadata and the provenance of a metadata schema are also meta-metadata.

An information resource (or simply resource) means information content stored in a medium; a novel in a printed book, a movie stored in an analogue videotape, a web page are all information resources. The fundamental difference between digital and non-digital resources is that the information content of a digital resource which is expressed as a digital object can be copied or transferred to another digital medium without any loss of content. Digital objects are first-class objects that can be directly handled by computers and transferred via the internet. Primary resources, metadata and meta-metadata are all digital objects.

'What is information content?' and 'What is an information resource and how can we identify a resource for archiving?' are interesting questions. Data models defined by metadata standards provide very good hints when we consider issues raised by these questions. For example, Functional Requirements for Bibliographic Records (FRBR)[1] and a metadata standard for digital preservation named PREMIS (Preservation Metadata: Implementation Strategies)[2] define intellectual content and its instantiation as separate entities in their data models. Both electronic texts contained in a digital book and printed texts in a physical book are an instantiation of an intellectual content. Memory institutions adopt metadata standards to build databases and digital archives of their holdings in accordance with the requirements that they have.

This chapter is aimed at discussing metadata issues for digital resources and archives in the networked information environment based on the studies by the authors. The rest of this chapter is organized as follows. 'Metadata in contents flow' introduces a metadata-oriented view of contents flow. 'A metadata model for comic books' shows a metadata framework for manga (i.e., graphic novels, comics) and discusses metadata issues for digital contents. 'Meta-metadata as an infrastructure' discusses digital archives as an infrastructure to keep our community memory safe. 'Archiving digital resources' discusses metadata schema issues for resource sharing and archiving on the internet. 'Issues for the future' shows a few other studies by the authors related to digital archives and preservation. The chapter concludes with a Summary section.

Metadata in contents flow – from creation and publishing to archiving

Introduction

As defined in the previous section, metadata are 'data about data', which is a very general definition. A book catalogue is a typical example of metadata. There are many different types of metadata – e.g., book reviews, ratings of movies, ingredients of foods, system requirements for software, geographical maps, railways maps, and so forth. A word dictionary is a collection of metadata about words. *Who's Who* is a collection of metadata about people. The name of a person is an important item of metadata about the person. Thus, even in the real world we use a variety of metadata.

It is obvious that we need to use many metadata of different types in our networked information environment. Metadata are designed in accordance with the purposes and target objects of description of a particular application, e.g., metadata to help access to books at libraries, or metadata to identify requirements to install software. There are important services that collect metadata for value-added services, e.g., database search across libraries, museums and archives. Therefore, we need a good infrastructure to make various metadata interoperable. The next section shows a conceptual publishing flow of books to illustrate the requirements for combining different metadata in the content flow.

A conceptual publishing flow and metadata interoperability

The following is a very simplified view of a flow of publishing of a book of creative works, e.g., graphic novels. We use a Japanese term, *manga*, which means graphic novel or comics. A manga creator collaborates with his/her editor at the publisher to publish a manga. The publisher instantiates the manga as a book and delivers it to bookstores and libraries via intermediaries. Bookstores and libraries make the book available for readers, i.e., end-users.

Figure 5.1 illustrates a generalized model of the contents flow. In this conceptual model, FRBR Group 1 entities are used to show instances produced and used by the players in the model (FRBR entities are explained in Figure 5.2):

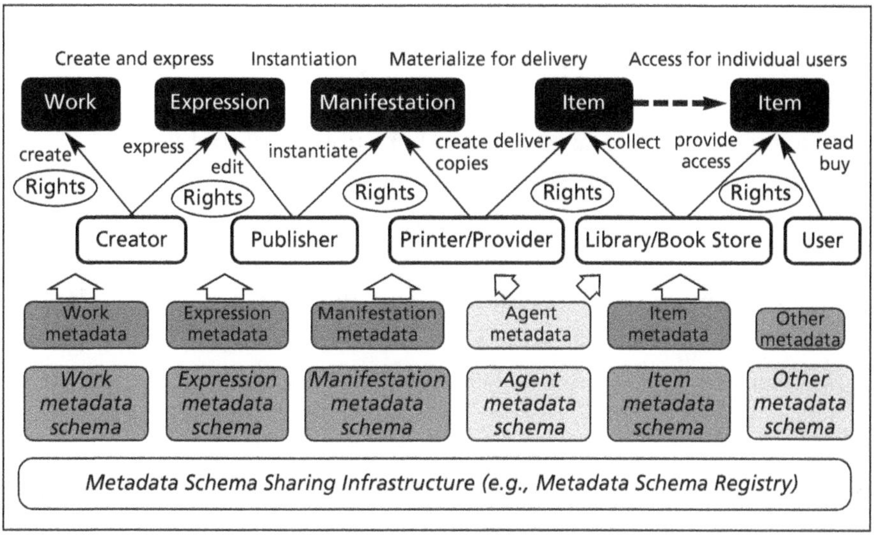

Figure 5.1 Conceptual model of content publishing flow

Group 1: The entities in the first group represent the different aspects of user interests in the products of intellectual or artistic endeavour. The entities defined as *work* (a distinct intellectual or artistic creation) and *expression* (the intellectual or artistic realization of a work) reflect intellectual or artistic content. The entities defined as *manifestation* (the physical embodiment of an *expression* of a *work*) and *item* (a single exemplar of a manifestation), on the other hand, reflect physical form.

Group 2: The entities in the second group represent those responsible for the intellectual or artistic content, the physical production and dissemination, or the custodianship of the entities in the first group. The entities in the second group include *person* (an individual) and *corporate body* (an organization or group of individuals and/or organizations).

Group 3: The entities in the third group represent an additional set of entities that serve as the subjects of *works*. The group includes *concept* (an abstract notion or idea), *object* (a material thing), *event* (an action or occurrence), and *place* (a location).

Figure 5.2 FRBR Group 1, 2 and 3 Entities. Quoted from *Functional Requirements for Bibliographic Records (section 3. Entities)*, www.ifla.org/publications/functional-requirements-for-bibliographic-records

1   The creator creates a Work of each graphic novel and expresses it as a graphic novel, i.e., creation of a manga Expression from a manga Work.
2   The creator collaborates with his/her publisher to publish the graphic novel as a single book. The publisher makes deliverable instances from the manga Expression, which may be in a print format or a digital format, i.e., a Manifestation and Items for the manga Expression. A Manifestation of the book is given an ISBN and Items are created for delivery.
3   Bookstores and libraries collects the Items and provide them to their customers.

The creator's creative work may be instantiated in a downloadable format. In that case, all products in the content flow may be digital and transferred online. Every instance in this process should be described by its metadata – the FRBR entities as well as the agents associated with them, e.g., creators and publishers. Agents would have rights in the manga and its book, e.g., intellectual property rights as a creator and an editor, rights related to publishing and delivery, and so forth. Agents interact with each other in the flow. The activities between agents may be recorded as transaction data. Transaction data are, in other words, metadata of the transaction. Thus, various types of metadata are created and used in the process – metadata about book resources, agents, transactions, rights and so forth.

Sharing information about the metadata used in the process is crucial for all of those agents involved in the flow. The information about the metadata that should be shared are the schemas of those metadata. The rules which define mapping between the schemas should be also shared. (See Figure 5.2 for FRBR entities.)

A simple model for interoperable metadata – a Dublin Core-based view

Interoperability of metadata is essential to improve information sharing among the agents involved in this process. Sharing information about metadata schemas is also essential to enhance metadata interoperability among the agents.

Every community has its own demands in metadata description. For example, publishers and libraries have different demands for describing books. Publishers would want to identify a book as a published entity and a commercial product, whereas libraries would want to identify a book as an entity owned by or accessible via a library. On the other hand, they have demands to make their metadata interoperable with each other in order to reduce costs and improve business environments by sharing their metadata. Thus, it is important to allow each community to include the community-specific requirements in the metadata and, at the same time, it is important to make the metadata interoperable across communities. A solution to this problem is to build a comprehensive standard which satisfies all requirements by all communities, but such a super-rich standard is not realistic.

The most difficult issue in achieving metadata interoperability is bridging the semantic gap between metadata schemas. Metadata mapping, the semantic mapping of term by term between schemas, is frequently carried out to use two or more different schemas in a single system but it is an expensive process. A solution is to use layered approach as described below. A metadata schema is composed of the following three components:

1   implementation syntax of metadata instances (i.e. concrete syntax)
2   structure and constraints of metadata instances (i.e. abstract syntax)
3   semantic definition of terms and vocabularies used in metadata instances (i.e. metadata vocabulary).

In addition to the three components above, we need guidelines and functional requirements for the creation and use of the metadata to understand the contexts and deep semantics of metadata, which may be invisible in the metadata instances and the schema. These components are modelled in the *Singapore Framework of Dublin Core Application Profiles*[3] but are not discussed here.

Figure 5.3 shows the three components of metadata schemas arranged in layers. Splitting a metadata schema into three layers is advantageous in understanding general interoperability issues – representation of metadata for data exchange among computers, structural constraints of metadata, and semantics of metadata terms and vocabularies. The examples below show typical semantic gaps. Here, '*title* of a book' and '*author* of a book' are typical descriptive elements, and *title* and *author* are an attribute (or property).

- '*Title* of a book' and '*title* of a person' have different meanings even if both of them are named 'title'.
- '*Description* about a resource', '*annotation* given to a resource' and '*notes* attached to a resource' have the same meaning – a description given to the resource.
- '*Author*' (e.g. *author* of a book) and '*photographer*' (e.g. *photographer* of a photograph) have different meanings but they may be merged to 'creator' as a term representing a broader meaning if we do not need the precise meanings.

The meanings of the terms defined in the bottom layer are shared among the metadata schemas A and B defined in the middle layer. The structures of the metadata defined in the middle layer are implemented in RDF/XML

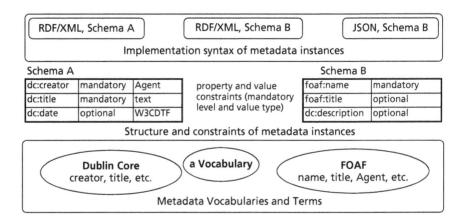

Figure 5.3 Layered view of metadata schema components

and JSON in the top layer. The layered view of metadata schemas helps us understand levels of interoperability and where the barrier for metadata interoperability exists. The Dublin Core Metadata Initiative (DCMI) defines a model for interoperability levels which is slightly different from the model here.[4] These models are based on the DCMI Application Profile, which is one of the most significant achievements of DCMI.

Metadata issues in contents flow – summary

Many players with different roles in the flow collaborate in the networked information environment. All players need to know the target resources and purposes of metadata description by other players, and they need to share information about metadata schemas to make their metadata interoperable.

Many metadata standards define their base data models to clearly define the target instances of description. For example, the FRBR entities of Group 1, 2 and 3 are useful to identify those entities produced in the content publishing flow, agents contributed in the flow and other intellectual entities, respectively. PREMIS, which is a metadata standard for digital preservation, defines a data model composed of Intellectual Entity, Digital Object, Event, Rights, and Agent.

These base data models define classes of instances which are the target of metadata descriptions. A class defines attributes (or properties) of the class instances. Mapping between metadata schemas, i.e., mapping between classes and between attributes, is a basic task to make the metadata interoperable. Therefore, it is important to collect information about the classes and attributes and provide the information in a machine-interpretable form for all players in the flow to help use the information to make their metadata interoperable.

A metadata model for comic books in networked information environment – manga metadata framework

Introduction – why metadata for manga?

Creating and publishing manga in the networked digital information environment has a large potential for changing not only the publishing business but also our reading behaviour. Metadata plays important roles in the transformation of publishing from print/analogue to digital for several reasons; metadata can be embedded in a digital manga and delivered to end-users via the internet, the contents may be linked to each other by metadata, browsers use metadata embedded in the content to adjust functions for rendering and reading, and so forth. This change is common in many other genres, such as novels, animations and videos. More importantly, the border between the genres is becoming unclear and the importance of metadata is becoming more evident.

The fundamental change caused by this transformation is that any entity identifiable as a single instance in the information space can be given a unique identifier. In the case of print publishing, it is not realistic to identify every identifiable component in a manga – for example, a single page, a single frame, a single character, onomatopoeia, and so forth. On the other hand, it is not expensive to make these components identifiable in a born-digital manga provided that we are given appropriate tools to create manga. Moreover, logical and physical structural features can be extracted from born-digital books automatically.

An interesting feature of digitally published books is that their contents may be linked to each other over the internet, which may be done not only by authors but also by readers. Once entities contained in a book are represented as an instance in the digital information space, those instances may be described and linked to each other by metadata. All of the digital instances are a first-class instance, regardless of whether an instance is a primary resource or a metadata instance.

Manga Metadata Framework

Manga Metadata Framework (MMF) was designed to describe not only bibliographic features, but also structural features and intellectual entities of manga.[5] MMF was designed based on two major standards – FRBR and TV-Anytime. FRBR defines requirements in bibliographic description. TV-Anytime is a standard for on-demand broadcasting of video programmes and based on MPEG-7. Figure 5.4 shows MMF, which has three categories – Bibliographic Description, Structural Description and Intellectual Entities. The bibliographic description and intellectual entities are defined based on FRBR entities of Group 1 and Group 3, respectively. The structural description is based on the programme structure defined in TV-Anytime. A manga is a graphic representation of a story, which is a sequence of scenes. Each scene is composed of one or more visual frames. These visual frames and scenes are presented in a page and an instance of manga is a sequence of pages. This structure is similar to the structure of video, because a video programme is a sequence of scenes and each scene is a sequence of shots, and a single title of TV drama may represent a series of dramas. Thus, this similarity helps us re-use existing standards and to avoid defining another new scheme.

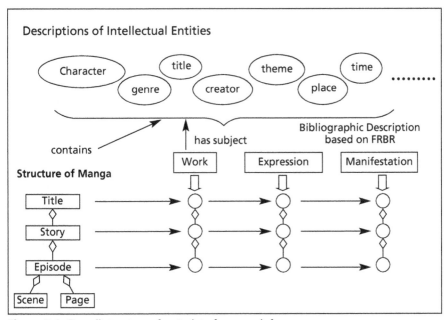

Figure 5.4 Overall structure of metadata framework for manga

The paragraphs below show two usage scenarios of MMF.

1   *Virtual bookshelf for manga*
    Bookshelves are a crucial user-interface to help users organize, find
    and access books although these bookshelves need not look like
    conventional two-dimensional bookshelves. Vocabularies to describe
    Intellectual Entities are natural candidates for categorizing books
    and lay them out on a virtual bookshelf, e.g., sorted by story genres,
    illustration genres, target ages, genres of creators, and so forth.
2   *Supporting reuse of products and bi-products during manga creation process*
    Comic books, which may be print or digital, are published as final
    products and maintained by publishers, libraries and readers. Many
    materials are created in the production process but they are not
    maintained well, even though the creators and publishers admit their
    values for later use and re-use. Those materials may be linked from
    the structural description and/or defined as an intellectual entity for
    reuse in the future.

A creative work expressed in a digital form may be read in various
environments – PCs, tablets, smartphones and digital book readers. The
accessibility issues for people with any disabilities urge us to make creative
works readable by anyone. In our networked information environment,
several people connected on the internet may collaboratively read a single
book. Their reading activity may be synchronous or asynchronous. The
collaborating readers share the content of the book but not a particular
instantiation of the book.

MMF defines the framework that covers all entities included in manga
as a creative work and as its instantiation. All of these entities are a first-
class object as well as the primary contents expressed in a digital format.
Those first-class objects may be linked to each other, shared among
datasets over the network and preserved for future use.

Identification of works of manga – an experimental study

Work and Expression of FRBR are crucial access points for users to find a Manifestation and an Item. For example, typical search demands are 'I want to find a comic book titled *One Piece* expressed in German', or 'I want to find an animation of *Doraemon* for my four-year-old son.' Here, *One Piece* and *Doraemon* are a title of a series of popular manga and a leading character name of manga, respectively. Each has many spin-off products that should be linked to an instance of Work and/or Expression.

Even though conventional bibliographic records are created primarily for Items and Manifestations, it is advantageous to provide users with access points based on Works and Expressions. However, there are no well established dictionaries or authority records for manga titles and characters. Wikipedia provides a large set of manga titles and characters in manga but it is not created as an authority. Therefore, we need to develop a technology to identify Works of manga using existing bibliographic records provided in order to help create authority records of manga.

Fiction Finder at OCLC helps aggregate bibliographic information of fiction books to create a Work set based on FRBR.[6] The authors studied an identification method of FRBR Work instances for manga using a bibliographic database and web resources.[7] In our study, we used a bibliographic database maintained at Kyoto International Manga Museum (KMM) and Wikipedia. We also used DBpedia as a Linked Open Data (LOD) resource created from Wikipedia. The outline of the identification process is as follows:

1 Create sets of bibliographic records where bibliographic records in each set have the same author(s) and a title text. Then, create an instance of Work tentatively for each set.
2 Search Wikipedia for a manga article which has the same author and title with the tentative Work instance. If a manga article is found in Wikipedia the tentative Work instance is regarded as a Work instance.
3 Give the Work instance a minimum set of information required as an authority data using the KMM bibliographic database, Wikipedia and other resources.

In the experiment, we identified 749 Work instances from roughly 6100 bibliographic records. Here, Wikipedia is used as a quasi-authority dictionary of Works. The limitation of this approach is that the granularity of Work is defined by the granularity of bibliographic descriptions, but not by the content of the books. Because the bibliographic records at libraries are created for a book but not for each story in a book, it is hard to identify a Work for each story of a manga.

Metadata for non-traditional resources – summary

There is no widely accepted metadata standard for bibliographic description designed for manga because manga was recognized as sub-culture content in the past and was not included in the standard collections of public libraries. On the one hand, this means we do not have a rich set of metadata and controlled vocabularies about manga. On the other hand, there is a large opportunity to study metadata for manga. In particular, the fundamental changes of the production and dissemination process of manga caused by the progress of electronic book technologies have significantly large potential to change the creation and usage of the metadata.

We often read and write annotations of a digital resource on the internet, e.g., reviews of a book, tags attached to a picture, a memorandum attached to a video, etc. These metadata may be embedded in the resource or created as a first-class object. Linking these resources by metadata may provide users with better environments to access and enjoy the contents. The metadata may provide new access points to the contents. For example, a manga which contains ancient European history may be linked to a cultural resource accessible via Europeana.

Archiving digital resources – keep community memory safe
Digital archiving at memory institutions

Museums, libraries and archives, or MLAs, which are so-called memory institutions, are responsible for keeping our memory resources safe for the future. Digital archiving and preservation is a key service for the memory institutions. They have been keenly working to organize traditional tangible resources and non-traditional digital resources to develop their internet-oriented services. Those digital resources can be generally classified into 'born-digital' or 'converted-to-digital'. Memory institutions have been working in both aspects; they have been creating a vast number of converted-to-digital cultural resource collections since the 1990s, and they have been collecting born-digital cultural resources, e.g., electronic books, games, web pages, electronic records of governments, and so forth.

There are various types of converted-to-digital resources – different types of original resources or different quality of digitization. For example, Toppan Virtual Reality site has introduced a digitized collection of large historical objects in very high quality.[8] Europeana provides a large collection of digital images created by collaborating memory institutions in Europe.[9] Cultural Heritage Online and Digital Library from the Meiji Era hold a large-scale digital collection of cultural heritage objects hosted by Japanese museums and a large collection of books published in the Meiji Era (1868–1912) and after, respectively.[10, 11]

A frequently asked question on digital archives is about the longevity of digital resources, because the development of new information technology never stops. Longevity of digital resources cannot be achieved without the proper management of archived objects. Once we lose control of the management of archived resources by natural or man-made disasters, recovery cost is very high, regardless of whether the resources are digital or non-digital.

Digital archives for communities

Community memory resources are important for the future, as well as those heritage resources maintained at major memory institutions. However, many community memory resources are facing higher risks of damage or loss. Digital archiving of community resources seems to be an appropriate solution to avoid the risks. However, in reality, there are barriers to communities building their digital archive of cultural resources.

A study group on digital archives organized by the Ministry of Internal

Affairs and Communication (MIC) of the Japanese government in early 2011 discussed the roles of digital archives. The Great East Japan Earthquake, which happened in March 2011, greatly affected the discussion of the group. The group agreed that making digital copies of our important memory resources is a reasonable solution for keeping our community memory safe for the future. A common barrier for regional communities is the cost and human resources. Resource and knowledge sharing is key to promoting the development of digital archives. The report suggests the following issues:

* promotion of digitization and open access
* human resource development
* system infrastructure for memory institutions
* information-sharing infrastructure (metadata).

The underlying issue common to these four points is sharing – sharing knowledge and skills to make the memory resources open to the public, sharing the know-hows for human resource development, sharing robust system infrastructure to keep digital resources safe, and sharing infra-structure to promote interoperable metadata.

Digital archives of the Great East Japan Earthquake

Right after the Great East Japan Earthquake happened on 11 March 2011, several institutions and organizations in Japan started to archive resources about the disaster.[12] Hinagiku, hosted at the National Diet Library, is a portal to the digital archives of the Great East Japan Earthquake.[13] As of April 2014, 33 databases are searchable via Hinagiku.

Creators of the databases of disaster resources are diverse – university research centres, newspaper and broadcasting companies, regional public sectors, information industries, and so forth. Content types of the databases are also diverse: photos, videos, news articles, documents, etc. The resources collected in the databases are valuable for the communities not only to keep the memory of the disaster but also to use the memory resources for disaster risk management in the future. There are still several open issues in these archives – how to manage resources that include privacy content and shocking scenes, how to use regional terms and connect them to standard terms, and what is a good service for the general public who do not have information skills but want to see the resources and contribute their experiences as content to the archives.

Meta-metadata as an infrastructure for digital contents flow and archiving

Metadata as a first-class object on the internet

New aspects of metadata on the internet are as follows:

- Metadata may be used as a first-class object like primary digital resources on the internet.
- Metadata may be embedded in a digital resource, not only to describe a property of the resource but also to connect the resource with other resources via the internet.
- The internet and world wide web provide identification schemes and implementation syntax of metadata, i.e., URI and Resource Description Framework (RDF), as the platform for metadata sharing and interoperability.

Metadata are key objects to sharing resources on the internet, and at the same time, metadata are shareable resources. This means meta-metadata are key to sharing metadata. Figure 5.5 explains the concept of meta-metadata through bibliographic metadata and its schema. The figure explains how a metadata schema can import terms defined in standard metadata vocabularies, which is the base model for DCMI Application Profiles.

Metadata schema registry as a hub for metadata schema sharing

Digital archives at memory institutions have been greatly influenced by the Semantic Web and Linked Open Data (LOD) activities by the World

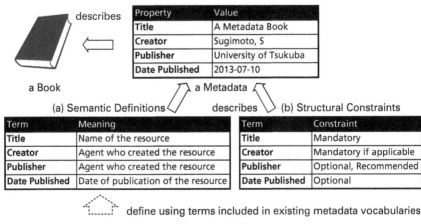

Property	Value
Title	A Metadata Book
Creator	Sugimoto, S
Publisher	University of Tsukuba
Date Published	2013-07-10

a Book

(a) Semantic Definitions

describes

a Metadata

(b) Structural Constraints

Term	Meaning
Title	Name of the resource
Creator	Agent who created the resource
Publisher	Agent who created the resource
Date Published	Date of publication of the resource

Term	Constraint
Title	Mandatory
Creator	Mandatory if applicable
Publisher	Optional, Recommended
Date Published	Optional

define using terms included in existing metadata vocabularies

Term	Meaning
Title	Same as Title element of DCMI terms See http://purl.org/dc/terms/title
Creator	Same as Creator element of DCMI terms See http://purl.org/dc/terms/creator
Publisher	Same as Publisher element of DCMI terms See http://purl.org/dc/terms/publisher
Date Published	Sub-property of Date element of DCMI terms See http://purl.org/dc/terms/date

(c) Semantic Definitions
referring external terms

As the meaning of each term
refers a definition given in
DCMI terms the terms of this
schema can be semantically
linked to other terms that
share the meaning defined by
DCMI terms.

Figure 5.5 Metadata and meta-metadata

Wide Web Consortium (W3C). The US Library of Congress and the National Diet Library of Japan have made their authority files in RDF available on the internet. The layered model discussed earlier in this chapter shows that shared metadata vocabularies enhance semantic interoperability of metadata.

Metadata schema information is indispensable for developers in using LOD resources. There are websites that provide vocabulary information – Linked Open Vocabulary[14] and Schema.org.[15] Metadata Schema Registry is a service which provides information about metadata schemas. The Dublin Core Metadata Schema Registry provides definitions of all terms defined by DCMI in RDF. MetaBridge provides metadata vocabularies and description set profiles defined according to DCMI

Application Profile.[16] These services are the basis of metadata sharing and metadata interoperability on the internet.

Metadata interoperability across communities and over time

Metadata vocabularies created by different communities are likely to be different even if their purposes are similar. Semantic mapping between metadata terms of different schemas is a crucial task in making the metadata interoperable. We need to build a mapping table that covers all metadata terms of the schemas. Thus, metadata vocabulary mapping is expensive and tends to be ad hoc. DCMI Application Profile suggests re-using existing metadata terms and vocabularies for a new application in order to lower the cost for vocabulary mappings. On the other hand, metadata mappings may use semantic relationships which are defined independently from the mapped vocabularies, e.g., term A *is equal to* term B, A *is broader/narrower than* B, and so forth. Sharing these relationships is also crucial to reducing the cost not only of creation of the mapping but also of its maintenance.

Metadata interoperability over time is also a crucial issue. Longevity of digital resources cannot be realized without metadata being consistently maintained. Long-term maintenance of metadata schemas is unavoidable in keeping the metadata consistent over time.

Long-term maintenance of metadata and metadata schemas has two aspects – preservation of metadata and metadata schemas as digital objects to keep them interpretable by computers, and maintenance of metadata and metadata schemas as a logical instance to keep their semantic consistency. Provenance description is crucial to keeping the change history traceable in an open environment across communities and over time.

Issues for the future – some lessons learned
Digital archives and metadata – case studies and lessons learned

Since the development of the world wide web in the early 1990s, many cultural resources have been digitized and many historical and cultural resources have been born digital. Digital archives which collect, organize, preserve and provide access to digital resources have very important roles to preserve our community memory and cultural resources for the future. The following paragraphs show some case studies at the authors' laboratory – a digital archive for a Daoism resource *Dao-Fa Hui-Yuan*, a task-centric model for archival metadata, and a cloud-oriented model for archiving.

A digital archive of Dao-Fa Hui-Yuan[17]

Dao-Fa Hui-Yuan is an important item of Daoism literature. This study organized the components of *Dao-Fa Hui-Yuan* into a database using digitized images of *Dao-Fa Hui-Yuan*. *Dao-Fa Hui-Yuan* is a compilation of *Fu*s and their descriptions. *Fu* is a graphic expression of charms used in Daoism ceremonies. The main component in this database is *Fu*. We have applied the database for the relationship analysis of the components – *Fu*s, their parts and volumes of *Dao-Fa Hui-Yuan*.

An important lesson learned in the study is that domain-specific rich description of the resources is necessary for scholars to find new facts using the database. The domain specificity is, however, disadvantageous for extensibility of the usage and longevity of the database. Scholars who are not included in the database design process would want to extend the database for their research, which may happen 10 years after the initial development. Metadata interoperability is very important for the functional extension of digital archives in the future.

Task-centric model for archival metadata[18]

Data models of conventional metadata standards for record keeping and archiving are resource-centric even if the resource lifecycle is well defined. This study proposed to see descriptive elements of metadata from the viewpoint of the resource lifecycle and analysed semantics of the elements based on 5W1H (Who, What, Where, When, Why and How) categories. The model provides a framework of mapping between metadata terms with semantics characterized by the 5W1H categories.

As the lifetime of a document and its metadata may well be long, maintenance of metadata and its metadata schema from the lifecycle's viewpoint is crucial. Both metadata schemas and contextual information such as usage of a term in the lifecycle need to be maintained in order to avoid misuse of metadata.

Cloud-oriented layered model for archiving[19, 20]

Cloud storage is a natural place to keep important documents and records for organizations which cannot afford an expensive robust archival system. Cloud computing environments are generally explained using a layered model.[21] The proposed model defines functions for archiving in accordance with the layered model for the cloud. Those functions are formally defined as an ontology. Allocating archival functions into layers is advantageous for both clear functional requirements and packaging information of archived objects in each layer.

Metadata schema sharing – lessons from metadata schema registries

The authors have been involved in the development and maintenance of the DCMI metadata registry and MetaBridge. The DCMI metadata registry provides the terms defined by DCMI. On the other hand, MetaBridge, developed as a metadata information infrastructure to support the content flow shown in Figure 5.1, provides not only metadata term definitions but also application profile definitions. Compared to metadata vocabularies and terms, application profiles are not well shared in machine interpretable formats. Application profiles are obviously a crucial resource for metadata schema designers to efficiently design a good schema for a given application service and for better metadata interoperability. Another crucial issue is long-term maintenance of metadata schemas. Application profiles are defined application by application, which means they are easily lost. Metadata schema registries have a significant potential for the long-term maintenance of metadata schemas and longevity of metadata. In practice, not many application profiles are provided on the web formally described. Metadata developers are encouraged to open their schemas on the web.

Summary

The internet and world wide web have brought cultural and historical resources closer to our daily lives. Since the 1990s, many cultural resources have been digitized for preservation and better access. We can view world cultural heritage from home and classrooms at a low cost and the development of new business and technology for digital publishing is boosting cultural resources born on the internet. Those resources online give us chances to add values to those resources – linking the resources, annotating the resources, etc. Metadata is key for us not only to publish and access cultural resources but also to add value to the resources.

There is wide variety of digital cultural resources that should be kept safe for the future. Governmental or business resources retained in archives for a long time have cultural value. Sub-culture and pop-culture resources, which may be excluded in traditional collections at memory institutions, have values as a culture resource worth archiving for the future. The networked information environment enables us to add values to the archived resources and helps us create new resources.

Perfect archiving is not an easy task. Metadata, which may not be visible on the surface of a cultural resource, is representing information and knowledge about the resource in many aspects – subject, technology, management, and so forth. The volume of metadata is increasing, which means the volume of knowledge expressed as a first-class object in the internet is increasing. We need to explore the new ways for the better use of first-class objects on the internet.

Acknowledgements

The authors give special thanks to Drs Jan Ashkoj, Jaeeun Baek and XiaoXiao Feng, and to Ms Wenling He, who contributed the studies presented in this chapter. We would like to express their gratitude to Profs Atsuyuki Morishima and Tetsuo Sakaguchi for their thoughtful comments on the studies. We would like to thank all students who have contributed to the studies.

References

1 IFLA (2009) *Functional Requirements for Bibliographic Records Final Report – Current Text*, http://archive.ifla.org/VII/s13/frbr/frbr_current_toc.htm. [Accessed 6 October 2014.]

2 PREMIS Editorial Committee (2012) *PREMIS Data Dictionary for Preservation Metadata (ver.2.2)*, www.loc.gov/standards/premis/v2/premis-2-2.pdf. [Accessed 6 October 2014.]

3 Nilsson, M., Baker, T. and Johnston, P. (2008) *The Singapore Framework for Dublin Core Application Profiles*, http://dublincore.org/documents/singapore-framework. [Accessed 6 October 2014.]

4 Nilsson, M., Baker, T. and Johnston, P. (2009) *Interoperability Levels for Dublin Core Metadata*, http://dublincore.org/documents/interoperability-levels. [Accessed 6 October 2014.]

5 Morozumi, A., Nomura, S., Nagamori, M. and Sugimoto, S. (2009) Metadata Framework for Manga: a multi-paradigm metadata description framework for digital comics. In *Proceedings of Dublin Core and Metadata Applications, October 2009*, 61–70.

6 OCLC Research, *FictionFinder: FRBR-based Prototype for Fiction in WorldCat*, www.oclc.org/research/activities/fictionfinder.html?urlm=159758. [Accessed 6 October 2014.]

7 He, W., Mihara, T., Nagamori, M. and Sugimoto, S. (2013) Identification of Works of Manga Using LOD Resources: an experimental FRBRization of bibliographic data of comic books. In *Proceedings of 13th ACM/IEEE Joint Conference on Digital Libraries 2013*, 253–6.

8 Toppan Printing Co. Ltd, *Toppan Virtual Reality*, www.toppan-vr.jp/bunka/en/content_works.shtml. [Accessed 6 October 2014.]

9 Europeana, Home page, www.europeana.eu. [Accessed 6 October 2014.]

10 Agency for Cultural Affairs, *Cultural Heritage Online*, http://bunka.nii.ac.jp/Index.do (in Japanese). [Accessed 6 October 2014.]

11 National Diet Library, *Digital Library from the Meiji Era*, http://kindai.ndl.go.jp/?__lang=en. [Accessed 6 October 2014.]

12 Sugimoto, S. (2014) Digital Archives and Metadata as Critical Infrastructure to Keep Community Memory Safe for the Future – Lessons from Japanese Activities, *Archives and Manuscripts, The Journal of the Australian Society of Archives, Inc.*, **42** (1), 61–72.

13 National Diet Library, *NDL Great East Japan Earthquake Archive*, http://kn.ndl.go.jp/node?language=en. [Accessed 6 October 2014.]

14 Vatant, B. and Vandenbussche, P.-Y., *Linked Open Vocabularies (LOV)*, http://lov.okfn.org/dataset/lov. [Accessed 6 October 2014.]

15 Schema.org, *Home – Schema.org*, http://schema.org. [Accessed 6 October 2014.]

16 MetaBridge, https://www.metabridge.jp/infolib/metabridge/menu/?lang=en. [Accessed 6 October 2014.]

17 XiaoFeng, X., Matsumoto, K. and Sugimoto, S. (2012) Digital *Dao-Fa Hui-Yuan*: developing a digital archive of Daoism documents, *Journal of Library and Information Science*, **38** (2), 24–38.

18 Baek, J. and Sugimoto, S. (2012) A Task-Centric Model for Archival Metadata Schema Mapping Based on the Records Lifecycle, *International Journal of Metadata, Semantics, and Ontologies*, **7** (4), 269–82.

19 Askhoj, J., Sugimoto, S. and Nagamori, M. (2011) Preserving Records in the Cloud, *Records Management Journal*, **21** (3), 175–87.

20 Askhoj, J., Sugimoto, S. and Nagamori, M. Developing an Ontology for Cloud-based Archive Systems, *International Journal of Metadata, Semantics, and Ontologies* (forthcoming).

21 Mell, P. and Grance, T. (2011) *The NIST Definition of Cloud Computing*, NIST Special Publication 800-145, http://csrc.nist.gov/publications/nistpubs/800-145/SP800-145.pdf. [Accessed 6 October 2014.]

CHAPTER 6

Managing cultural heritage: information systems architecture

Lighton Phiri and Hussein Suleman
University of Cape Town, South Africa

Introduction

This chapter is about the architecture of systems that store, preserve and provide access to digital cultural heritage objects. It presents some major design considerations for implementing cultural heritage system architectures and some existing architectural patterns currently in use. Then, a simpler architectural design is proposed; this new architecture could potentially have a positive impact on digital preservation.

Digital library systems (DLSs) are specialized information systems designed to store, manage and preserve digital content over long periods of time. With the increase in the number of historical artefacts being digitized, the cultural heritage space is one of many application domains where DLSs are currently used, in an effort to foster easy access to this information and additionally preserve the digital content for future use.

While the motivation for using cultural heritage DLSs (hereafter also referred to as cultural heritage systems) is common across systems, the architectural choices made when designing cultural heritage tools and services varies. The variation in the architectural designs are, in part, influenced by the type – video, audio, digital scans, multi-dimensional models, etc. – of cultural heritage artefacts that will be subsequently digitally preserved and how the digital objects will be subsequently accessed. The next section highlights these requirements further.

The high-level design of these systems takes the form of an architectural framework composed of three main components: a repository layer that stores and manages the digital objects; a service layer with necessary services required to access and manipulate the digital objects; and a user interface layer used by end-users to access the digital objects (Arms, 2000). This is illustrated in Figure 6.1, with specific examples of content and services indicated at each layer.

The remainder of this chapter is organized as follows: 'Resource requirements of cultural heritage systems' describes the major resource requirements for cultural heritage systems; 'Major design constraints and patterns' describes some design constraints and architectural patterns associated with cultural heritage systems; and, finally, 'Designing for preservation: simplicity' presents a proposed architectural design aimed

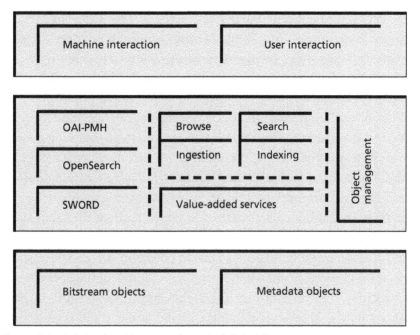

Figure 6.1 High-level architecture of a typical digital library system

at ensuring that the resulting tools and services simplify the overall preservation lifecycle.

Resource requirements of cultural heritage systems

The general technological requirements for designing and implementing cultural heritage systems were summarized in the RLG/OCLC report *Trusted Digital Repository: Attributes and Responsibilities* (RLG/OCLC Working Group on Digital Archive Attributes, 2002). This comprehensive list of issues includes: roles and trust; financial issues; organization/legal responsibility; preservation; collections and content; designated communities; and certification. In addressing these issues, organizations with limited resources need to specifically pay attention to the following aspects:

Routine maintenance

The preservation lifecycle of digital objects is an ongoing process that typically involves the management of digital content and its associated representational information. This routine maintenance is a crucial task in long-term digital preservation for both small- and large-scale preservation projects (Beagrie and Jones, 2001). However, smaller organizations involved in curation and preservation of information often do not have sustainable funding models, making it difficult to effectively manage the preservation lifecycle, as most data and services require regular maintenance.

Technical expertise

Like other systems, the hardware and software stack used to host cultural heritage systems requires constant and active monitoring. Such activities require specific technical expertise and this effectively raises the management and maintenance costs.

Technological resources

The vast majority of modern cultural heritage systems are internet-based and require storage and computational resources, whether local or remotely hosted. In addition, multimedia applications (such as image/video archives) make intensive use of internet bandwidth. These requirements may not pose much of a challenge to well established cultural heritage organizations, but smaller organizations with fewer resources need to plan for this. In addition, when cultural heritage systems are deployed in regions where internet bandwidth is unreliable and mostly very expensive, it is difficult to guarantee widespread accessibility to services offered.

Major design constraints and patterns

There are a number of design constraints and patterns associated with cultural heritage systems in particular, and DLSs in general. Some of the key aspects are as follows:

Scalability

Scalability refers to the ability of a system to expand in order to handle an increasing load. Scalability is an important characteristic for information management systems, and especially DLSs, since there is always a likelihood of adding additional digital objects/collections. It is thus imperative that the architectural design of such systems take into account the potential future growth of content being stored in them.

The scalability of a system can be achieved in two ways: vertical scalability and horizontal scalability. Vertical scalability involves adding resources within an existing logical unit so as to increase capacity. For instance, expanding storage would involve additional hard drives. Horizontal scalability, on the other hand, involves combining multiple logical units of resources to make them function as a single unit (Bondi, 2000).

In the context of cultural heritage systems, the architectural design must be scalable enough to handle different content types that could potentially be placed in the system; the number of users who will be accessing the system at a given time; and also the different ways through which the content will be accessed.

While the overall decisions made in order to facilitate scalable architectures might be system-specific, scalability requirements are design-time decisions.

Preservation

One of the core functions of cultural heritage systems is centred around digital preservation – ensuring that the stored content will be accessible over a long period of time.

A particularly challenging design consideration for cultural heritage systems is ensuring that the architecture is appropriately designed to support potential migration and emulation techniques that might be employed to recover and subsequently access the digital content in the future (Becker et al., 2009). However, this eventual access of digital content is hampered by digital obsolescence – a situation in which software and hardware used to store digital content becomes obsolete due to the rapidly changing hardware and software environments.

While the effects of digital obsolescence manifest themselves at varying levels of the infrastructure used to store digital content, a cheaper and potentially effective alternative involves using architectures that place an emphasis on ensuring that data formats persist into the future. One example where such an approach has proven viable is that of Project Gutenberg (Hart, 1992). Its success is in part attributed to one of its core principles, that all electronic texts are made available in the simplest, easiest-to-use forms, independent of software and hardware platforms used to access the texts.

Federated architectures

In a connected society, information sharing is pivotal in ensuring the success of this connectedness. Federated information system archi-tectures, coupled with interoperability protocols like the Open Archives

Initiative Protocol for Metadata Harvesting (OAI-PMH) (Lagoze et al., 2002), have been particularly instrumental in facilitating the sharing of information among cultural heritage systems.

Federated architectures function through the seamless integration of distributed independent services that communicate with one another using standardized protocols.

The Europeana project presents a classic example of a large-scale cultural heritage federated system. Europeana is a large-scale cultural heritage portal that offers a single access point to European cultural heritage collections. The portal provides access to millions of digital objects from across Europe via a multilingual interface (Purday, 2009). Being a federated service, resource metadata from disparate data providers and aggregators is periodically loaded into a central database so as to provide a globally consistent view of cultural heritage digital objects for potential end-users of the portal. Dublin Core is used as the resource metadata format, making it easier for standard metadata elements to be put into a Solr search engine (Dekkers, Gradmann and Molendijk, 2011).

Portable architectures

The vast majority of publicly accessible cultural heritage systems are set up as web accessible services. However, some environments do not have the necessary infrastructure required to host such services. In addition, such internet infrastructure, if available, is expensive.

A number of portable architectures have been proposed to help facilitate universal access to cultural heritage systems. Greenstone[1] is an example of a widely used software application for heritage systems that are based on a portable architecture. Greenstone is an open-source software tool that was specifically designed for building and distributing digital collections. The architecture of the tool makes it possible for digital content to be organized and published on the internet, or optionally on self-installing CD-ROMs (Witten, Bainbridge and Boddie, 2001). The software's ability to redistribute collections on a self-installing CD-ROM has made it a popular tool in regions with limited internet connectivity.

The digital Bleek and Lloyd collection[2] is another example of a cultural heritage system implemented using a portable architecture. It is an online catalogue that was developed to store and enable access to digitized manuscripts depicting the life of the |Xam and !Kun speakers of Southern Africa. The system was designed to be XML-centric, and is based on an implementation strategy that involves pre-generating scalable hyperlinked XHTML pages using XSLT (Phiri and Suleman, 2012; Suleman, 2007).

Designing for preservation: simplicity

Motivation

Digital libraries were initially designed, to meet the above objectives and address the complex identified issues, as an abstraction layered over databases to provide higher-level services (Arms, Blanchi and Overly, 1997; Baldonado et al., 1997; Frew et al., 1998). They have subsequently become more complex (Janée and Frew, 2002; Lagoze et al., 2005), and thus difficult to maintain, extend and re-use. The difficulties resulting from the complexities of such tools are especially prominent in organizations and institutions that have limited resources to manage such tools and services. Some examples of organizations that fall within this category include cultural heritage organizations and a significant number of other organizations in developing countries found in regions such as Africa (Suleman, 2011).

The majority of existing tools for cultural heritage curation are arguably unsuitable for resource-constrained environments due to the reasons outlined earlier in this chapter. Thus, an alternative architectural design was pursued, based on a set of defined design principles.

Principles

A grounded theory qualitative analysis of successful architectures for DLSs, and other systems to manage digital content, was conducted. The fundamental outcome of this analysis, and interaction with organizations needing to preserve digital content, is a set of guiding design principles, as described in the following sections.

Principle 1: Hardware and/or software platform independence

It should be possible to operate tools and services on a wide variety of hardware and software platforms. The rationale behind this principle is to ensure that the least possible cost associated with technological infrastructure is incurred during the collection management lifecycle.

The preservation lifecycle of digital objects is an ongoing process that typically involves the management of digital content and its associated representational information. The cost implications of long-term digital preservation is a crucial task for both small- and large-scale preservation projects (RLG/OCLC Working Group on Digital Archive Attributes, 2002). However, the vast majority of organizations involved in the curation and preservation of digital information usually do not have adequate funding to support this process, which often includes migration of tools and/or content.

A reduction in the cost associated with the collection management process could be achieved in various ways including, but not limited to, the following:

- designing tools that require minimal technical expertise to manage
- designing tools capable of being run on popular operating systems
- designing tools capable of being operated on hardware platforms with minimal specifications.

Principle 2: Heterogeneous object, metadata and service integration

There should be explicit support for integration of any digital object type, metadata format or new service. The proliferation of both born-digital and digitized information has given rise to various data formats and metadata standards. In addition, there is a growing demand for DL (digital library) services in order to facilitate ubiquitous access to information. It is therefore necessary that the design of DL tools be flexible enough to accommodate heterogeneous objects, metadata and services.

Principle 3: Support for community and international standards

The design of tools and services should take into account community-based standards and international standards in order to facilitate interoperability. The increase in the amount of digital content generated and made available publicly has brought about a need to standardize processes in the digital curation workflow. Incorporating standards in the initial stages of the design process would effectively ensure that the resulting DL services become interoperable with other external services. It also makes it easier for services to be customized.

Principle 4: Flexible design to facilitate extensibility

The design should be flexible enough to enable end-users to adapt the tools and services to their own needs. DLSs are increasingly being used in a wide array of application domains, e.g., institutional repositories and cultural heritage systems. The services offered by these different application domains vary and the overall design must be flexible enough to facilitate customization and extensibility.

Principle 5: Minimalist design approach

There should be minimal use of external software components, in order to simplify the overall design. This would arguably result in tools that are easier to manage. The design of services should, at a minimum, only be composed of the least number of components that are required for it to function. Auxiliary external components should be made optional, making them available only when required. In addition, mandatory components should be critically analysed to ensure that they make use of simplest possible solutions and/or technologies.

Principle 6: Simplified preservation process

The preservation process should be simplified as much as possible to make it easy to migrate digital content. The preservation lifecycle is an ongoing process that requires dedicated staff. The majority of contemporary DL services require technology experts to perform the routine preservation tasks. The overall design should thus be made as simple as possible so that relatively novice users are able to perform at least basic preservation tasks.

Principle 7: Structured organization of data

There should be explicit support for hierarchical logical organization of information. The majority of data that is curated and made publicly accessible has some form of logical organization of information. In addition, data consumers usually visualize information using varying logical views. The design should thus explicitly support the logical organization of information, and make it flexible enough for users and/or administrators to define the desired logical views and structures.

Principle 8: Design for least possible resources

There should be support for access to digital collections in environments with resource constraints. One of the major motivating factors for advocating for a minimalist approach to the overall design of DL tools and services is the apparent unavailability of DL tools that can effectively operate in resource-constrained environments. This is still an issue for most environments in developing countries, such as those found in Africa. The design of DL services should thus be based on the least possible resources to enable resulting services to operate in environments with limited resources.

Repository design overview

The principled design approach, resulting from the principles described above, is applicable to the different architectural components of DLSs –

user interface layer, service layer and repository sub-layer. The emphasis in this discussion is on the repository layer.

Design decisions

The repository design decisions are a result of a direct mapping of the principles set out previously and requirements of the different components of a typical DLS repository sub-layer (Arms, Blanchi and Overly, 1997). These design decisions are presented here in a series of tables. Table 6.1 presents the storage design of digital objects. Table 6.2 presents the storage design of metadata objects. Table 6.3 presents the

Table 6.1 Persistent object storage design decision

Element	Description
Requirement	Persistent object storage
Issues	Principles 1, 2, 6 and 8
Decision	Store bitstreams on the local operating system file system
Assumptions	None
Alternatives	Store bitstreams as blobs in a database; store bitstreams in the cloud
Rationale	Backup and migration tasks associated with repository objects can be potentially simplified; operating system commands can be used to perform repository management tasks
Implications	None; most conventional tools and services use the same approach
Notes	None

Table 6.2 Repository metadata storage design decision

Element	Description
Requirement	Metadata records storage
Issues	Principles 1, 2, 5, 6 and 8
Decision	Native operating system file system is used as storage for metadata
Assumptions	None
Alternatives	Relational database; NoSQL database; embed metadata into digital objects
Rationale	Storage of metadata in plain text files ensures platform independence; complexities introduced by alternative third-party storage solutions is avoided through the use of the native file system
Implications	No standard method for data access (e.g. SQL); transaction process support only available via simple locking; non-availability of complex security mechanisms
Notes	None

scheme for object and metadata naming. Finally, Table 6.4 presents the object structuring scheme.

Table 6.3 Repository object naming scheme design decision	
Element	Description
Requirement	Object naming scheme
Issues	Principle 5
Decision	Use actual object name as unique identifier
Assumptions	Native operating systems
Alternatives	File hash values; automatically generated identifier
Rationale	The native operating system ensures file naming uniqueness at directory level; in addition, it is a relatively simpler way of uniquely identifying objects, as object naming control is given to end-users, rather than imposed on them
Implications	Object integrity has the potential to be compromised; objects could potentially be duplicated by simply renaming them
Notes	None

Table 6.4 Repository object storage structure design decision	
Element	Description
Requirement	Object storage structure
Issues	Principles 6 and 7
Decision	Bitstreams are stored alongside metadata records, at the same directory level on the file system; file system directory is to be used as a container structure for repository objects
Assumptions	The other sub-layers of the Digital Library System have read, write and execute access to the repository root node
Alternatives	Separate storage locations for bitstreams and metadata records
Rationale	Storage of bitstreams and corresponding metadata records alongside each other could potentially make migration processes easier; container structures could potentially make it easier to move repository objects across different platforms
Implications	None
Notes	None

Repository architecture

The architectural design is centred around designing a simple repository. At a bare minimum this should be capable of facilitating the core features of a DLS, such as long-term preservation and ease of access to digital objects. The repository design is file-based and makes use of a typical native operating file system as the core infrastructure. Table 6.5 shows the main components that make up the repository sub-layer, with all the components residing on the file system, arranged and organized as normal operating system files – regular files and/or directories – as shown in Figure 6.2.

Table 6.5 Repository component structural composition

Component	File Type	Description
Container Object	Native OS Directory	Structure used to store digital objects
Content Object	Native OS regular file	Content/bitstreams to be stored in repository
Metadata Object	Native OS regular file	XML-encoded plain text file to store metadata

A typical DLS repository would be located in an application-accessible base root directory node, and is composed of two types of digital objects – Container Objects and Content Objects – both of which are created and stored within the repository with companion Metadata Objects that store representational information associated with the objects. Figure 6.2 illustrates how Container and Content Objects are stored on a typical file system.

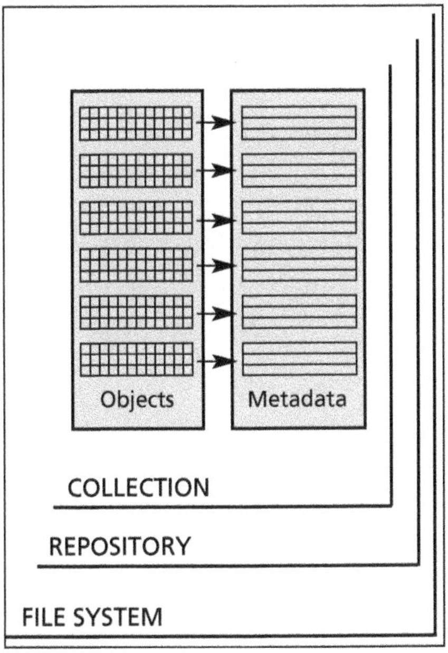

Container Objects can be recursively created within the root node as the repository scales, and enable the creation of additional Container Objects within them. As shown in Figure 6.3, the Metadata Object associated with a Container Object holds information that uniquely identifies the object; optionally it describes the object in more detail, including relationships that might exist with other objects within the repository; and a detailed log of objects is contained within it, referred to as the manifest.

Content Objects represent digital

Figure 6.2
Repository object organization

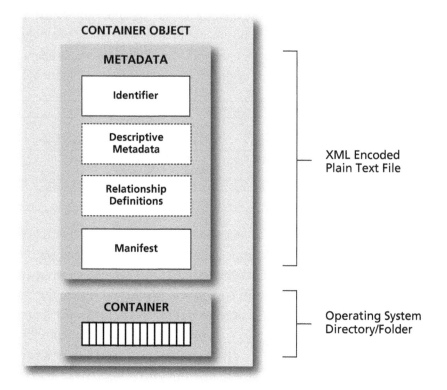

Figure 6.3 Simple repository container object component structure

objects to be stored within the repository. As shown in Figure 6.4, the representational information stored in the Metadata Objects associated with Content Objects is similar to that of Container Objects, with the exception of manifest-related information.

Case studies

This repository architecture was implemented in two case studies, described in the following, to assess feasibility and examine the impact of these design decisions on real-world data.

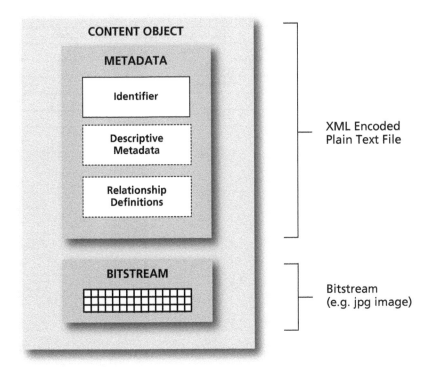

Figure 6.4 Simple repository content object component structure

Case study: The Bleek and Lloyd collection

The Bleek and Lloyd collection (Skotnes, 2007) is a 19th-century compilation of notebooks and drawings comprising the linguistic and ethnographic work of Lucy Lloyd and Wilhelm Bleek on the life of the |Xam and !Kun speakers of Southern Africa. In 2003, the Lucy Lloyd Archive and Research Centre at the University of Cape Town embarked on a large-scale digitization project of all the artefacts and corresponding representation information was generated. Table 6.6 shows the current composition of the digitized objects and Figure 6.5 shows a sample page from one of the digitized notebooks.

A repository for this collection was implemented using the hierarchical architectural design previously described. The container and digital content metadata records are encoded using qualified Dublin Core for descriptive metadata tags and relationships that exist within the different resources.

Table 6.6 The Bleek and Lloyd collection profile	
Collection theme	Historical artefacts; museum objects
Media types	Digitized
Collection size	6.2GB
Content type	image/jpeg
Number of collections	6
Number of objects	18,924

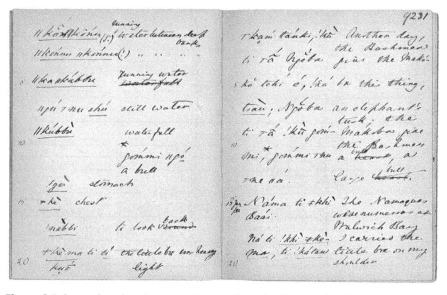

Figure 6.5 Screenshot showing a sample page from the 'Posts and trading' story in the Lucy Lloyd !Kun notebooks

A prototype web-based DLS, that makes use of this repository as the data storage layer, was subsequently implemented (Phiri et al., 2012) using the Java programming language. The prototype DLS is made up of two main components: a curator interface for performing digital object management tasks and administrative functions, and an end-user interface, through which end-users can access the digital content stored in the repository. Evaluation of these interfaces confirmed that their usability, utility and performance were acceptable. There was no discernible impact on user experience.

Case study: SARU archaeological database

The Spatial Archaeology Research Unit (SARU), in the Department of Archaeology[3] at the University of Cape Town has been compiling archaeological collections since the early 1950s. These collections are predominantly in the form of site records and corresponding artefacts within the vicinity of the sites. Table 6.7 shows the composition of collections that have been compiled thus far, and Figure 6.6 shows an image of a rock art motif from one of the archaeological sites.

Table 6.7 SARU archaeological database collection profile	
Collection theme	Archaeology artefacts; museum objects
Media types	Born digital
Collection size	283GB
Content type	image/jpeg; image/tiff
Number of collections	110
Number of objects	72,333

Figure 6.6 Screenshot showing the Die Mond South plant fossil from the Eastern Cederberg rock art site

Owing to the growing number of collections and a growing need by a number of researchers to access this information, an archaeological database was designed in 2005, in part to produce layers suitable for integration with geographic information systems. The site records are originally accessible only via a Microsoft Access[4] database-based desktop application (Wiltshire, 2011).

Using the repository architectural design described earlier, a hierarchical file-based repository was implemented to store artefacts for the SARU collection. However, unlike the Bleek and Lloyd collection outlined above, a custom metadata scheme for the digital content had to be devised due to the complex nature of the metadata records associated with the artefacts.

The School of Rock Art cultural heritage educational portal (Crawford, Lawrence and Marston, 2012) was implemented as a layered service on top of the file-based repository. The portal is composed of three main components: a Cave Navigation module to enable end users to navigate three-dimensional models of caves, annotated with repository images; a Guided Tours module for sequencing the viewing of repository images; and a Story Telling module that integrated stories with images from the repository. This case study demonstrated usability, flexibility and extensibility of the core repository design.

Summary

Architectures for digital library systems to preserve cultural heritage artefacts have much in common with other forms of DLSs, but also some requirements that are different. In designing such cultural heritage systems, system architects need to focus on the needs of curators as well as the ever-present preservation imperative. Such a preservation-focused effort leads to specific design goals that are arguably well served by an architectural model based on the concept of simplicity.

This chapter has presented the motivation and details behind such a simple architecture, based on a set of design principles that were derived from an analysis of successful aspects of existing architectures. This repository architecture was then used as the basis for two case studies, which suggest that it is a feasible model. Various user studies and performance experiments have been conducted to prove the flexibility and scalability of such simple architectures, in the context of these case studies and others.

Ultimately, there is no silver bullet in DLS architecture. However, simple architectures may have advantages for some types of systems; and some elements of simple architectures may have wide applicability for all systems. It is clear, though, that the architecture of systems needs to be planned and based on specific goals, as that can have a profound impact on the architectural design and therefore the content being curated and its long-term preservation and access.

Notes

1 www.greenstone.org.
2 http://lloydbleekcollection.cs.uct.ac.za.
3 http://web.uct.ac.za/depts/age.
4 http://office.microsoft.com/en-us/access.

References

Arms, W. Y. (2000) *Digital Libraries*, 2nd edn, Cambridge, MA, MIT Press, 344, www.cs.cornell.edu/wya/DigLib.

Arms, W. Y., Blanchi, C. and Overly, E. A. (1997) An Architecture for Information in Digital Libraries, *D-Lib Magazine*, **3** (2). DOI: 10.1045/february97-arms.

Baldonado, M., Chang, C.-C. K., Gravano, L. and Paepcke, A. (1997) The Stanford Digital Library Metadata Architecture, *International Journal on Digital Libraries*, **1** (2), 108–21, http://ilpubs.stanford.edu:8090/270.

Beagrie, N. and Jones, M. (2001) *Preservation Management of Digital Materials: the handbook*, Digital Preservation Coalition, 31–47, www.dpconline.org/component/docman/doc_download/299-digital-preservation-handbook.

Becker, C., Kulovits, H., Guttenbrunner, M., Strodl, S., Rauber, A. and Hofman, H. (2009) Systematic Planning for Digital Preservation: evaluating potential strategies and building preservation plans, *International Journal on*

Digital Libraries, **10** (4), 133–57. DOI: 10.1007/s00799-009-0057-1.

Bondi, A. B. (2000) Characteristics of Scalability and Their Impact on Performance. In *Proceedings of the Second International Workshop on Software and Performance – WOSP '00*, New York, NY, ACM Press, 195–203. DOI: 10.1145/350391.350432.

Crawford, K., Lawrence, M. and Marston, J. (2012) *School of Rock Art*, Cape Town, http://pubs.cs.uct.ac.za/honsproj/2012/crawford_lawrence_marston.zip.

Dekkers, M., Gradmann, S. and Molendijk, J. (2011) *D3.4: Final Technical and Logical Architecture and Future Work Recommendations*, Europeana Working Group, 1–29, http://pro.europeana.eu/c/document_library/get_file?uuid=d0327b50-2e86-45bd-81c1-7bff4b9a449b&groupId=10602.

Frew, J., Freeston, M., Freitas, N. and Hill, L. (1998) The Alexandria Digital Library Architecture. In Nikolaou, C. and Stephanidis, C. (eds), *Research and Advanced Technology for Digital Libraries*, Lecture Notes in Computer Science, **1513**, Springer, 61–73. DOI: 10.1007/3-540-49653-X_5.

Hart, M. (1992) *Gutenberg: the history and philosophy of Project Gutenberg*, Project Gutenberg, www.gutenberg.org/wiki/Gutenberg:The_History_and_Philosophy_of_Project_Gutenberg_by_Michael_Hart.

Janée, G. and Frew, J. (2002) The ADEPT Digital Library Architecture. In *Proceedings of the Second ACM/IEEE-CS Joint Conference on Digital Libraries – JCDL '02*, New York, NY, ACM Press, 342. DOI: 10.1145/544220.544306.

Lagoze, C., Van de Sompel, H., Nelson, M. and Warner, S. (2002) *Open Archives Initiative – Protocol for Metadata Harvesting – v. 2.0*, www.openarchives.org/OAI/openarchivesprotocol.html.

Lagoze, C., Payette, S., Shin, E. and Wilper, C. (2005) Fedora: an architecture for complex objects and their relationships, *International Journal on Digital Libraries*, **6** (2), 124–38. DOI: 10.1007/s00799-005-0130-3.

Phiri, L. and Suleman, H. (2012) In Search of Simplicity: redesigning the Digital Bleek and Lloyd, *DESIDOC Journal of Library and Information Technology*, **32** (4), 306–12, http://pubs.cs.uct.ac.za/archive/00000780/.

Phiri, L., Williams, K., Robinson, M., Hammar, S. and Suleman, H. (2012) Bonolo: a general digital library system for file-based collections. In Chen,

H.-H. and Chowdhury, G. G. (eds), *14th International Conference on Asia-Pacific Digital Libraries,* Taipei, Springer-Verlag, 49–58. DOI: 10.1007/978-3-642-34752-8_6.

Purday, J. (2009) Think Culture: Europeana.eu from concept to construction, *The Electronic Library,* **27** (6), 919–37. DOI: 10.1108/02640470911004039.

RLG/OCLC Working Group on Digital Archive Attributes (2002) *Trusted Digital Repositories: attributes and responsibilities,* Research Libraries Group and Online Computer Library Center Report, Mountain View, CA, www.oclc.org/resources/research/activities/trustedrep/repositories.pdf.

Skotnes, P. (2007) *Claim to the Country – the archive of Wilhelm Bleek and Lucy Lloyd,* Johannesburg, Jacana Media.

Suleman, H. (2007) Digital Libraries Without Databases: the Bleek and Lloyd Collection. In Kovács, L., Fuhr, N. and Meghini, C. (eds), *Proceedings of Research and Advanced Technology for Digital Libraries, 11th European Conference (ECDL 2007), Budapest,* Berlin/Heidelberg, Springer, 392–403. DOI: 10.1007/978-3-540-74851-9_33.

Suleman, H. (2011) An African Perspective on Digital Preservation. In Munshi, U. M. (Indian Institute of Public Administration) and Chaudhuri, B. B. (Indian Statistical Institute) (eds), Multimedia Information Extraction and Digital Heritage Preservation, *Statistical Science and Interdisciplinary Research,* **10**, 295–306.

Wiltshire, N. (2011) *Spatial Analysis of Archaeological Sites in the Western Cape Using an Integrated Digital Archive,* University of Cape Town.

Witten, I. H., Bainbridge, D. and Boddie, S. J. (2001) Greenstone: open-source digital library software with end-user collection building, *Online Information Review,* **25** (5), 288–98. DOI: 10.1108/14684520110410490.

CHAPTER 7

Cultural heritage information: users and usability

Sudatta Chowdhury
University of Strathclyde, UK

Introduction

The main goal of an information system or service is to facilitate discovery and access to relevant information, thereby meeting the requirements of users. User studies or human information behaviour studies, which focus broadly on how people seek and use information, have remained a major focus of the research and professional activities in information science over the past six decades. Initial research focusing on information needs and information behaviour began in the 1950s with users in science and technology disciplines (Wilson, 1999, 2008); it continued through the 1960s and grew significantly in the 1970s onwards. The field of research has been designated or referred to by various names, such as information behaviour studies, user studies, information needs studies, information seeking and retrieval studies, and so on (Bawden and Robinson, 2012). Several theories and models have been developed in course of the research activities during the past few decades (for details see Wilson, 1994). However, during the first few decades, the focus of user studies remained limited to the information systems and users in the STEM (science, technology, engineering and medicine), and in some cases social sciences, disciplines, and 'only during the 1990s did attention turn to the information behaviours of academics and practitioners in the arts and humanities' (Bawden and Robinson, 2012, 191).

In today's digital world users can play a key role in the entire lifecycle of information – from the creation of information to the design and usability of information systems and services that facilitate access to, and use of, information. While user studies focus on information behaviour, information needs, information seeking and retrieval, etc., usability studies focus on the role of users in the design and evaluation of information systems, products and services (Chowdhury and Chowdhury, 2011). The overall aim of both these sets of studies is to facilitate better and easier access to information that are relevant to a user in a specific context.

With the advancement of ICT, web and mobile technologies the scope of user and usability studies has increased significantly because:

- An information service may include one or more specific types or format of information – text as well as images of objects and artefacts, data, music, video, etc.
- The service may collect and manage information and data from a variety of information creation, distribution and management systems, e.g., information and data can be generated and distributed through a formal publishing and peer review process, they may come from the existing collections of a variety of institutions, or they can also be self-published and self-distributed through the web.
- Users may use a variety of computing devices; information systems and services are increasingly becoming device-independent, and they are increasingly being accessed and used through mobile devices.
- Users may be distributed across a number of different institutions or countries and they may come from a variety of different communities or cultures.
- There is a common push, and a general move, towards open access where anyone can access information free at the point of use.
- Information services are increasingly using various Web 2.0 and social networking technologies for publishing information as well as for gathering user-generated content and data.

As stated earlier, research on users and usability of information systems and services in digital humanities and digital culture began much later – in the 1990s as opposed to 1950s – and there have been relatively fewer projects and publications in this area. Based on an analysis of some literature and practical research projects, this chapter discusses various issues and challenges of users and usability studies in digital humanities and digital culture. It also briefly discusses some emerging trends in the context of users and usability studies of cultural heritage information systems and services.

Users of cultural heritage information

Research shows that information needs, information seeking and retrieval, information and use and interactions, etc., are significantly influenced by the culture and context of users, as well as the nature of the domain and information itself; and a large number of models and theories have appeared discussing these issues over the past few decades (see, for example, Case, 2012; Ingwersen and Järvelin 2005; Ruthven, 2007; Ruthven and Kelly, 2011). However, most of these information behaviour models were developed based on studies on users from STEM and social science fields that may or may not be appropriate for information users in cultural heritage.

Cultural heritage information users can be quite diverse, for example they may be:

- cultural heritage institutions organizing or providing content to users or other institutions or services (for example, librarians, archivists, digitization centres and digital libraries that provide information services to the public, but at the same time contribute to, and interact with, larger or different information services like Europeana
- cultural heritage institutions creating content (for example, museums, theatres, art galleries, publishers and database providers)
- cultural heritage professionals creating content (for example, artists, musicians, photographers and journalists)

- researchers, scholars and academics studying or teaching objects or cultural heritage in different disciplines (for example, art, architecture, history, language and literature, social sciences and sciences)
- tourism users interested in cultural heritage objects or sights (tourists, travel agents, government tourism departments and information centres, etc.)
- members of the general public interested in art and culture, and so on.

Each user category has different requirements and skills that have implications for how information should be organized, accessed and used; and these need to be multiplied by age, language, educational, socio-economic and cultural factors.

Looking specifically at the information behaviour of humanities users, Warwick et al. (2005) note that they:

- have sophisticated information needs and yet often they do not have a clear idea of what they are looking for
- often look for a wide range of information resources
- often look for information resources that are older
- often look for original information resources rather than a surrogate.

Terras (2012) points out that the information needs and information-seeking behaviour of humanities scholars are quite different from those in the sciences or social sciences, and these should be taken into account for the design and delivery of cultural heritage information services. Warwick comments that:

> - Humanities scholars have a complex repertoire of information skills that allow them to evaluate traditional information resources;
>
> Warwick, 2012, 13

and

- we cannot and must not try to tell digital humanities users what they ought to like, need or use. We also cannot expect people to abandon working practices instantly when they have suited them well over many years and in some humanities fields, generations.

Warwick, 2012, 18

These characteristics of users reinforce the importance of understanding 'the behaviours of humanities researchers and the users of cultural heritage resources, in the context of digital tools and resources so that they may be designed to be more usable and sustainable in the future' (Warwick, 2012).

Although digital versions of content can facilitate better and easier access, many serious researchers prefer to access and use the original sources. Warwick (2012) comments that users are more likely to trust an information resource as they get more information about it. It is observed that digital humanities users prefer more structured documentation as opposed to the more informal, community-based approach of folksonomies (Warwick et al., 2009). Historians rely mainly on institutional or published sources for images because metadata attached to images is expected to adhere to standards with required fields and controlled vocabulary, leading to improved reliability of the collections, as opposed to images through social networked collections with natural language tagging (Harris and Hepburn, 2013). Therefore, trustworthiness and context-specific access to the original information resources are some of the top priorities of humanities users. Furthermore, Harris and Hepburn suggest that historians value texts over visual resources, and this should be taken into consideration for digitization and providing information services. However, gaining intellectual control has always remained a challenge for historians, and in today's networked world anxiety about comprehensiveness of information is growing (Rutner and Schonfeld, 2012).

Design and usability of cultural heritage information systems

People use digital resources if they fit their needs, and yet as Warwick, Terras and Nyhan (2012) note, many digital resources are still designed without reference to the users and their requirements, and often this means that expensive digital resources remain unused or unappreciated by their intended audience. Kachaluba, Brady and Critten (2014) point out that interactivity features, such as note-taking and copying, and navigability and general ease of use are some of the essential attributes of a user-centred design of cultural information services. User-centred design focuses on methods directly involving the users with the rationale that this will help to develop systems that meet users' expectations and needs. User-centred design involves two approaches: user analysis in the early stages of a project, and usability research during the later stages (Normore, 2009).

Apart from technical, legal, economic and social issues such as licensing agreements and long-term preservation (Kachaluba, Brady and Critten, 2014), other issues, such as design (architecture, interfaces and search tools) and usability (globalization *v.* localization, language – mono- *v.* multi-lingual systems – cultural issues, content and human behaviour) (Chowdhury, Landoni and Gibb, 2006) and the environmental issues such as green IT (Chowdhury, 2010) are important considerations for making user-centred and usable information systems and services.

'Know Thy User' is the mantra of any user-centred design, and yet most digitization activities for building digital libraries and digital preservation systems have been developed without proper considerations of user current and future needs, culture, context, etc. Warwick (2012) argues that it is extremely important 'to seek to understand the behaviours of humanities researchers and the users of cultural heritage resources, in the context of digital tools and resources, so that they may be designed to be more usable and sustainable in the future.' Similar views have been expressed by other researchers, too. For example, Sinn (2012) comments that which materials users demand and how users will use the materials can also be important qualifications for inclusion of resources in digital projects. One of the major challenges facing information system designers and managers is to design systems that can meet the needs of users – many of whom may be unknown and unseen, and often have a different physical location – characteristics and nature of activities, language and culture, and so on (Chowdhury and Chowdhury, 2011).

Furthermore, there are some practical problems for user-centred design of large and transnational digital libraries and information services. Let's take the example of the European digital library. The main impediment for creating a clear vision of what users would expect from Europeana arises from the extremely broad user scope set out for Europeana by the European Commission: to provide a platform for the use of 'The European Citizen'. Thus Europeana has an extremely broad and unspecific target user group. Who is the European Citizen and what would a user-centred design for such a user look like?

Broadly speaking, a European citizen is a person residing in a country in Europe. As of 2010 the European Union had 27 member states with about half a billion people comprising about 20% children and young people (0–19 years), 60% adults of working age and around 20% retired or elderly people (65 years or older) (Eurostat, 2010). Figures from 2013 report that around 28% of the European population have a lower secondary education, 47% have upper secondary education, and 23% have tertiary education (Eurostat, 2014). Designing an information service that can meet the information needs of this diverse set of population in itself is a big challenge, but there are other associated challenges too.

In Europe there are 24 officially recognized languages, more than 60 indigenous regional and minority languages, and many non-indigenous languages spoken by migrant communities (European Commission, 2012). Most European citizens speak at least one more foreign language beside their native mother tongue. With the inclusion of Croatia into the European Union in 2013, the most conservative estimate of the number of cultures would take the number of nation states or countries as its baseline, that is, 28 cultures are represented in the EU. But anyone from England will say that people from Scotland, Northern Ireland or Wales have a different culture, and this is true for every region in every country;

and even a major city like London or Rome has different cultures in its different parts. So, the question remains: is there such a thing as the European user? Europeans live in different countries and regions, speak different languages, have different ages, different educational background, different levels of digital and information skills, and – most of all – many different cultures. It goes without saying that they have many different information needs or, at worst, sometimes they may not have any specific information need but yet they may intentionally or unintentionally (e.g., through referral from a search engine) want to access the Europeana site. Research into information literacy and people's information behaviour can have implications for the design of information services and products and they can also understand and build appropriate information literacy interventions (Hepworth and Walton, 2013).

Furthermore, there are the rapid developments in the ICT, web and mobile technologies that are significantly influencing user information behaviour and culture. Sula observes that 'the 21st century has seen a dramatic rise in social networks and crowdsourcing, access to digitized cultural heritage materials, and interfaces for archives and collections that exploit the capabilities of linked data and visualization' (Sula, 2013).

In addition to the diverse sets of users and their information needs and behaviour, there are other issues, too. For example, cultural heritage information resources have some inherent attributes that pose usability challenges when they are digitized and are made accessible through a digital information system or service. While a large part of content and data in science and technology is born digital, much of the cultural heritage information resources are digitized and attributes of such digitized objects play an important role on the overall usability of a cultural heritage information service. Accuracy, clarity, resolution, look and feel, file sizes, etc., are some of the major features of digitized objects that may affect the usability.

There is also the issue of digital divide (Chowdhury and Chowdhury, 2011). Brandtzaeg, Heim and Karahasanovic (2011) observe that 60% of European citizens from the countries investigated in their study lag alarmingly behind others in their internet usage, out of which 42% are non-users and 18% are sporadic users. The study predicted the presence of a 'rich get richer' effect in which the divide between the different types will increase in connection with the growing development and distribution of the internet and its technologies.

One of the objectives of usability and evaluation studies is to measure the impact of a digital information product or service. However, in general, impact studies of information services are few and far between. Sinn (2012) argues that access cannot reflect the quality and relevance of the digital resources to users. Warwick (2012) suggests that digital humanities projects should from the beginning have a clear idea of who the expected users might be and accordingly the project team should consult them as soon as possible and maintain contact through the project. In the context of archival collections and historians, Sinn (2012) comments that it is extremely important to understand how historians, who are arguably the major group of users for archival collections, use digital archives. Kachaluba, Brady and Critten (2014, 92) comment that we are in a period of transition not only in academic publishing practices in digital humanities and culture but also in research methodologies, as different formats of cultural heritage content facilitate 'different behaviors for reading, analyzing, and discovering information'.

Proper project documentation is very important in terms of usability, and especially re-use, of cultural heritage content. Research shows (Warwick et al., 2009) that it was almost impossible to re-use digital resources due to lack of documentation. Warwick et al. emphasize that technical documentation should describe:

> the rationale for the creation of the mark up scheme and the way that individual tags are applied or function as a detailed codebook for a database showing how fields were allotted and explaining relationships between fields. This allows anyone who wishes to reuse the data to understand the rationale for its creation and is especially useful if there are any problems with the consistency of how the scheme has been applied.
>
> Warwick et al., 2009, 35

Procedural documentation is more general and describes the way a digital humanities or digital culture project was created and run. It should include details and completeness of sources, selection methods and the details of any important decisions taken in the project (Warwick et al., 2009).

Rutner and Schonfeld (2012) point out that the ever-expanding landscape of digital resources facilitates the collection and analysis of more and more information during the research process, but at the same time this has increased the challenge of engaging with all of the material. Therefore, user training is important to reduce the challenges, but it is also necessary to develop new and more effective discovery mechanisms to effectively support research and discovery (DeRidder and Matheny, 2014).

Emerging trends

One of the major objectives of user studies research is to identify new trends and patterns in the seeking, access and use of digital information. Based on the analysis of some research projects and literature, some emerging patterns of user behaviour and usage of cultural heritage information are discussed in the following sections.

Access patterns: mobile devices and search engine referrals

Digital natives are the young people living in the age of Web 2.0, where social networking and text messaging are the preferred channels for sharing and communicating ideas. In the context of the usability of Europeana, the largest digital library of cultural heritage information in Europe, it was noted that there is a significant difference among younger and older generations of users and an earlier research notes that some simple search-engine-like features are preferable for younger users (Dobreva and Chowdhury, 2010). Other researchers also noted that most people do not like or need the complicated functionality and difficult interface to make the search possible (Warwick et al., 2008a; Warwick et al., 2008b). Many digital natives will have little experience of traditional online information services such as online scholarly databases, and they prefer the most commonly used interfaces and functionalities of popular search engines as a way into the cultural heritage information systems and services (Nicholas et al., 2013). Similar observations about the information behaviour of young users have been made by other researchers. For example, Cunningham (2010) points out that digital natives are now making their way into the workplace and live with the technology: they have different understanding and expectations of technology in a business environment. Research shows that the digital natives are significantly influencing the design and delivery of information services, including cultural heritage information services (Nicholas et al., 2013).

As in other areas of web information, use of mobile devices is also becoming common in cultural heritage information services. It is noted that mobile devices are a very fast-growing market segment for the Europeana digital library: mobile use has quadrupled in one year, and the real change for Europeana has been in the increasing use of tablets (CIBER, 2011). It was also noted that some mobile users make relatively brief visits of just under two minutes, typically conducting a single search and viewing several pages of content.

The way people access cultural heritage information services is also changing. Many cultural heritage information services are now accessed through what is known as referrals, where the users are referred to them by search engines. While studying the mobile user behaviour of Europeana, Nicholas et al. (2013) note that search engines, and predominantly Google, are the key drivers, sending as much as 80% of Europeana's traffic, and also fixed and mobile users do not differ much in terms of their referral patterns for the Europeana service. This indicates that search engines are the first port of call and users are referred to the respective digital information services by the search engines in response to a query.

The above two sets of observations raise a number of questions for cultural heritage information systems and services (Nicholas et al., 2013). For example:

- Does it mean that cultural heritage information services will be better placed to act as a storehouse of digital information, leaving the access part to the search engine services?

- What changes will be brought by the fast-changing mobile technologies in terms of the design and delivery of cultural heritage information services?
- Given the proliferation of the use of mobile technologies, how are the information industry and the information services sector going to be influenced by the 'apps' industry? Are we going to see specific 'apps' developed for user- and context-specific use of cultural heritage information?

Crowdsourcing, user-generated content and collaborations in digital culture

Cultural heritage information services often integrate their services with user-generated content using Web 2.0 – social media and crowdsourcing techniques (Warwick, 2012). Web 2.0 describes a new generation of web-based services that facilitate a number of hitherto impossible activities: for example, information consumers can now easily become information creators; and it is now possible to share content, add comments and re-use content, and thus generate new information based on existing cultural heritage content. Warwick (2012) stresses that social networks, blogs, podcasts and crowdsourcing are now central to work in digital humanities because these technologies facilitate information sharing, collaboration, participation and community engagement. While reviewing 36 crowdsourcing projects in digital humanities, Carletti et al. (2013) observe that one of the major challenges for crowdsourcing is how to integrate institutional and crowd-contributed content. They also point out the need for developing appropriate socio-technological systems that can support the collaboration between cultural institutions and their users.

Nevertheless, as in the case of other Web 2.0 services and user-generated content, major challenges persist in the context of crowdsourcing of digital cultural content, such as the lack of clarity and trust surrounding the digital content, experiences and competencies of information users, information overload, and so on (Ross, 2012; Research Information Network, 2011; Conole and Alevizou, 2010). There are also various legal and ethical issues with regard to the use/re-use of user-generated content. More research is needed to capture information on who is accessing and using social media and crowdsourcing applications and for what purpose, in an academic or cultural heritage context. As pointed out in the UK government-sponsored *Hargreaves Review* (Hargreaves, 2011) and the subsequent Finch Report (Finch, 2012), appropriate business models for supporting seamless transactions of user-generated content have also to be developed and tested.

Conclusion

Just as in any information system or service, users should be the focal point of the design, management and delivery of any cultural heritage information service. Chowdhury and Chowdhury (2011) emphasize that 'a usable website should allow users to perform all the functions necessary to meet their information requirements with the minimum amount of time and effort.' However, going for a user-centred design can be a challenging task, especially for a large cultural heritage information service like Europeana.

Wickett et al. (2014) comment that cultural heritage collections are a fundamental feature of information organization systems, providing technical capabilities for retrieval and evaluation of content within large aggregation. However, access and use of digital heritage information, like other resources, also heavily depend on trust issues, such as the authenticity and quality of content. Users of cultural heritage information are often unique and have some characteristics that are different from those of other disciplines.

Along with the fast-moving technological shifts such as information on mobiles, tablets and so on, users' behaviours, users' expectations and the nature of digital content are constantly evolving. It is becoming an increasingly challenging task to keep up with the rapid changes both in digital resources and users' expectations. Keeping in mind the needs of the 'future' users of the society who are so-called 'digital natives', analogue content should be digitized, and the overall cultural heritage information services should be managed to match the rapidly changing ICT, web, mobile and social networking technologies. Myers and Sundaram (2012) propose that a set of five interrelated dimensions – namely, personalized, interactive, intuitive, attractive and social – should be considered to guide the design of ubiquitous information systems for digital natives.

References

Bawden, D. and Robinson, L. (2012) *Introduction to Information Science*, London, Facet Publishing.

Brandtzaeg, P. B., Heim, J. and Karahasanovic, A. (2011) Understanding the New Digital Divide: a typology of internet users in Europe, *International Journal of Human–Computer Studies*, **69**, 123–38.

Carletti, L., Giannachi, G., Price, D. and McAuley, D. (2013) Digital Humanities and Crowdsourcing: an exploration. In Proctor, N. and Cherry, R. (eds), *Museums and the Web 2013*. Silver Spring, MD, Museums and the Web, http://mw2013.museumsandtheweb.com/paper/digital-humanities-and-crowdsourcing-an-exploration-4.

Case, D. (2012) *Looking for Information: a survey of research on information seeking, needs and behaviour*, 3rd edn, Emerald.

Chowdhury, G. G. (2010) Carbon Footprint of the Knowledge Sector: what's the future?, *Journal of Documentation*, **66** (6), 934–46.

Chowdhury, G. G. and Chowdhury, S. (2011) *Information Users and Usability in the Digital Age*, London, Facet Publishing.

Chowdhury, S., Landoni, M. and Gibb, F. (2006) Usability and Impact of Digital Libraries: a review, *Online Information Review*, **30** (6), 656–80.

CIBER (2011) *Europeana: culture on the go*, www.ciber-research.eu/download/20111007-Europeana_Culture_on_the_Go-mobile_report.pdf.

Conole, G. and Alevizou, P. (2010) *A Literature Review of the Use of Web 2.0 Tools in Higher Education 2010*, Higher Education Academy.

Cunningham, J. (2010) New Workers, New Workplace? Getting the balance right, *Strategic Directions,* **26** (1), 5–6.

DeRidder, J. L. and Matheny, K. G. (2014) What Do Researchers Need? Feedback on use of online primary source materials, *D-Lib Magazine,* **20** (7/8).

Dobreva, M. and Chowdhury, S. (2010) A User-centric Evaluation of the Europeana Digital Library. In *The Role of Digital Libraries in a Time of Global Change, 12th International Conference On Asia-Pacific Digital Libraries,* ICADL 2010, Gold Coast, Australia, 21–25 June 2010. LNCS 6102, Springer, 148–57.

European Commission (2012) *Europeans and Their Languages: report,* http://ec.europa.eu/public_opinion/archives/ebs/ebs_386_en.pdf.

Eurostat (2010) *Demography Report: older more numerous and diverse Europeans,* European Commission, http://epp.eurostat.ec.europa.eu/cache/ ITY_OFFPUB/KE-ET-10-001/EN/KE-ET-10-001-EN.PDF .

Eurostat (2014) *European Commission: education and training data,* http://epp. eurostat.ec.europa.eu/portal/page/portal/education/data/database.

Finch, J. (ed.) (2012) *Accessibility, Sustainability, Excellence: how to expand access to research publications,* report of the Working Group on Expanding Access to Published Research, www.researchinfonet.org/wp-content/uploads/2012/ 06/Finch-Group-report-FINAL-VERSION.pdf.

Hargreaves, I. (2011) *Digital Opportunity: a review of intellectual property and growth,* www.ipo.gov.uk/ipreview-finalreport.pdf.

Harris, V. and Hepburn, P. (2013) Trends in Image Use by Historians and the Implications for Librarians and Archivists, *College & Research Libraries,* **74** (3), 272–87

Hepworth, M. and Walton, G. (eds) (2013) *Developing People's Information Capabilities,* Bingley: Emerald.

Howard, J. (2011) Social Media Lure Academics Frustrated by Journals, *Chronicle of Higher Education,* 20 February, http://chronicle.com/article/Social-Media-Lure-Academics/126426.

Ingwersen, P. and Järvelin, K. (2005) *The Turn: integration of information seeking and retrieval in context,* Springer.

Kachaluba, S. B., Brady, J. E. and Critten, J. (2014) Developing Humanities Collections in the Digital Age: exploring humanities faculty engagement with electronic and print resources, *College & Research Libraries,* **75** (1),

91–108.

Myers, M. D. and Sundaram, D. (2012) Digital Natives: rise of the social networking generations, *University of Auckland Business Review*, **15** (1), 29–37.

Nicholas, D., Clark, D., Rowlands, I. and Jamall, H. R. (2013) Information on the Go: a case study of Europeana mobile users, *Journal of the American Society for Information Science and Technology*, **64** (7), 1311–22.

Normore, L. F. (2009) Characterizing a Digital Library's Users: steps towards a nuanced view of the user, *Proceedings of the American Society for Information Science and Technology*, **45** (1), 1–7.

Research Information Network (2011) *Social Media: a guide for researchers*, a Research Information Network Guide, RIN.

Ross, C. (2012) Social Media for Digital Humanities and Community Engagement. In Warwick, C., Terras, M. and Nyhan, J. (eds), *Digital Humanities in Practice*, London, Facet Publishing, 23–45.

Ruthven, I. (2007) Interactive Information Retrieval, *Annual Review of Information Science and Technology*, **42** (1), 43–91.

Ruthven, I. and Kelly, D. D. (eds) (2011) *Interactive Information Seeking, Behaviour and Retrieval*, London, Facet Publishing.

Rutner, J. and Schonfeld, R. C. (2012) *Supporting the Changing Research Practices of Historians*, Ithaka S+R technical report for the National Endowment of the Humanities, US Department of Commerce National Technical Information Service.

Sinn, D. (2012) Impact of Digital Archival Collections on Historical Research, *Journal of the American Society for Information Science and Technology*, **63** (8), 1521–37.

Sula, C. A. (2013) *Digital Humanities and Libraries: a conceptual model*, http://chrisalensula.org/digital-humanities-and-libraries-a-conceptual-model.

Terras, M. (2012) Digitization and Digital Resources in the Humanities. In Warwick, C., Terras, M. and Nyhan, J. (eds), *Digital Humanities in Practice*, London, Facet Publishing, 47–70.

Warwick, C. (2012) Studying Users in Digital Humanities. In Warwick, C., Terras, M. and Nyhan, J. (eds), *Digital Humanities in Practice*, London, Facet Publishing, 1–21.

Warwick, C., Blandford, A., Buchanan, G. and Rimmer, J. (2005) User Centred

Interactive Search in the Humanities. In *Proceedings of 5th ACM/IEEE-CS Joint Conference on Digital Libraries*, New York, NY, ACM Press, 400.

Warwick, C., Terras, M., Galina, I., Huntington, P. and Pappa, N. (2008a) Library and Information Resources and Users of Digital Resources in the Humanities, *Program-Electron Library*, **42** (1), 5–27.

Warwick, C., Terras, M., Huntington, P. and Pappa, N. (2008b) If You Build It Will They Come? The LAIRAH Study: quantifying the use of online resources in the arts and humanities through statistical analysis of user log data, *Literary and Linguistic Computing*, **23** (1), 85–102.

Warwick, C., Galina, I., Rimmer, J., Terras, M., Blandford, A., Gow, J. and Buchanan, G. (2009) Documentation and the Users of Digital Resources in the Humanities, *Journal of Documentation*, **65** (1), 33–57.

Warwick, C., Terras, M. and Nyhan, C. (2012) Introduction. In Warwick, C., Terras, M. and Nyhan, J. (eds), *Digital Humanities in Practice*, London, Facet Publishing, xiii-xix.

Wickett, K. M., Doerr, M., Meghini, C., Isaac, A., Fenlon, K. and Palmer, C. (2014) Representing Cultural Collections in Digital Aggregation and Exchange Environments, *D-Lib Magazine,* **20** (5/6).

Wilson, T. (1994) Information Needs and Uses: fifty years of progress. In Vickery, B. C. (ed.), *Fifty Years of Information Progress: a Journal of Documentation review*, London, Aslib, 15–51.

Wilson, T. (1999) Models in Information Behaviour Research, *Journal of Documentation*, **55** (3), 249–70.

Wilson, T. (2008) The Information User: past, present and future, *Journal of Information Science*, **34** (4), 457–64.

CHAPTER 8

A framework for classifying and comparing interactions in cultural heritage information systems

Juliane Stiller and Vivien Petras
Humboldt-Universität zu Berlin, Germany

Introduction

For centuries, cultural heritage institutions have acted as guardians of the society's cultural memory, guiding visitors and researchers through historic and contemporary assets while explaining their significance and value. Through digitization of cultural heritage and online access to it, memory institutions such as museums, libraries and archives have the opportunity to unlock the potential of their material. Recent technological developments enable organizations to reach a broad spectrum of people with different backgrounds and to facilitate contextualization of cultural heritage artefacts in an unprecedented way, thus opening up new horizons in experiencing cultural heritage.

Most institutions seized the opportunity to revive their hidden heritage by digitizing objects and publishing and displaying a digital surrogate on a website or information system. They seek meaningful presentations of their digitized cultural heritage data with regard to display of context and purposeful interactions, but transferring context and significance of objects in a digital environment is not a trivial task. In most cases, the digital representations do not reflect the context the original artefacts were embedded in. This leads to a loss of meaningful, and often expensively curated, information and the question of what purposeful interactions with digital cultural heritage should entail.

Cultural heritage information systems need to be differentiated from systems accessing pure textual content. The main differences between a generic information system and one storing and accessing cultural heritage are the potential interactions with the digital content. First, the information system needs to offer appropriate access functionalities that bring meaningful objects to the surface and ensure important information does not get buried in a pile of low-quality metadata. Second, they need to enable the users to immerse themselves in the historic situation an object gained significance from and make clear in which context it was created. In the best case, context and digital objects are so interweaved that they transport the user back in time, simulating the historic setting. Presenting and showcasing cultural heritage and striving for enthusing users about their heritage through the means of the digital medium should be the goal of memory institutions.

One might consider these to be dreams of the future, because a lot of steps need to be taken for this vision to become a reality. Defining purposeful interactions with cultural heritage online and giving users guidance on exploring new functionalities in experiencing digital artefacts are certainly among the most important aspects memory institutions should take into account. It is essential to identify the potential benefits of displaying and providing cultural heritage in a digital medium, with its unique affordances allowing for different interactions from those commonly practised with physical objects (Murray, 2011). The goal is to build systems for interacting with memory artefacts that are able to evolve and can adapt to interaction and usage patterns that are not yet foreseeable. Many recently developed cultural heritage information systems are lacking a strategy for user involvement and the purpose of such an engagement.

This chapter[1] deals with the strategies of cultural institutions to provide users with means for purposeful interactions with digital cultural heritage while maintaining their mandate to offer universal access to curated content. It presents a conclusive framework for evaluating interactions and critically analysing them with regard to serving users and cultural institutions alike. This systematic approach supports the assessment of interactions with digital cultural heritage in their entirety. The objective is to share insights about the nature of purposeful interactions in this domain and strategically improve and enhance them to serve the needs of institutions while being open to future developments and use cases. A particular focus will be on aggregators, especially Europeana,[2] and their interactions. They often accumulate material from libraries, museums and archives and serve as good examples of cultural heritage information systems.

Defining interactions in cultural heritage information systems

In contrast to natural heritage, cultural heritage consists of objects created or interpreted by humans. These objects are products which inherit a purpose and are defined by their use (Bearman and Trant, 2002). Intangible objects such as dances or language explicitly extend this definition.

Recently, the shift of memory institutions from being gatekeepers to becoming facilitators and mediators of knowledge exchange (Freedman, 2000) involves complementing cultural artefacts with digital surrogates and their metadata in information systems. Cultural heritage information systems collect, organize and display cultural heritage objects, including their metadata, in a digital environment providing information about the contextual background of the object (Petras, Stiller and Gäde, 2013). This requires the information system to offer interactions that go beyond the common known-item search experience, including contextualization and collaboration.

Interactions are a crucial component in the architecture of an information system. Here, the view of human–computer interaction and interaction design (e.g., Cooper, Reimann and Cronin, 2007; Rogers, Sharp and Preece, 2011) is adopted to define the concept: an *interaction* includes one or more actions a user can complete in a cultural heritage information system, such as searching or browsing items. It also describes actions that support collaborative engagements, for example editing a user profile, uploading objects and creating collections. In the foreground of this definition is the underlying purpose of the action that is taken by a user.

In digital libraries, not only do users interact with the system but also the system components interact with other layers of the system. Bates' model of cascading layers of interactions suggests that each strategic part influences the design of the following component. On their basic level, digital libraries consist of content and a database to organize it. The last part in this model consists of the user's expectations and interactions with the system (Bates, 2002). A much more simplified model derived from Bates' assumptions determines that every information system (including those outside the cultural heritage domain) strives for seamless inter-actions between the users and the content. The layers in between – on the one hand, the system which enables access to the content in all its facets and, on the other, the interaction patterns and interface functionalities which enable the user to interact – should be transparent and intuitive to the user. Figure 8.1 illustrates this simplified model. Murray (2011, 10) calls this concept *transparent*, meaning that the interface should not distract the users from their tasks but offer them interactions they can intuitively execute.

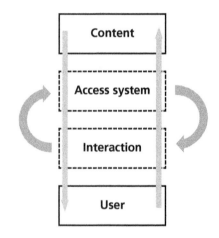

Figure 8.1
Simplified model of an ideal information system

Modes of information access

User interactions with the content are based upon and support the different access modes a system provides. These can be broadened and further enriched by the user, who creates more access points. From a generic perspective, interactions with the system provide access to information encompassing all aspects, from finding a resource and using it to making sense of it. Information access consists of three main modes – *Search*, *Browse* and *Engage* – which are similarly described in Petras, Stiller and Gäde (2013).

Search

In most information systems, Search is the most important access mode. It can be defined as a bundle of techniques and methods for identifying relevant documents which are likely to satisfy a user's information need (Agosti, 2008). The user interacts with the content of an information system by inputting a query into a search box. It is an access mode characterized by interactions to find the objects users are looking for. It includes all interactions that help support the users in retrieving facts and objects that match their input, such as a query. Search is an access mode that can be further broadened through interactions of users, creating more points of access.

Browse/explore

Browse is considered to be an access mode that is distinguished from Search as it does not require a query to find information or get a general idea about the collection or items offered in an information system. Browsing is often described as being cognitively easier to perform than searching with a query and retrieving relevant results from a list (*recognition over recall paradigm*) (Hearst, 2009, 74, but also Cove and Walsh, 1988). Through user interactions, structuring and grouping, data can be introduced easily. This requires more interaction opportunities in a system than a simple search box. But often new structures and contextual groupings of the data unfold once users interact with a system. Compared to Search, Browse presumes more complex interactions. In return, these interactions create more access points to the material.

Engage

Engage is the most complex access mode; it encompasses interactions that are not based on pure consumption, such as searching and browsing. When searching or browsing, the user consumes information items as provided by the information system. If users interact with an information system's content in the Engage access mode, they edit existing content or add new content collaboratively with others or alone (Frieseke et al., 2011, 18). How cultural heritage institutions deal with user-contributed data and use it to engage users on the one hand and enrich their content on the other will be the key factor determining the success of their information systems. They will be judged by their ability to maintain a discourse involving experts and novice users about cultural material that excels in quality and relevance (Proctor, 2010).

The new approach presented here links the modes of access, Search, Browse and Engage, to the interactions offered by a system. The access to information and cultural heritage content is influenced by the interactions and their ability to create valuable access points. The interrelatedness between interactions and access modes is the basis for the development of the framework of interactions introduced in the next section.

A framework of interactions

The framework of interactions in cultural heritage information systems combines a categorization of interactions with their degree and their interplay with the access modes.[3] It is a means to express complexity and variability of interactions in a system in relation to the modes of access it provides. It enables comparison and evaluation of interactions in cultural heritage information systems. The framework offers the opportunity to assess systems from a different perspective, deriving new insights on how system design influences access points.

The framework was developed on the basis of a review of 50 cultural heritage information systems, analysing the interaction features and interaction patterns that were found in this sample. The framework consists of two dimensions. The first dimension is a taxonomy that allows all user interactions within the system to be systematized into different interaction classes. The second dimension describes the complexity within a class and its relation to the different access modes.

Categorizing interactions

In a first step, the different interactions and interaction patterns found in the sample information systems were clustered into groups. By analysing these interactions, different classes of interactions emerged. The classes spanned by meta-classes form the first dimension of the framework, creating a taxonomy of common interaction patterns in cultural heritage information systems:

Content interaction meta-class

The content is the basis of an information system and guides its design and functionalities. In cultural heritage information systems, either the institution or the user provides content. Interactions with content aim at discovery through search or browsing, deep-zooming into pictures or paging through a curated online exhibition. The content's origin is often reflected in the interactions offered with it.

Curation interaction meta-class

Curation can be institutional or applied by the user. Institutional curation is often applied prior to feeding the objects into the information systems, e.g., through acquisition of an object. This type of curation is usually carried out in the information system, but users can interact with its results, for example curated exhibitions. The user-driven interactions are characterized by the customized and personalized way in which the user can experience the digital cultural heritage material. The goal is to involve users on the one hand and to contextualize the digital material by engaging a user or a group of like-minded people on the other.

Support interaction meta-class

To offer a meaningful and sustainable system with a rich user experience, some supporting interactions are necessary. They are often neglected, as they revolve around user management and user identities. They invite the user to revisit a particular system and identify with its content. The Support classes take the Curation interactions to the next level, engaging the user and providing incentives to contribute and visit regularly. These interactions make the experience in a cultural heritage information system meaningful and sustainable.

The interaction classes described above are interrelated. Curation classes are not possible without Support classes, and the content is just a lifeless structure without any activities targeted towards interacting with it. Table 8.1 shows the taxonomy of interactions with a detailed description of every class and the interactions which were clustered in these classes.

Within an interaction class, there are several options for how to

Meta-class	Class	Description of the clustered interaction patterns
Content	Institutional Objects	Interaction patterns related to the institutional content aggregated in information systems. Examples are searching full-text, looking at a full-view item or browsing thematic exhibitions.
	User Objects	Same as above, but the content is user-provided, therefore different functionalities are applied, such as upload features.
Curation	Annotations	Interaction patterns that allow users to add additional information to content, such as writing comments, tagging or other free text. It also includes the linking of other digital objects to existing content.
	User Exhibition	Interaction patterns that allow users to curate customized exhibitions and collections of content.
	Storytelling	Interaction patterns that allow users to add their own point of view through directed and chronological narration.
Support	User Representation	Interaction patterns that let users represent themselves and connect with each other, e.g. creating user profiles and following other users' contributions across the site. Depending on the implementation of the Curation class, this can have different implications.
	User and Content Reputation	Interaction patterns that present the reputation of content and users alike. This implies rating and starring favourite objects, but also leadership boards.

Table 8.1 Classes of interactions with descriptions of the interaction patterns

implement a certain feature, e.g., a social tagging functionality in the *Annotations* class. Not all of these options prove to be useful, so a means to express the complexity and quality of the interactions within a class is required. Consequently, a second dimension is added, which can describe the degree of the interactions of a certain class and links them to the access modes.

Degree and complexity of interactions

The classification of interactions is not yet adequate to compare cultural heritage information systems and their implemented features with one another. It lacks an essential ingredient which fuels the interactions and determines how sustainable and useful an offered interaction is. From the interaction classes alone, one cannot evaluate the implications and dependencies for improving access to cultural heritage content. Tasks such as adding a tag to a resource can be implemented in different ways, and it is often not obvious what intention different implementations have. For example, it makes a difference whether a tag is visible on the full view page of the object that was tagged or whether the tag is hidden in the user's account. In the first case, the tag can be searched and browsed; in the latter the tag is invisible to other users. In one information system, interactions of the *Annotations* class might stimulate social collaboration among users; in another, social tagging is no more than an annotated list of bookmarks. To distinguish between these different degrees of interactions within a class, a second dimension is introduced which assesses the degree and complexity of interactions.

For interactions to become purposeful, they need to attract users to participate and revisit the system, ideally also supporting the institution's mission. The degree to which interactions achieve this can be illustrated in a second dimension of the framework. The degree of interactions can be considered as development stages, as each stage builds upon the preceding one. At each stage, the interactions become more complex, but also more purposeful, creating more access points for the material the user is interacting with. In general, institutions should strive for a higher degree of interactions, as it grants more purpose to the users' interactions. Figure 8.2 shows a model of the interaction degrees and their influence on shaping different access points in the Search, Browse and Engage modes. In general, the more complex and user-oriented an information system is, the more interaction features it offers.

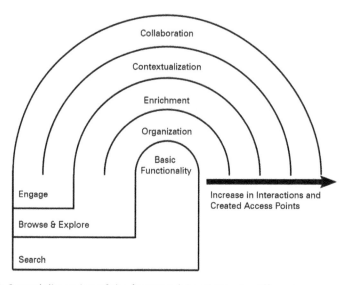

Figure 8.2 Second dimension of the framework in relation to different access modes

Driven by the complexity of interactions, five development stages can be identified, as described in Table 8.2. The different degrees of interactions are interwoven with the access modes offered to the material. The higher the degree of interaction, the greater the complexity of the possible interaction patterns and the access points created.

The combined dimensions presented above form a rich framework of interactions in cultural heritage information systems. It allows classifying interaction patterns by their goal within the system. Additionally, each interaction class can be complemented by an assessment of its degree and complexity. This dimension is closely related to the access modes offered by the system and the new access points, which are created through interactions. In general, interactions should focus on being purposeful for the institution and its users. This framework helps to understand the purpose a cultural heritage information system offers through its interactions from the users' point of view.

Evaluating interactions

The framework is a tool for evaluating interactions in cultural heritage information systems. The best way to achieve this is visualizing the framework and mapping the interactions of each system or a group of

Table 8.2 Degrees of interactions and their descriptions with regard to the meta-classes

Degree level	Description	Access Mode
Basic Functionality	For the *Content* classes, this degree is characterized by textual search as the most basic form of accessing content; in many cases in form of a simple search box. For the *Curation* classes, it means the basic module of a given feature is provided. For example, in the *Annotations* class, the user can add a tag or a comment. How this user addition is used and processed in the system is not part of this stage. For the *Support* classes, basic features for user representation, such as an account, or rating objects, are present. On this level some structure might exist but it is not used.	Search
Organization	This degree level enables more complex interaction patterns. In the *Content* classes, this means adhering to best practices in metadata standards such as the use of rich, domain-specific data models. An example of the benefits of more structured metadata is the provision of faceted search to reduce the number of results for a query. In the *Curation* classes, it means that curated content is stored in a structured way, thus allowing simple browsing and content exploration beyond search. For the *Support* classes, this often means that representation and reputation are made visible, creating recommendations for other users.	Search and Browse
Enrichment	Enrichment provides users with more entry points for retrieving and exploring particular content. It enables targeted browsing and search, as ambiguous terms can be differentiated and named entities and the like identified. For the *Content* classes, it can mean the provision of semantic enrichment within the metadata. In the *Curation* classes, it refers to any form of additional semantic information that is added to the content. In the *Support* classes, enrichment adds an additional layer of complexity which might be reached through the transparent exposure of user-object relationships.	Search and Browse
	Continued on next page	

Table 8.2 *Continued*

Degree level	Description	Access Mode
Contextualization	With contextualization, the Engage access point is activated, as contextualization can be a product of links between users and resources. The content gets embedded into richer and more diverse contexts. In the *Content* classes, this means that users contextualize cultural heritage objects and add their meaning and interpretations drawn from a number of different sources, including external ones, to them. In the *Curation* classes, the product of the interaction can be contextualized with linked data from third-party sources. Users can embed their tags, exhibitions or uploaded objects into the broader perspective by adding them to a map or grouping them by different viewpoints, placing the resource into a broader context. For the *Support* classes, contextualization often means the creation of further pivot points for grouping data. At this stage, workflows become very complex and possible interactions increase. They get intermixed with the need to set the right incentive for the user to participate. The technical implications for implementing contextualization are manifold; user-generated content needs to be stored, upload functionalities provided and a quality assurance system deployed. Cultural heritage information systems rarely offer contextualization through user-driven data.	Search and Browse and Engage
Collaboration	The most complex degree of an interaction class is collaboration. The focus is on working together in groups of like-minded people and sharing the product of the experience with a broader audience. For the *Content* classes, collaboration means working together on activities related to institutional or user objects. To implement this, complex group functionalities and rights management need to be set up. Furthermore, getting users to interact with each other requires multifaceted user management and representation features. The *Curational* classes at this level are characterized by a social and collaborative effort in, for example, creating user exhibitions in groups. The *Support* classes assist the collaborative activities through simplifying communication and updates, e.g. follow features for other users. In the cultural heritage domain this is still a long way off, but something cultural institutions should strive for.	Search and Browse and Engage

systems to it. For a visual representation, the framework and its two dimensions are reflected in a radar model (Figure 8.3). The edges of the radial lines in the radar graph represent the interaction classes, whereas the different rings represent the complexity and degree of interaction. With each outgoing ring from the centre to the edge of the graph, the

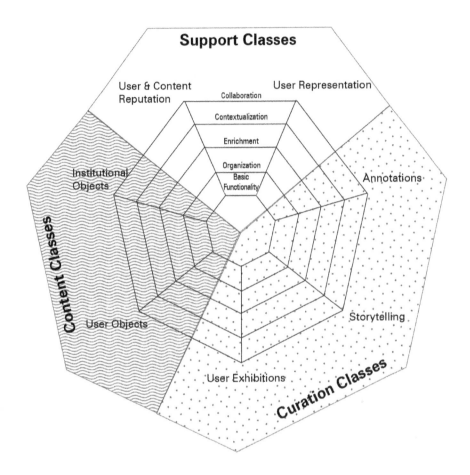

Figure 8.3 The framework visualized in a radar graph

degree of interaction develops from *Basic Functionality* to *Collaboration*. The further away an interaction class is from the central point, the closer it is to support Collaboration, i.e., the largest degree of interaction a system can provide. Wider rings correspond to more access points that are created with more complex interactions. The more the interaction is implemented towards Collaboration, the more access points are produced. Each interaction of an information system can be positioned on this grid to easily identify its nature.

Evaluation of cultural heritage aggregators

As a practical example, the following section will apply the framework for an assessment of interactions in one type of cultural heritage information system, the aggregators. Aggregators accumulate digital cultural heritage material across institutions, languages or domains. A special focus lies on Europeana, the single access point for digital cultural material in Europe. It will be shown that the framework can be used to evaluate a group of systems or single systems and compare their interactions. For that, interactions were pinned to the framework to reveal characteristics and derive recommendations.[4]

Twelve aggregators were included in the analysis (Table 8.3). They either cover a single domain or aggregate content across domains. Aggregators measure their success by the size of their collection and often display this on the home page. Size and number of records differs considerably across the different systems. This is due to the different missions of the aggregators and what they want to achieve. The European

Table 8.3 Sample of aggregators, their originating country and number of objects

Name	URL[5]	Country	Number of Objects
Archives Portal Europe	www.archivesportaleurope.net	ES	48 million records
ArtBabble	www.artbabble.org	USA	1,500 videos
DPLA	http://dp.la	USA	7.4 million records
Europeana	www.europeana.eu	NL	32 million records
Gallica	http://gallica.bnf.fr	FR	3 million records
Google Art Project	www.googleartproject.com	USA	70,000 artworks
HathiTrust	www.hathitrust.org	USA	11 million volumes
Project Gutenberg	www.gutenberg.org	USA	45,000 books
Smithsonian Collections Search Center	http://collections.si.edu/search/index.htm	USA	8.6 million records
The European Library	www.theeuropeanlibrary.org	NL	22 million objects, 150 million records
World Digital Library	www.wdl.org	USA	10,000 records
Your Paintings	www.bbc.co.uk/arts/yourpaintings	UK	210,000 paintings

Library, for example, joins together the collections of 48 national libraries and research libraries in Europe. Your Paintings, on the other hand, is a project funded by the BBC and The Public Catalogue Foundation aggregating all oil paintings in the UK and making them accessible to the public through crowdsourced tags that describe these paintings.

Case study I: evaluating aggregators

Figure 8.4 shows the percentage of the systems within the sample of aggregators that implemented an interaction class to a certain degree. In general, it can be observed that aggregators are focused on improving and standardizing metadata, embedding additional information to them. As

	Basic Functionality	Organization	Enrichment	Contextualization	Collaboration
Institutional Objects	100%	100%	92%	17%	0
User Objects	8%	0	0	0	0
Annotations	50%	17%	8%	8%	0
User Exhibitions	58%	25%	17%	8%	0
Storytelling	0	0	0	0	0
User Representation	50%	0	0	0	0
User and Content Reputation	17%	8%	0	0	0

Figure 8.4 Percentage of systems among aggregators that provide interactions per class and degree (the darker the cell the more systems provide interactions in this class)

aggregators are not affiliated with a single physical institution but rather act as independent digital libraries, they need to offer innovative ways to discover content. This sets them apart from the online presence of other memory institutions and ensures that providers are willing to contribute content. Their main task is driven by the challenges that arise when aggregating content from different sources. Moreover, they target their services toward offering customized user experiences, although the social part does not play such a big role here. Their services are not focused on user collaboration. Nevertheless, they strive for meaningful representation of their material.

As the aggregated material is often very heterogeneous, aggregators need to solve problems of metadata standardization and display before focusing on user interactions. Their unifying goal is to offer users a single access point that refers to the locations where the digital object resides. Most aggregators are not hosting the digital objects themselves but only their metadata records; digital objects stay with the provider. They redirect the traffic to the content provider, making it more visible in return. They legitimate their funding and hereby their existence through discovery tools and means which integrate heterogeneous data. In the following section, the meta-classes and their characteristics within the sample of aggregators systems will be discussed.

Content interaction classes

For aggregators, the interaction class Institutional Objects is shaped by their tools for content discovery and browsing (degree: Enrichment). In most cases (eight in the sample), aggregators do not have the digital objects to offer deep-zoom functionalities or other features that would require the computational analysis of the underlying content. They focus on discovery tools that built on the metadata of the artefacts leveraging fields for coverage and date. Almost all systems allow the user to discover data through geospatial or timeline browsing.

Aggregators are focused on providing a rich search experience; they need to guide the users to huge amounts of data providing them with powerful tools to refine search results. All of them offer advanced search and facets to refine the search results. Here, they are not as innovative as, for example, museums and mostly rely on the information in the metadata to construct the facets.

Curation interaction classes

Aggregators implement hardly any interactions from the Curation classes. They often do not have the digital objects and only host the metadata. Their efforts concentrate on making the content more retrievable with search and browsing functionalities. Many implement user exhibitions and half of the systems allow the users to add annotations. Some aggregators (e.g., Europeana and Gallica) implement tagging in the personal space of users, allowing them to tag saved items for later revisits. These annotations are not intended to be social or shared publicly but rather have the function of organizing the user's information space.

Out of the eight systems that offer interactions in the User Exhibitions class, six let users only save searches and favourite items for later revisits (degree: Basic Functionality). One system allows the user additionally to share these personalized lists (degree: Organization). In these cases, exhibitions or collections serve the research purpose of the user. Saving searches and revisiting them, the same as frequenting a list of saved items, is targeted towards users who are researching specific areas of the collection. Interactions in the Storytelling class are not implemented in any of the aggregator systems.

Aggregators implement user curation on a limited scale. One reason is that they have access only to the metadata and do not have rich digital objects. One exception in this group is the Google Art Project, which lets users contextualize their user exhibitions and the items in it. It can afford this type of interaction as it has high-resolution images of the art works, allowing the user to zoom in and annotate certain parts of the objects.

Support interaction classes

Half of the aggregators offer a user account, where users can customize their experience and save favourite items and searches. In general, the user account is not used to add a social aspect to the user experience. None of the user accounts let the user have a public profile or transparently link the users to activities they have taken within a given system. This might be due to the prevailing uncertainty of what a successful social experience with aggregated content might look like. There is the facility to save searches and items. This feature accommodates the workflow of researchers who often construct complex queries and might need to revisit them again. With regard to the public user, the purpose of such a feature needs to be challenged. The user accounts in aggregator systems often do not fulfil a specific purpose and are therefore rarely used.

To summarize, for aggregators, engagement plays only a marginal role. They are characterized by the provision of personalized experiences with the content rather than collaborative ones. The user curation of objects is limited to the personal space and not for public consumption.

Case study II: evaluating Europeana

One aggregator that will be further evaluated is Europeana. The Europeana portal offers a single access point to the digitized cultural heritage coming from museums, archives, libraries and galleries in Europe. It is an aggregator and provides access to the metadata of the objects and a thumbnail, and enables the user to go to the hosting institution accessing the digital object in full size or the full text of the required document.

Presently, Europeana aggregates over 32 million objects[6] coming from more than 2000 different European institutions. This aggregation of digital cultural heritage data is unique in its scale. It not only unifies millions of heterogeneous digital cultural objects but it is also characterized by European-wide collaboration of providers, researchers and other stakeholders which want to enable access to Europe's cultural heritage. Europeana fosters research in the area of digital cultural heritage and is pioneering new approaches to improving access, for example the contextualization of the material by semantic enrichment of the metadata (Isaac, 2013).

A visualization of Europeana's interactions in the framework compared to the ones of the Aggregators group can be found in Figure 8.5. For none of the interaction classes does Europeana reach more than the *Enrichment* level. The biggest task it is facing is the aggregation of heterogeneous data created without cross-institutional standards. This data needs to be homogenized to offer equal access to all objects and ensure transparency. Therefore, Europeana pays particular attention to data aggregation, while presentation display and engagement is of secondary concern. This is shown in the degrees of their interaction classes. Interactions in the Institutional Objects (degree: Enrichment) are more highly developed than in the Curation classes, where the degree does not exceed Basic Functionality.

Europeana offers search and browsing functionalities for its users to find and discover *Institutional Objects* and *User Objects*. For example, it has

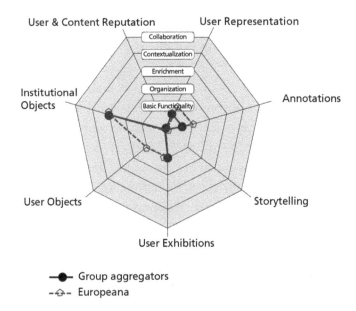

Figure 8.5 Radar graph of Europeana and all aggregators in comparison

curated exhibitions that highlight parts of the collection and tell a story about a specific topic. Furthermore, the standardized metadata fields are used as facets that allow the user to refine search results. The fact that Europeana enriches its metadata with external multilingual vocabulary allows the user to find more objects even if they are in languages that users do not understand. Europeana strives for the integration of objects contributed by users. The different satellite projects funded by the EU, which contribute technology, content and expertise to Europeana, aggregate user content and find ways of engaging the users with cultural heritage. Several storytelling platforms targeting different themes were created which let users tell their stories and upload their material (e.g., Europeana 1914–1918[7]). Some of this content finds its way into Europeana and there it can be searched by default with the opportunity to exclude it from the results via a tick box. Search is enabled for the user objects but no upload functionality is offered, so the degree of Basic Functionality is reached in the User Objects class. User-contributed objects serve as additional content source for Europeana but they only aggregate, not create, this content on their platform. In this class, Europeana differs from the rest of the aggregators, as they normally do not provide the searching of user objects.

In the User Curation section of the interaction classes, Europeana is rather weak. One reason is that Europeana does not have the original digital objects and can only present thumbnails, which limits interactions. The users can annotate objects and save favourite items but they are hidden in the user's private area and these features have no social component associated with them. Therefore, the level for Annotations and User Exhibitions is the Basic Functionality. These low levels can be explained by the interactions in the Support interaction classes. Europeana offers a user account which falls into the class User Representation but it has no other functionality than to set preferences and to edit saved lists of objects and tags. This private area, called 'my Europeana', stores user data and has no social component; thus users cannot present themselves in a profile or similarly. This equates to the degree of Basic Functionality in the class User Representation. Interactions in the classes Storytelling and User and Content Reputation are not implemented in Europeana.

Europeana concentrates on the aggregation of data and access provision on a large scale. Therefore, the implementation of curational activities is on a low level. Several problems need to be solved before these curational activities can be developed more. For example, there is yet no way of feeding changes in the metadata back to the source data, as Europeana does not own the data.

Although Europeana does not aggregate the original source data, there are ways to improve user interactions and construct better models to serve users and institutions alike. First, interactions within the Curation interaction classes, i.e., User Exhibitions and Annotations, should become social, so more people can profit from other users' tags and saved searches. A first step here is to make user annotations publicly visible or allow users to share them with like-minded people in social networks or within Europeana. The other necessary change is to improve the tagging feature within the Annotations class. For now, each tag creates one entity consisting of one digital object with one or more tags. Adding another tag to the same object creates a separated object that is not related to the previous one. This construction makes it impossible for the users to manage their tags and the tagged objects. This also limits the use of the tags for other users if they might become part of the metadata at some point.

Furthermore, the existing user accounts, interaction class User Representation, can be used to personalize the users' experiences and enable them to set preferences which influence the search experience. Multilingual preferences can be offered which would allow searching a collection in a specific language or automatically translating all results to the users' preferred ones.

As an aggregator, Europeana should focus its efforts on improving the interactions in the Institutional Object class by embedding the content into broader contexts and allow users to experience it from different perspectives. Aggregators display the objects of several hundreds or even thousands of individual institutions. This offers the opportunity to display objects from different viewpoints and create relationships that an individual institution cannot establish. Due to the thematic heterogeneity of the providers, aggregators can highlight the different dimensions of one topic. For that, it is essential to further enrich the metadata[8] to be able to regroup objects based on characteristics other than their creator, title or providing institutions. The most valuable asset of aggregators is the data they are providing; therefore, the core task is the accessibility of these objects, creating links between them that would have not been possible in the providing institution.

Conclusion

This chapter presented a framework to evaluate, discuss and assess implemented interactions in cultural heritage information systems. It combined the interactions with modes of access provided for the material and argued that collaborative interactions will lead to the creation of more access points. The framework helps stakeholders of information systems in the cultural heritage domain to identify weaknesses in their provided interactions and define points where an improvement strategy could be effective. The framework is a holistic approach to understanding interactions offered by the system and utilized by users and their relation to the access modes Search, Browse and Engage. In general, several points can be concluded from the development of the framework:

1   The content drives the type of curational activities provided by the institution.
2   Curational activities develop from individual participation to group collaboration.
3   The more collaborative the curational activities are, the more users are engaged and new access points for the content are established.
4   Additional access points are in turn leveraged through Search, Browse and Engage.

It is necessary not only to provide certain features, and consequently interactions, but also to be aware of their influence on the access modes. Each interaction can provide more access points, which can be leveraged by other users to access the content. The more these considerations affect the system design, the more likely a system is going to offer purposeful interactions – benefiting users and institutions alike.

Notes

1   This chapter is extracted and adapted from Stiller (2014).
2   www.europeana.eu.
3   An earlier version of the framework appeared in Stiller (2012).
4   The codebook and coding form for pinning interactions to the framework can be found in the appendix of Stiller (2014).
5   All URLs were last accessed on 29 July 2014.
6   32,273,993 on 29 July 2014.
7   www.europeana1914-1918.eu.
8   A study on the semantic and multilingual enrichments of Europeana has shown that they can be misleading and erroneous if no enrichment strategy is applied (Olensky et al., 2012).

References

Agosti, M. (2008) Information Access Using the Guide of User Requirements. In M. Agosti (ed.), *Information Access Through Search Engines and Digital Libraries*, Springer, 1–12.

Bates, M. (2002) The Cascade of Interactions in the Digital Library Interface, *Information Processing and Management*, **38** (3), 381–400.

Bearman, D. and Trant, J. (2002) *Issues in Structuring Knowledge and Services for Universal Access to Online Science and Culture*, Paper presented at the Nobel Symposium (NS 120) 'Virtual Museums and Public Understanding of Science and Culture', Stockholm, Sweden, www.nobelprize.org/nobel_organizations/nobelfoundation/publications/symposia/ns120-lectures/bearman.pdf.

Cooper, A., Reimann, R. and Cronin, D. (2007) *About Face 3: the essentials of interaction design*, John Wiley & Sons.

Cove, J. F. and Walsh, B. C. (1988) Online Text Retrieval Via Browsing,

Information Processing & Management, **24** (1), 31–7.

Freedman, G. (2000) The Changing Nature of Museums, *The Museum Journal*, **43** (4), 295–306.

Frieseke, M., Gäde, M., Petras, V. and Stiller, J. (2011) *Report – Interaction Patterns in Cultural Heritage Information Systems*, Project Promise – Participative Research labOratory for Multimedia and Multilingual Information Systems Evaluation, unpublished.

Hearst, M. A. (2009) *Search User Interfaces*, Cambridge University Press.

Isaac, A. (2013) *What is Europeana Doing With Semantic Web and Linked Open Data?*, http://lodlam.net/2013/06/18/what-is-europeana-doing-with-sw-and-lod.

Murray, J. H. (2011) *Inventing the Medium: principles of interaction design as a cultural practice*, MIT Press.

Olensky, M., Stiller, J. and Dröge, E. (2012) Poisonous India or the Importance of a Semantic and Multilingual Enrichment Strategy. In Dodero, J., Palomo-Duarte, M. and Karampiperis, P. (eds), *Metadata and Semantics Research: 6th Research Conference, MTSR 2012, Cádiz, Spain, November 28–30, 2012. Proceedings*, Springer, 252–63.

Petras, V., Stiller, J. and Gäde, M. (2013) Building for Success (?): evaluating digital libraries in the cultural heritage domain. In Cool, C. and Ng, K. B. (eds), *Recent Developments in the Design, Construction, and Evaluation of Digital Libraries: case studies*, IGI Global, 141–63.

Proctor, N. (2010) Digital: Museum as Platform, Curator as Champion, in the Age of Social Media, *Curator: the museum journal*, **53** (1), 35–43.

Rogers, Y., Sharp, H. and Preece, J. (2011) *Interaction Design: beyond human-computer interaction*, 3rd edn, John Wiley & Sons.

Stiller, J. (2012) A Framework for Classifying Interactions in Cultural Heritage Information Systems, *International Journal of Heritage in the Digital Era, Proceedings of Euromed 2012: Progress in Cultural Heritage Preservation*, **1**, 141–46.

Stiller, J. (2014) *From Curation to Collaboration: a framework for interactions in cultural heritage information systems*, Doctoral thesis, Humboldt-Universität zu Berlin, http://edoc.hu-berlin.de/dissertationen/stiller-juliane-2014-02-13/PDF/stiller.pdf.

CHAPTER 9

Semantic access and exploration in cultural heritage digital libraries

Ali Shiri
University of Alberta, Canada

Introduction

Cultural heritage information collections and repositories are becoming increasingly visible on the web. The prevalence and popularity of digitization and digital preservation initiatives have given rise to numerous projects focusing on the development of sustainable cultural heritage digital libraries and collections. One of the central components of any such initiative is the conceptualization and implementation of information organization and representation strategies and tools to facilitate information access and interaction. Solid and well established cultural heritage digital libraries address informatio n organization and representation in their business, strategic and sustainability plans for effective and efficient information access and retrieval. The variety of digital objects, digital formats and digital artefacts found in cultural heritage collections make this task a challenging undertaking that requires proper planning, including not only indexing and tagging of materials but also the ways in which indexes and tags can be effectively incorporated into the information architecture and search functionalities of the underlying systems and architectures. Knowledge organization systems (KOS) have been widely used in digital libraries, subject repositories and open archives. The term 'knowledge organization systems' refers to a broad range of schemes for organizing information and facilitating resource description and discovery. KOS may include general classification schemes, special classification systems, thesauri, subject headings, taxonomies, ontologies, gazetteers, synonym rings and other types of standardized controlled vocabularies (Hodge, 2000). Effective and efficient organization, representation and retrieval of information on the web in general and in digital libraries in particular call for the different ways in which KOS can be utilized. KOS have the potential to provide various perspectives of a collection in the digital environment and to offer users a rich conceptual and semantic structure to facilitate search term selection for query formulation, reformulation or expansion. The use of these tools becomes increasingly relevant and important when considering the variety of information sources and formats and the need to create accessible and easy-to-use web-based search systems (Shiri and Molberg, 2005). Digital libraries, digital archives and virtual museums have made use of knowledge organization systems and controlled vocabularies. Recently, more attention has been paid to user-centred approaches to knowledge organization systems (Tudhope and Lykke Nielsen, 2006) and their integration into search user interfaces of digital libraries (Shiri, 2006; Shiri and Chase-Kruszewski, 2009) and institutional repositories (Mondoux and Shiri, 2009).

This chapter provides an overview of knowledge organization systems and metadata standards used in cultural heritage digital libraries. It reviews the literature of information search behaviour as it relates to humanities and cultural heritage information. It will examine and analyse the ways in which three selected cultural heritage digital libraries have incorporated controlled vocabularies in their search user interfaces to support the information exploration and access. Specific attention is paid to the search user interface features of the cultural heritage digital libraries to establish the extent to which they have taken into account evidence from the recent research on the information search strategies of cultural heritage information seekers.

Context

Knowledge organization systems have served as information representation and retrieval tools in a broad range of digital libraries and repositories. Previous research has documented the different types of knowledge organization systems in new information environments. This entails the use of thesauri, classification systems, subject headings lists, ontologies and taxonomies in numerous open archives, digital libraries, content management systems and institutional repositories. It should be stressed that the use of a particular knowledge organization system is not an end, but rather a means, to facilitate effective and timely access to cultural information in its broad sense. Therefore, it is argued that at least there are two aspects to the application of knowledge organization systems in cultural heritage digital libraries: (a) organizing and representing information and (b) an organized presentation of the information for the purpose of supporting users' interaction and engagement with that information. The latter is clearly advocating the use of knowledge organization systems as user interface affordances and functionalities. This delineation is particularly important, as many cultural heritage digital libraries tend to give preference to the organization of information and not to the ways in which users' interaction can be facilitated or enhanced. In this chapter we argue that the choice and application of knowledge organization systems should not only take into account information organization but also user interaction and engagement with information through the proper integration of knowledge organization systems into search user interfaces.

With the rise of cultural heritage digital libraries as new information organization and representation platforms, the need to make effective use of knowledge organization systems becomes more pressing than ever before. Baca (2003) notes that cultural heritage institutions are rushing to make their collections available online, but the decisions that must be made in order for online resources to be truly useful are often misunderstood. It is not enough to use some metadata standard. A metadata standard appropriate to the materials in hand and the intended end-users must be selected. Even the right choice of a metadata schema will not ensure good end-user access.

Controlled vocabularies and metadata standards for cultural heritage digital libraries

In order to provide a clear context for the discussion of knowledge organization systems in cultural heritage digital libraries, it would be useful to provide a definition for cultural heritage and cultural works as the representation of cultural heritage. Harpring defines these concepts as follows:

> *Cultural works* are the physical artefacts of *cultural heritage*, which encompasses broadly the belief systems, values, philosophical systems, knowledge, behaviours, customs, arts, history, experience, languages, social relationships, institutions, and material goods and creations belonging to a group of people and transmitted from one generation to another. The group of people or society may be bound together by race, age, ethnicity, language, national origin, religion, or other social categories or groupings. The works discussed in this book are cultural works, but they are limited to fine arts, architecture, and other visual art as described below.
>
> Harpring, 2010, 2

Examples of cultural heritage digital collections may include fine arts, architecture, crafts, decorative arts, textiles, clothing, ceramics, needlework, woodworking, furniture, metalwork, decorative documents and vehicles. In terms of the context and creators of these collections, a wide range of organizations may be responsible for these collections, including museums, visual resources collections, libraries, archival collections, special collections and private collections.

Doerr (2009) stresses the diversity of cultural heritage, proposing the following list of major kinds of collections:

- history of arts and modern arts (graphics, painting, photography, sculpture, architecture, manuscripts, religious objects)
- historical heirloom (treaties, letters, manuscripts, drawings, photos, films, personal objects, weapons)
- archaeology (sherds, sculptures, tools, weapons, household items,

human remains)
- design (furniture, tableware, cars, etc.)
- science and technology (machinery, tools, weapons, vehicles, famous experiments, discoveries)
- ethnology (costumes, tools, weapons, household items, religious objects, etc.)
- immobile sites (architecture, sculpture, rock art, caves)
- to a certain degree, natural history collections, such as paleontology, biodiversity, mineralogy are also evidence of human activities (i.e. research) and hence culture.

Doerr (2009), 464–5

A considerable number of controlled vocabularies and metadata standards have been utilized for organizing and representing cultural works in libraries, museums and archives. Item-level and collection-level metadata as well as subject metadata have been adopted by many cultural collections. In the following, a brief overview of these tools and standards will be provided to demonstrate the variety of tools used. Among the most widely used metadata standards for cultural materials are Dublin Core, Visual Resources Association (VRA Core), Encoded Archival Description (EAD), Getty Categories for the Description of Works of Arts (CDWA) and CIDOC (Centro Intercultural de Documentación Coceo) Conceptual Reference Model (CRM). A significant number of knowledge organization systems have been used as sources of subject metadata in various cultural and memory institutions. The widely adopted and used controlled vocabularies are listed below:

- Getty Art and Architecture Thesaurus (AAT)
- Getty Thesaurus of Geographic Names (TGN)
- Getty Union List of Artist Names (ULAN)
- Getty Cultural Objects Name Authority (CONA)
- Getty Conservation Thesaurus (CT)
- Library of Congress Thesaurus for Graphic Materials (LCSH/TGM)

- Library of Congress Subject Headings (LCSH)
- Library of Congress Authorities
- IconClass
- Virtual International Authority File (VIAF).

Some of the above knowledge organization systems are more widely used than others. Shiri and Chase-Kruszewski (2009) found that the AAT thesaurus was the most commonly used thesaurus for art collections in North American digital libraries. The AAT thesaurus was also the second most widely used controlled vocabulary following the LCSH in American digital repositories and collections (Park and Tosaka, 2013). Doerr (2009) views the AAT thesaurus as the largest and most stable thesaurus in the cultural heritage sector. The diversity and variety of knowledge organization systems in the cultural heritage area has instigated research into the alignment, reconciliation and maintenance of multiple vocabularies to support searching and browsing (Isaac et al., 2008; Van der Meij et al., 2010; Van Hooland et al., 2013) and into semantic interoperability within the context of cultural heritage digital collections (Harsányi, Rozinajová and Andrejčíková, 2012). The High Level Thesaurus (HILT) project, for example, investigated the subject interoperability among various knowledge organization systems, including the AAT thesaurus (Nicholson and Shiri, 2003). Binding and Tudhope (2004) reported a project that investigated the use of the AAT thesaurus for semantic query expansion in the context of the UK National Museum of Science and Industry.

In addition to the above knowledge organization systems, a number of other controlled vocabularies have been in use in European cultural heritage information collections. For instance, the HEREIN (the European information network on cultural heritage policies) project produced an interlingua as a thesaurus consisting of terms derived from reports on cultural heritage policies in Europe. The thesaurus was created without direct reference to the terms or structure of any pre-existing thesaurus (Zeng and Chan, 2004). The Netherlands Institute for Sound and Vision employs the GTAA (Gemeenschappelijke Thesaurus

Audiovisuele Archieven) or the Common Thesaurus [for] Audiovisual Archives to index and disclose their audiovisual documents. SVCN (Stichting Volkenkundige Collectie Nederland) is an ethnographic thesaurus developed and used by several Dutch ethnographic museums (Hollink et al., 2008). A useful and analytical discussion of the ontologies used in cultural heritage is provided by Doerr (2009).

With the development of semantic web technologies such as Simple Knowledge Organization System (SKOS) for encoding various types of knowledge organization systems and linked data, new opportunities have arisen to allow libraries, archives and museums to share, exchange, interconnect, re-use and re-purpose their knowledge organization systems. Shiri (2012) enumerates some of the advantages of SKOS and linked data as follows:

- link several different thesauri
- expand search functionalities through federated searching of multiple controlled vocabularies and linked data sources
- allow for the integration of thesauri into many web-based search engines and services
- provide semantically rich visualization of thesauri and links between and among thesauri
- facilitate multilingual information access and retrieval
- provide easy access to thesauri for indexing and information representation purposes.

A number of the above-mentioned controlled vocabularies are available as linked data resources. For instance, all of the Library of Congress controlled vocabularies are available as linked data on the LC Linked Data Service website (http://id.loc.gov). The Getty Research Institute is currently planning for the future publication of the Getty vocabularies as Linked Open Data.

Information search behaviour and user interaction with KOS in cultural heritage digital libraries

As was argued earlier in this chapter, many metadata schemas and application profiles have suggested the use of well established controlled vocabularies for subject metadata in the area of cultural heritage. Very few focus on the usability and user access elements of these vocabularies. Also, a significant number of digital library projects and initiatives emphasize the importance of using consistent subject metadata for various digital heritage collections. However, there is little information as to how the applied subject metadata can be made accessible to the user for exploring, browsing and navigating digital collections. In order to make cultural digital collections more usable and accessible, it is essential to link users' interaction and search behaviour research with the ways in which knowledge organization systems can be incorporated into search user interfaces. One of the effective ways of doing so is to draw upon the evidence found in information search behaviour studies. Wildemuth (2006) proposes the notion of evidence-based practice in search interface design. She argues that results of many user search behaviour studies can form the basis on which designers can support people's 'natural' searching behaviours or on which designers can support the remediation of less effective search strategies.

In line with Wildemuth's notion of evidence-based practice in search user interface design, in this section we provide a review of the information search behaviour studies of the humanities and cultural heritage information seekers in order to set the context for the evaluation of a select number of cultural heritage digital library interfaces. In our evaluation, which will be presented in the next section, we will try to map how individual information search strategies can be supported using knowledge organization systems incorporated into search user interfaces.

In the discussion of the development of the Perseus digital library, Crane highlights the importance of the needs both present and potential of various communities within the humanities. He notes that:

> students of the ancient world, for example, work intensively on relatively

small, very fragmentary data sets in complex languages (e.g., Latin, classical Greek, Sumerian, Sanskrit); students of modern industrial cultures, by contrast, have extraordinarily detailed records and sources. Those working with pre-modern, typically sparse materials spend much of their time extrapolating from imperfect sources, while those working with recent and often vast data sources have a greater need to filter and visualize their data.

Crane, 2002, 628

This quotation demonstrates some of the information-seeking patterns of students of humanities. In particular, it sheds light on the variety of resources and search strategies with which information seekers of various disciplinary backgrounds in humanities may approach cultural heritage digital collections.

In a comprehensive review of the digital information resources on heritage, Chaudhry and Jiun (2005) conclude that the development of KOS for cultural heritage networks must focus heavily on user behaviour, the facilitation of browsing (in addition to searching as a mode of navigation) and the presence of relationships (between different resources), as well as intuitive labelling systems (terminology). Bates, Wilde and Siegfried (1993) and Siegfried, Bates and Wilde (1993) investigated the search terms used by humanities scholars searching DIALOG databases. The results of the study showed that the terminology used by humanities researchers was remarkably different from the vocabulary used in other fields, as were aspects of the information-seeking and online searching behaviour. The humanities scholars searched for more named individuals, geographical terms, chronological terms and discipline terms. Buchanan et al. (2005) studied the information-seeking behaviour of humanities academics and scholars using digital libraries. They found that browsing in the digital environment was noted as a particular problem and that search proved an ineffective replacement for browsing. Chaining, namely using references and citations (Ellis, 1989), was a dominant form of behaviour. In terms of query terms, proper names such as names of places and people were common. Simple keyword searching was not effective at all and users conducting conceptual searches had difficulties.

In an investigation of the physical and digital qualities of humanities research, Rimmer et al. (2008) note that new means of browsing in digital libraries could improve scholars' perceptions of serendipity when working with digital documents. Toms and O'Brien (2008) investigated the information and communication needs of e-humanists and found that in order to get access to primary and secondary sources using the web or library catalogues to locate e-texts, the scholars identified access points such as genre and publication date as key, in addition to traditional title, author and subject searches. Amin et al. (2008) studied the information-seeking needs and behaviour of cultural heritage experts and identified a number of information-seeking tasks, namely fact finding, information gathering and keeping up to date. Furthermore, they identified sub-tasks for each search task. These sub-tasks included: topic search, comparison, related search, exploration and combination. They also found that the current tools provided insufficient interface support for query formulation. Among the issues they identified that could be used as design guidelines for better search systems were: searching multiple sources, communication, information maintenance and provenance and trust.

In relation to the integration of knowledge organization systems into search user interfaces, Shiri (2012) provides a categorization of design guidelines for thesaurus-enhanced search user interfaces. This categorization of information search strategies can be used as a framework for the evaluation of user interfaces enhanced with other types of knowledge organization systems as well. The categorization is presented below:

- query formulation
- term suggestion
- query reformulation
- browsing
- search or query history
- results presentation along with KOS display
- visual representations

- integration of querying and browsing
- general search process.

In the next section of this chapter, we will draw upon the above information search behaviour studies and search interface design guidelines to create an analytical framework for the evaluation of three case studies of cultural heritage digital libraries.

Case studies

In this study we aim to evaluate how search interfaces to three cultural heritage digital libraries support different information-seeking tasks. Given that this study places a particular emphasis on semantic and conceptual searches using knowledge organization systems, the evaluation will focus on this particular aspect of search user interfaces.

In this section, three cultural heritage digital library cases are selected for examining the implementation of knowledge organization systems as searching, browsing and navigating mechanisms. As was stated earlier in the review of controlled vocabularies used for cultural heritage collections, the AAT thesaurus was one of the most widely used knowledge organization systems in the cultural heritage digital collections. In this study we examine the following three cultural heritage digital collections that have all made use of the semantic structure of the AAT thesaurus:

- *ARTstor Digital Library*. The ARTstor Digital Library makes available more than 1.5 million images in the arts, architecture, humanities, and sciences from outstanding museums, photo archives, photographers, scholars, and artists.
- *The J. Paul Getty Museum*. The museum houses collections of European paintings, drawings, sculptures, illuminated manuscripts, decorative arts, and European and American photographs.
- *The Victoria and Albert Museum (V&A)*. The Victoria and Albert Museum in London is the world's largest museum of decorative arts and design, housing a permanent collection of over 4.5 million objects.

The choice of the above digital collections lies in the broad-ranging nature of these collections and in their use of a well established controlled vocabulary. The three selected collections contain digital representations of various cultural heritage artefacts.

Drawing upon the findings reported by Kellar, Watters and Inkpen (2007) and Amin et al. (2008) and the design guidelines proposed by Shiri (2012), a conceptual framework was developed for the analysis and evaluation of the selected cultural heritage digital library search interfaces. The evaluation aims to take an evidence-based approach to examine how search user interface design for cultural heritage digital libraries can be improved. To this end, the information search tasks and sub-tasks identified by Amin et al. (2008) in examining cultural heritage experts' search behaviour were combined with best practices and design guidelines suggested by Shiri (2012) and were grouped and defined to provide an evaluation framework as presented below.

- *Fact finding*: users ask goal-oriented and focused questions; they look for specific factual pieces of information
- *Information gathering*: find information on a topic rather than for a specific fact
- *Query formulation*: construct queries using search topics and terms
- *Term suggestion*: suggestion of similar or alternative search terms
- *Query reformulation*: making changes and/or additions to the initial search statements
- *Comparison*: involves gathering information to compare differences and similarities between objects or sets of objects
- *Relationship search*: is about finding relationships between individual pieces of information
- *Browsing*: hierarchical and alphabetical browsing
- *Faceted browsing*: using facets and sub-facets for browsing and searching purposes
- *Exploratory search*: is typically not goal directed; a searcher may associatively follow one train of thought after another
- *Integration of querying and browsing*: integration of the associated

knowledge organization system in the searching and browsing at all stages of the search

- *Combination*: is about finding matches among pieces of information, most likely from different sources
- *Search or query history*: previous search terms and strategies
- *Result presentation along with KOS display*: concurrent display of results and the associated knowledge organization system
- *Communication*: an information exchange task, either face to face or through technology, such as e-mail
- *Information maintenance*: include saving, printing, e-mailing, bookmarking and keeping notes
- *Keeping up to date*: receiving news about new collections, exhibitions, developments etc.

Each of the three selected digital library user interfaces was examined and analysed on the basis of this analytical framework to establish the extent to which each accommodates various information search tasks suitable for cultural heritage digital information seekers.

Table 9.1 provides a comparative view of the information search tasks that are supported by the search user interfaces of the selected cultural heritage collections. As can be seen from the list of features, parts of this analysis will focus on the effective use of the AAT thesaurus for information architecture and presentation and parts of the analysis will focus on various aspects of the information search process.

Discussion

A comparative examination of the three cultural heritage digital libraries above demonstrates the variety of approaches to integrating knowledge organization systems in support of searching, browsing and exploration of digital content. Each of the three libraries supports some of the information search tasks proposed by previous researchers. ARTstor, with its rich collection, makes use of subject categories for searching and browsing. However, the depth of subject browsing is limited to a

Table 9.1 Information search task support in cultural heritage digital library interfaces

Search Tasks	Digital libraries		
	ARTSTOR	The J. Paul Getty Museum	Victoria and Albert Museum
Fact finding	Supported through basic and advanced search modes	Supported through Basic search mode	Supported through Basic search mode
Query formulation	Keyword search and faceted search	Keyword search	Keyword search
Term/query suggestion	Not supported	Not supported	Partially supported
Query reformulation	Supported through faceted search using 16 high-level facets	Limited support	Supported
Comparison	Supported through image groups and folders; display image group on a single page	Not supported	Not supported
Relationship search	Not supported	Not supported	Supported
Browsing	By country, classification and collection	By object type and medium By artist name By theme or topic	By subject and period and style
Faceted browsing	By 16 high-level facets	9 high-level facets and 2 levels of sub-facets	23 subject facets and 11 period and style facets
Exploratory search	Limited support	Limited support	Supported
Integration of querying and browsing	Limited support	Limited support	Limited support

maximum of two levels. The library provides some sophisticated and well thought-out functionalities to support users' information-seeking tasks, such as combination, comparison and sharing. Creating image folder and image group as well as image URL and image group URL are among the features that support these information-seeking tasks.

The J. Paul Getty Museum has a smaller collection and provides a useful set of browsing functionalities. One of the main advantages of subject browsing in this library is that it allows users to immediately view the next two levels of subject specificity so that they can quickly view and narrow down a specific aspect or facet of a term. Browsing in this library is simple and straightforward. The library does not support term suggestion or sophisticated query formulation and reformulation strategies. It is also

Table 9.1 *Continued*			
	Digital libraries		
Search Tasks	ARTSTOR	The J. Paul Getty Museum	Victoria and Albert Museum
Combination	Supported through image groups and folders	Not supported	Not supported
Search or query history	Both query and strategies supported	Not supported	Limited support
Result presentation along with KOS display	Limited support	Not supported	Supported
Communication	Generate image or image group URL	Facebook Twitter LinkedIn E-mail YouTube Tumblr Flickr	Facebook Twitter LinkedIn E-mail Tumblr
Information maintenance	Save Download Print current view Rotate Save citations for image group	Bookmarking Printing Multiple view options	Download image Download PDF version of a record Print
Keeping up to date	Supported through a blog	Discover recent acquisition feature E-newsletter Subscription Blog	E-newsletter

limited in its ability to allow users to create, combine and compare personalized collections for various information use cases, such as teaching and research.

The V&A library makes effective use of subject browsing both at collection and item levels. Subject browsing of the collection is well supported through high-level and specific subject terms. Some of the useful features of the V&A search user interface include faceted searching and browsing, relationship search and automatic completion of search terms and search term suggestion. However, the interface does not accommodate analytical search strategies such as the combination and comparison of selected items in a personalized fashion.

Based on the above evaluation of the three libraries, a number of useful features can be suggested to support users in their interaction with cultural heritage digital libraries – use of KOS systems to provide:

- search term and query suggestion
- faceted searching and browsing
- collection-level and item-level browsing
- cross-browsing and cross-searching various collections through linked and open KOS
- query formulation and reformulation
- relationship search through subject and other metadata elements
- enhanced view of result presentation along with facets and sub-facets.

In addition to the above features, cultural heritage digital information collections should offer support for creating, combining and comparing personalized collections in order to enhance the applicability and usefulness of these digital libraries in various contexts, namely education, work and hobby. Examples of ways in which combination, comparison and communication can be modelled for search user interface design purposes may include the use of cloud computing infrastructure and services to allow large storage capacity with extensive computational power to accommodate and support various information seeking, use and analysis of cultural heritage digital library resources. The provision of image processing tools and environments as well as digital publishing platforms for personal and professional purposes can provide new frontiers for extending the usability, accessibility and usefulness of cultural heritage information.

Conclusion

In this chapter, a review of knowledge organization systems and information search behaviour studies for cultural heritage digital libraries was presented. An analytical framework was proposed for the examination and evaluation of cultural heritage digital library search user interfaces.

This framework was developed based on: (a) the previous research into information search behaviour of web searchers and cultural heritage digital library users and (b) previous research on the best practices and guidelines for incorporating knowledge organization systems into search user interfaces. An evaluation of three cases of cultural heritage digital libraries was conducted to empirically demonstrate the suitability and relevance of this analytical framework. The evaluation study reported here provided evidence for the functionality and suitability of the elements of the proposed analytical framework. Future research may utilize this framework to evaluate the usability and usefulness of cultural heritage digital library search user interfaces in support of various information search behaviours and strategies.

References

Amin, A., Van Ossenbruggen, J., Hardman, L. and Van Nispen, A. (2008) Understanding Cultural Heritage Experts' Information Seeking Needs. In *Proceedings of the 8th ACM/IEEE-CS Joint Conference on Digital Libraries*, ACM, 39–47.

Baca, M. (2003) Practical Issues in Applying Metadata Schemas and Controlled Vocabularies to Cultural Heritage Information, *Cataloging & Classification Quarterly*, **36** (3–4), 47–55.

Bates, M. J., Wilde, D. N. and Siegfried, S. L. (1993) An Analysis of Search Terminology Used by Humanities Searchers: the Getty online searching project report No 1, *Library Quarterly*, **63** (1), 1–39.

Binding, C. and Tudhope, D. (2006) KOS at Your Service: programmatic access to knowledge organisation systems, *Journal of Digital Information*, **4** (4).

Buchanan, G., Cunningham, S. J., Blandford, A., Rimmer, J. and Warwick, C. (2005) Information Seeking by Humanities Scholars. In Rauber, A., Christodoulakis, S. and Tjoa, A.M. (eds), *Research and Advanced Technology for Digital Libraries*, Berlin, Heidelberg, Springer, 218–29.

Chaudhry, A. S. and Jiun, T. P. (2005) Enhancing Access to Digital Information Resources on Heritage: a case of development of a taxonomy at the integrated museum and archives system in Singapore, *Journal of Documentation*, **61** (6), 751–76.

Crane, G. (2002) Cultural Heritage Digital Libraries: needs and components. In Agosti, M. and Thanos, C. (eds), *Research and Advanced Technology for Digital Libraries*, Berlin, Heidelberg, Springer, 626–37.

Doerr, M. (2009) Ontologies for Cultural Heritage. In Staab, S. and Studer, R., *Handbook on Ontologies*, Berlin, Heidelberg, Springer, 463–86.

Ellis, D. (1989) A Behavioural Model for Information Retrieval System Design, *Journal of Information Science*, **15** (4–5), 237–47.

Harpring, P. (2010) *Introduction to Controlled Vocabularies Terminology for Art, Architecture, and Other Cultural Works*, edited by Murtha Baca, Los Angeles, CA, J. Paul Getty Trust, www.getty.edu/research/publications/electronic_publications/intro_controlled_vocab/index.html.

Harsányi, Z., Rozinajová, V. and Andrejčíková, N. (2012) Identifying Semantic Relationships in Digital Libraries of Cultural Heritage. In Ioannides, M., Fritsch, D., Leissner, J., Davies, R., Remondino, F. and Caffo, R. (eds), *Progress in Cultural Heritage Preservation*, Berlin, Heidelberg, Springer, 738–45.

Hodge, G. (2000) Systems of Knowledge Organization for Digital Libraries: beyond traditional authority files, Washington, DC, CLIR, www.clir.org/pubs/abstract/pub91abst.html.

Hollink, L., Van Assem, M., Wang, S., Isaac, A. and Schreiber, G. (2008) Two Variations on Ontology Alignment Evaluation: methodological issues. In Bechhofer, S., Hauswirth, M., Hoffmann, J. and Koubarakis, M. (eds), *The Semantic Web: research and applications*, Berlin, Heidelberg, Springer, 388–401.

Van Hooland, S., Verborgh, R., De Wilde, M., Hercher, J., Mannens, E. and Van de Walle, R. (2013) Evaluating the Success of Vocabulary Reconciliation for Cultural Heritage Collections, *Journal of the American Society for Information Science and Technology*, **64** (3), 464–79.

Isaac, A., Schlobach, S., Matthezing, H. and Zinn, C. (2008) Integrated Access to Cultural Heritage Resources Through Representation and Alignment of Controlled Vocabularies, *Library Review*, **57** (3), 187–99.

Kellar, M., Watters, C. and Inkpen, K. M. (2007) An Exploration of Web-based Monitoring: implications for design. In *Proceedings of the SIGCHI*

Conference on Human Factors in Computing Systems, ACM, 377–86.

Van der Meij, L., Isaac, A. and Zinn, C. (2010) A Web-Based Repository Service for Vocabularies and Alignments in the Cultural Heritage Domain. In *The Semantic Web: Research and Applications*, Berlin, Heidelberg, Springer, 394–409.

Mondoux, J. and Shiri, A. (2009) Institutional Repositories in Canadian Post-secondary Institutions: user interface features and knowledge organization systems, *Aslib Proceedings: new information perspectives*, **61** (5), 436–58.

Netherlands Institute for Sound and Vision, http://portal.beeldengeluid.nl.

Nicholson, D. and Shiri, A. (2003) Interoperability in Subject Searching and Browsing, *OCLC Systems & Services*, **19** (2), 58–61.

Park, J. R. and Tosaka, Y. (2013) Metadata Creation Practices in Digital Repositories and Collections: schemata, selection criteria, and interoperability, *Information Technology and Libraries*, **29** (3), 104–16.

Rimmer, J., Warwick, C., Blandford, A., Gow, J. and Buchanan, G. (2008) An Examination of the Physical and the Digital Qualities of Humanities Research, *Information Processing and Management*, **44** (3), 1374–92.

Shiri, A. (2006) The Use of Controlled Vocabularies in Interfaces to Canadian Digital Library Collections. In *Proceedings of the American Society for Information Science and Technology (ASIS&T) 7th Information Architecture Summit*, 23–27 March 2006, Vancouver.

Shiri, A. (2012) *Powering Search: the role of thesauri in new information environments*, ASIS&T Monograph Series, Medford, NJ, Information Today Inc.

Shiri, A. and Chase-Kruszewski, S. (2009) Knowledge Organisation Systems in North American Digital Library Collections, *Program: electronic library and information systems*, **43** (2), 121–39.

Shiri, A. and Molberg, K. (2005) Interfaces to Knowledge Organization Systems in Canadian Digital Library Collections, *Online Information Review*, **29** (6), 604–20.

Siegfried, S., Bates, M. J. and Wilde, D. N. (1993) A Profile of End-User Searching Behaviour by Humanities Scholars: the Getty Online Searching Project report No 2, *Journal of the American Society for Information Science*, **44** (5), 273–91.

Toms, E. G. and O'Brien, H. L. (2008) Understanding the Information and

Communication Technology Needs of the E-humanist, *Journal of Documentation*, **64** (1), 102–30.

Tudhope, D. and Lykke Nielsen, M. (2006) Introduction to Knowledge Organization Systems and Services, *New Review of Hypermedia and Multimedia*, **12** (1), 3–9.

Wildemuth, B. M. (2006) Evidence-based Practice in Search Interface Design, *Journal of the American Society for Information Science and Technology*, **57** (6), 825–28.

Zeng, M. L. and Chan, L. M. (2004) Trends and Issues in Establishing Interoperability Among Knowledge Organization Systems, *Journal of the American Society for Information Science and Technology*, **55** (5), 377–95.

CHAPTER 10

Supporting exploration and use of digital cultural heritage materials: the PATHS perspective

Paul Clough, Paula Goodale,
Mark Hall and Mark Stevenson
University of Sheffield, UK

Introduction

> Cultural heritage involves rich and highly heterogeneous collections that are challenging to archive and convey to the general public.
>
> Hardman et al., 2009, 23

This statement describes two aspects that make access to cultural heritage information challenging: the heterogeneous nature of many cultural heritage collections and the growing need to provide non-specialist users with access to cultural heritage content. Cultural heritage institutions (libraries, museums and archives) hold an enormous and rich variety of digital content covering a broad range of subjects, such as natural history, ethnography, archaeology, historic monuments and fine and applied arts, which often cross national and linguistic boundaries. There is strong motivation to bring together content from different cultural institutions into centralized portals, which have typically offered access services based on traditional catalogues used in libraries, museums and archives. For example, Europeana[1] provides online access to over 32 million digitized cultural heritage artefacts provided by a range of European institutions. However, the size and lack of organization of these collections can be overwhelming for many users, who are provided with little or no guidance about how to access, interpret and use the information in them. There is a risk of 'overload' when users are presented with vast collections of information (Patterson, Roth and Woods, 2001).

This chapter discusses techniques to support information access to digital cultural heritage collections and, in particular, helping users explore and use the information they contain. In this chapter 'use' relates to assisting users with creating paths or trails with the items they find. To ground the discussion we focus on a particular system called 'PATHS' that aims to support multiple user groups with varying degrees of domain knowledge through the provision of state-of-the-art functionalities, such as recommendations and visualizations. A central theme of the system is the integration of 'paths' (sets of artefacts from the collection organized around a topic) into the system to assist users with navigating and interpreting the content. These paths may form access points to the collection, and the pathway metaphor is an effective way of guiding users through online digital collections (Shipman et al., 2000), as well as artefacts displayed in physical museums (Van Hage et al., 2010; Grieser et al., 2011). By adopting a 'user-centred approach' in the design of the system we have been able to gather feedback on the utility of the PATHS perspective on providing access to digital cultural heritage information. By describing the development of the PATHS system we aim to provide insights for those involved in developing similar systems.

Information access in cultural heritage

In cultural heritage, interpretation, meaning-making and constructivist approaches to learning are implicit in the provision of access to collections (Hein, 1998). In digital environments these processes are increasingly participatory and collaborative, with opportunities for novice users to actively engage in knowledge creation (Proctor, 2010). Indeed, at a high level, expert and novice users have somewhat similar requirements in this domain, engaging in a range of information-related tasks (Amin et al., 2008; Skov and Ingwersen, 2008). Common tasks include fact-finding (or known-item) searches, those of a more exploratory or information-gathering nature, and keeping up to date. Fact-finding and known-item tasks tend to revolve around search, whilst information-gathering tasks lend themselves more to browsing and exploration. Searching behaviours are often more prevalent, and searching may be a starting point that leads on to more exploratory behaviour (Skov and Ingwersen, 2008). Information-gathering tasks may involve a variety of sub-tasks, including comparison, relationship search, topic search, exploration and combination (Amin et al., 2008). For cultural heritage professionals and for arts and humanities scholars, the credibility of sources is also extremely important (Inskip, Butterworth and MacFarlane, 2006; Amin et al., 2008; Audenaert and Furuta, 2010), and there is evidence of a wide range of different types of sources, including more generic search tools, such as Google (Amin et al., 2008; Ross and Terras, 2011), and more esoteric domain-specific sources (Inskip, Butterworth and MacFarlane, 2006). There is also a marked preference for visual content from both heritage expert and scholarly information users (Amin et al., 2008; Ross and Terras, 2011), and from non-expert users (Skov and Ingwersen, 2008).

Traditionally tools to access digital cultural heritage have been geared towards subject specialists and experienced users; however, the environment in which cultural heritage institutions are operating has changed as they seek to make collections accessible and appealing to a wider audience with little or no domain knowledge (i.e., the general public). There has been increased research activity on helping citizens create, interpret and preserve cultural and scientific resources for recreational use, such as family history searching and learning, in the context of everyday life information seeking (Yakel, 2004; Darby and Clough, 2013). Cultural heritage institutions are seeking to provide richer user experiences that support connectivity between people, content and applications, to support writers as well and readers, and to enable collaborations with and between users. A new generation of cultural heritage portals is encouraging user participation by offering people opportunities to interact with content (for example encouraging them to tag resources), making recommendations to other users

(Carmagnola et al., 2007; Trant, 2009) and personalization (Cramer et al., 2008; Ardissono, Kufik and Petrelli, 2012; Hampson et al., 2012).

However, digital cultural heritage collections can often be difficult to navigate, especially for those without advanced levels of subject and domain knowledge (Skov and Ingwersen, 2008). Johnson (2008) highlights three main problems that users, especially novice users, have with accessing online cultural heritage materials: (1) knowing where to look (i.e., starting the search); (2) knowing what to say (i.e., putting the right words in the query box); and (3) making sense of archival material (i.e., interpreting the results). Many have argued that a keyword-based search 'is not sufficient because one is above all interested in relations, e.g., between artists, their works, the friends, their studies, who they inspired, etc.' (Benjamins et al., 2004, 433). In cultural heritage, people often use 'creative and exploratory thought processes involved in translating conceptual ideas to visual instantiations' (Jörgensen and Jörgensen, 2005, 1357). The limits of keyword-based search, particularly to support more diverse information activities such as exploration and learning, have also been noted by the wider information retrieval and seeking community within the field of exploratory search (White and Roth, 2009; Wilson et al., 2010). There is therefore a clear need for cultural heritage institutions to provide systems that go beyond information delivery and better support the navigation, interpretation and use of items in digital collections (Koolen, Kamps and De Keijzer, 2009; Van den Akker et al., 2013) and to support more generally users' analytical and sense-making processes (Marchionini, 2006).

Example: The PATHS project

The PATHS (Personalised Access To cultural Heritage Spaces) project,[2] funded under the European Commission's FP7 programme, explored alternative approaches to enhance information access as a means of discovery and exploration, and utilize pathways as a mechanism for navigation and interpretation in large and heterogeneous cultural heritage collections (Fernie et al., 2012; Agirre et al., 2013a). The project consisted of partners from multiple disciplines, including cultural heritage, library and information science and computer science, from both academic and non-academic institutions. A selection of artefacts from Europeana was used as a source of cultural heritage artefacts, but additional semantic enrichment was carried out on the content together with the development of user interfaces to support users in their exploration of digital cultural heritage.

A typical user-centred development process was followed (identify requirements, prototype and evaluate), whereby the foundations of the system are laid through reviewing past literature, gathering user requirements and developing a functional specification for the system (Goodale et al., 2012). A central aspect of the system was the use of paths or trails to allow digital content from the PATHS system to be organized into guided pathways resembling the exhibitions and tours commonly provided for physical collections such as those found in museums. Therefore, expert users, such as educators and curators, who typically create pathways through cultural heritage collections, were consulted during the gathering of user requirements and subsequent evaluations of prototype systems. We also explored different ways of supporting users, especially novices, with exploration and interpretation activities, accompanied by exploring existing users studies based on Europeana, in which prospective user groups were identified and described using personas and use cases (Rasmussen and Petersen, 2012). A clear understanding of the user's likely information needs and behaviour and the tasks they engage in is critical in developing systems that support good information access and interaction: 'research into user needs, tasks and resources is required before the design can begin' (Allen, 1996, 291).

Based on the analysis of past literature and user requirements, we defined potential user groups for the PATHS system and possible use cases, from which we derived functional requirements for the PATHS system (Goodale et al., 2011). Four generic user profiles were identified for the PATHS system: expert path creator (e.g., curator of researcher); non-expert path creator (e.g., family historian or student), path facilitator (e.g., teacher or museum educator) and path consumer (e.g., student, visitor or casual user). Specific behaviour profiles (i.e., details of typical user profiles, activities, tasks and processes) and use cases were then developed for each

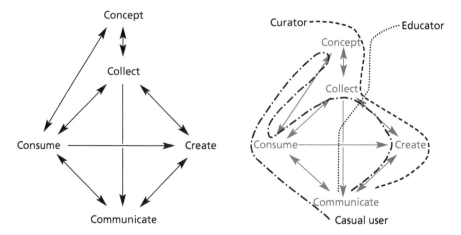

Figure 10.1 The PATHS conceptual model that identifies the activities of users as they create and consume paths

type of user and were used to define the functional requirements and inform user evaluation. In addition, we developed a conceptual model to describe the main activities of users in creating and interacting with paths (Figure 10.1). The model seeks to capture the main activities that users follow as they construct paths for use by others. The model also attempts to capture the activities of non-expert users, such as students, when consuming or following previously created paths. The PATHS system was then designed around this simple model with features implemented to aid users with each of the main activities. The model captures five key activities when interacting with paths: developing a *Concept*; *Collecting* relevant materials; *Creating* a path; *Communicating* and sharing the path and its content; and *Consuming* paths created by other users.

Figure 10.1 shows the sequence of activities different users may take in creating and consuming paths. For example, an expert path creator (e.g., curator or educator) is likely to begin with a concept around which to construct a path and move on to collecting materials and creating the path, while a non-expert path creator (e.g., casual user) might begin by consuming an existing path and then move to collecting materials as they identify other routes of interest off the initial path. Goodale et al. (2013a) compares the stages in the PATHS conceptual model with established models of user behaviour in complex information work tasks (see Table 10.1), including Marchionini's exploratory search model (Marchionini, 2006), the Information Journey model (Blandford and Attfield, 2010) and Shneiderman's model of creativity, the Genex Framework (Shneiderman, 2000). There is significant overlap between these models, which all address aspects of information seeking, exploration, sense making, creativity and information use to some degree.

Results from the user requirements formed the basis of a functional specification against which to develop the PATHS system. System functionalities were based around the five main activities of the conceptual model. The first column in Table 10.1 shows the PATHS user requirements in relation to our conceptual model and the design features within the user interface. The key functions of the system are different modes or approaches for exploring artefacts in the collection (e.g., navigating or browsing artefacts in the collection, map-based visualizations and recommendations), functions for creating and editing new paths and following existing paths, functionalities for searching for specific artefacts in the collection and additional functionality to support user registration and assistance (e.g., introductory tutorials and context-sensitive help/tips).

Following on from the specification of functional requirements, we developed both low- and high-fidelity prototypes that were used to investigate approaches for supporting users with exploration of the digital collection. In the end two high-fidelity prototype systems were developed in an iterative manner. Goodale et. al (2013b) describes both systems and observed differences in user behaviour with varying degrees of functionality. Creating the prototype systems required processing the content to undertake semantic enrichment and then utilizing and surfacing this enriched data through the user interface (see following sections). The final stage of evaluation was carried out to test individual components, as well as testing the completed prototype system using established methods in lab-based controlled evaluations (Kelly, 2009; Borlund, 2003) and more naturalistic field trials. Evaluation was carried out with a range of users (novices and experts) within the following scenarios: general museum visitors; university students using cultural heritage information during their

Table 10.1 Summary of user needs and the associated system and interface requirements in relation to the PATHS conceptual model and existing models of exploration, creativity and information use (Goodale et al., 2013a)

PATHS user requirements	PATHS UI model	PATHS design features	Exploratory search (Marchionini, 2006)	Information journey (Blandford and Attfield, 2010)	Genex framework (Shneiderman, 2000)
Explore opportunities Formulate ideas Develop overarching concept	Concept	Follow existing paths Explore modes *Background links* *Search*	Investigate *Learn*	Recognize need *Find info* *Use*	Relate
Explore available content Find suitable material Save artefacts for later use	Collect	Search Explore modes Add to workspace *Facets* *Similar artefacts* *External links*	Learn *Look up*	Find info *Validate/* *interpret*	Collect
Organize saved content Annotate saved content Use content to create new resources	Create	Create path *Re-arrange nodes* *Annotate nodes* *Add text node*	Learn Investigate	Validate/ *interpret* *Use*	Create *Relate*
View paths created by others Explore related content	Consume	Follow existing paths *Similar artefacts* *External links*	Learn *Investigate*	Use *Recognize need* *Find info*	N/A *Collect* *Relate*
Add information and comments Share content with others Annotate shared content	Communicate	Publish paths Share content/path *Annotate path* *Add comments*	Learn	Use *Validate/* *interpret*	Donate *Relate*

*Points in italic indicate secondary roles or features

degree; and researchers, lecturers and cultural heritage professionals using digital content for their work.

Semantic enrichment

The PATHS system was implemented with a subset of content from Europeana, the European Library. Europeana contains over 32 million artefacts, including paintings, films and books, with metadata in a range of European languages. Artefacts are provided by around 1500 cultural heritage institutions, including the British Library, the Rijksmuseum and the Louvre. The content in Europeana is an aggregation of different collections of cultural heritage objects and is not connected with any single institution. Dealing with an aggregation of datasets brings about its own challenges when processing the content and providing information access. For example, no single unified thesaurus or controlled vocabulary is used to index the content; the quality of metadata is variable; and the same metadata attributes may be used differently (e.g., 'date' might reflect acquisition date in one collection and creation date in another).

The PATHS system used content from Europeana with metadata in English and Spanish, with these languages being chosen as the ones which the project consortium had expertise in processing automatically. The content was selected from one collection with English (CultureGrid) and two (Cervantes and Hispana) with Spanish metadata (Agirre et al., 2013a). Analysis of this data showed that the amount of detail about each artefact varied considerably, with some containing very short descriptions of only a few words and large numbers of artefacts with identical descriptions. The content was therefore filtered to remove any artefacts with very short titles or titles which were repeated more than 100 times in the collection. This resulted in a final set of 1,701,672 artefacts, around 69% of the total of the three collections. The content typically consists of a thumbnail image representation of an artefact, together with associated metadata. Given the limitations of the metadata, we apply different Natural Language Processing (NLP) techniques to pre-process and enrich the data to enable the provision of various functionalities on the user interface to support users' search and exploration activities.

The first type of content enrichment was the identification of artefacts that are considered to be similar, even artefacts from different collections, and the type of similarity. This is useful for navigation and recommendation since it allows users to explore the content within the collection related to a particular area. The artefacts in Europeana are drawn from a diverse set of collections and, while they may contain related artefacts, this is not indicated in the metadata. To identify similar artefacts the description of each artefact was interpreted by a statistical model and the similarity between them determined by comparing these models (Aletras, Stevenson and Clough, 2012). Various types of similarity were also identified: similar author, similar people involved, similar time period, similar location, similar events, similar location and similar description. Similar pairs of artefacts for each type were identified using a range of techniques described in Agirre et al. (2013b). The majority of these were based on comparison of the text in the relevant fields of artefact's metadata, for example the <dc:Creator> field was used to identify similar authors.

In addition, 'background links' from Wikipedia were added to each artefact in the collection (Fernando and Stevenson, 2012). This helps to supplement the information available about the artefact when the metadata is limited and also provides background information to assist with interpretation, which may be of particular assistance to novice or casual users.

Finally, information from the background links was used to automatically create subject hierarchies through which the artefacts in the collection could be navigated. There is no single hierarchy shared by the various collections that contribute to Europeana: different hierarchies and vocabularies are used, but they are generally not compatible; others do not use any hierarchy at all. Consequently, inducing a hierarchy directly from the data was found to be a more suitable approach than attempting to adapt any of the ones on the collections. The hierarchy generated proved to be extremely useful for supporting browsing and navigation. The hierarchy is created using two approaches: the first is based on analysing the frequency with which Wikipedia articles appear in the background links. The second is based on the Wikipedia Taxonomy (Ponzetto and Strube, 2011), an existing hierarchy based on Wikipedia. The final hierarchy used within the PATHS system is a combination of these approaches which was shown to outperform the use of either approach alone (Fernando et al., 2013).

User interfaces and interaction

The user interface was designed to meet the requirements captured in the functional specification (see Table 10.1), but also taking into account existing design principles from HCI and interactive information retrieval (Hearst, 2009; Russell-Rose and Tate, 2013). The user interface was built around two main principles. First, it should not prescribe a certain way of interacting, but allow the user to choose the interaction patterns that they feel most comfortable with. Second, the individual components should be as tightly integrated as possible, to allow for a smooth interaction experience. In the following we describe features of the PATHS user interface for supporting users as they explore (search and navigate) the content and create/consume paths.

Figure 10.2 shows the main landing page for the PATHS system. The top of the screen shows navigational support including a history list, login/registration features, the workspace (which drops down when clicked) and a standard search box. The left-hand side of the screen shows facets for filtering the results and browsing the collection. The right-hand side of the screen shows links to paths previously created and artefacts from the collection (randomly selected). The centre of the screen provides a summary of the system and a link to an online video tutorial.

Exploration in the PATHS system is supported through the use of navigational aids and visualizations to provide overviews of the entire collection, together with recommendations and a workspace area. Navigation is built around two features: an automatically generated vocabulary that is organized hierarchically and supports top-down exploration, and links to related artefacts (including paths) that allow for

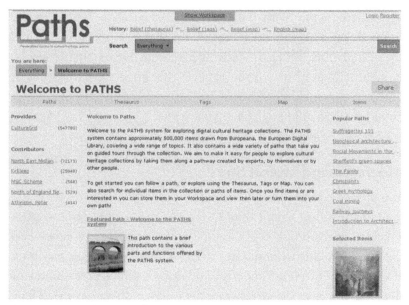

Figure 10.2 Landing page for the PATHS system

horizontal navigation between artefacts. These are created as a part of the semantic enrichment process.

The top-down exploration is visualized in three different ways (see Figure 10.3), which we hypothesized would meet the needs of users with differing cognitive information processing capabilities (Clough, Stevenson and Ford, 2011). A thesaurus provides a standard, text-based tree-structure, where the user can expand and collapse nodes in the tree and in that way explore the collection. Alternatively a term-cloud representation is provided, which only shows one level in the hierarchy, but which visualizes the amount of data available for each of the terms.

Finally a map-based visualization is provided (see Figure 10.4), which allows the user to explore the semantic space of the collection in the same way they would explore an online digital map, for example Google Maps. The visualizations are tightly coupled; thus if the user switches between them, they are always shown the same part of the hierarchy. Search is also integrated into all of these visualizations, with a single search box shown at the top of all pages (see Figure 10.2). The search functionality is also

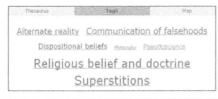
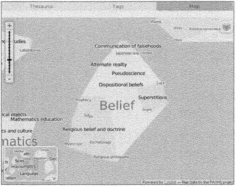

Figure 10.3 Different ways of navigating the PATHS hierarchy: standard tree-like structure (left), term-cloud view (top) and map-based visualization (bottom)

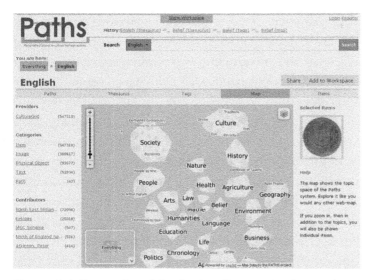

Figure 10.4 The map-based visualization allows users to inspect the contents of the entire collection

tightly coupled: if the user has explored into parts of the vocabulary and then initiates a search, the search will be executed within the area of the vocabulary the user is currently in.

The map-based visualization provides a novel way to explore large document collections (Hall and Clough, 2013). For the users of the PATHS system, the map-based view enables the content of the entire collection to be inspected, offering a visual overview of the cultural heritage collection. The map represents subjects in the hierarchy as clusters or 'islands' whereby similar artefacts (or subjects) are clustered together and placed physically nearer to each other, with their size representing the number of artefacts in the collection and layout approximating semantic relationship between clusters. The process of representing non-spatial information as maps or landscapes is known as 'spatialization' and in our visualization we apply a custom hierarchical spatialization algorithm to artefacts that have been previously mapped to a thesaurus (Fernando et al., 2012).

In addition to providing overviews of the collection, the system also allows the user to explore individual items through the interface, as shown in Figure 10.5.

In this example, a thumbnail of the artefact is shown along with the title and description and associated metadata. A link is also provided to locate the originating source, since this information is often important to users of cultural heritage portals. The right-hand side of the screen shows links for exploration of the collection in a more horizontal manner through recommendations (Clough et al., 2014). The type of recommendation provided by the system is general or 'non-personalized' recommendations (i.e., the same for all users). In this case the user is shown related artefacts based on the type of the similarity relation (e.g., creators, people and time period). At the bottom on the right are the links to related Wikipedia articles for the given artefact (in Figure 10.5 the articles entitled 'priory', 'abbey' and 'deanery') that aim to provide relevant background information.

As the user explores and searches the collection, they can add any page that they find interesting to their workspace. This area allows the user to store, organize, and annotate objects of interest, which they can later then

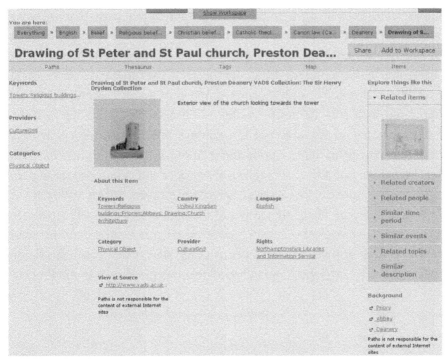

Figure 10.5 The PATHS user interface when viewing an artefact from the collection

organize into paths. Users can create new paths based on the artefacts they have gathered in the workspace or adding text-only nodes. The idea of these is to allow users to insert nodes that are not linked to artefacts in the collection, e.g., a node to describe a change in the theme of a path or a node with a learning assessment (e.g., a quiz).

The structure of paths resembles a tree-like structure in which nodes can have branches allowing users to follow multiple aspects of a topic. Path nodes can also be results pages, term cloud pages, views of the map, and artefacts associated with a concept in the hierarchy, rather than just artefacts, enabling richer types of paths. Functionality is provided that allows users to create paths by dragging artefacts from the workspace into a visual path editor in which nodes can be (re-)arranged, ordered as branches at the same level and additional descriptive text added. Registered users are then able to publish the paths they create for others to view and follow. Figure 10.6

shows an overview of a published user-generated path that includes branching to divide the narrative into themes or sections. In this path (about railways in the UK) the user has structured the path with branching at different levels to represent different aspects of the topic, e.g. at the second level 'the technology' and 'closures'. Artefacts from the collection are associated with sub-themes providing the user with a guide through the collection based on the subject of UK railways. When following a path users can either start from the first node and then select the next node in the path (at a branching point the user is given a 'signpost' indicating that more than one possible route can be followed); alternatively users can view the path as a whole (see Figure 10.6) and jump into the path at any point. The paths in themselves have proven interesting artefacts to analyse and demonstrated highly varied approaches to constructing narratives through digital collections and highlighted the utility of features developed in the PATHS

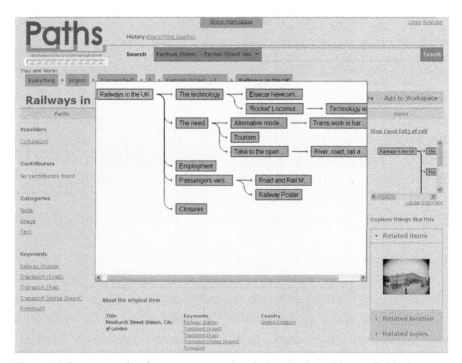

Figure 10.6 An example of a user-generated path showing branching to divide the content into themes or sections

system to construct and share pathways (Goodale et al., 2013b; Smith et al., 2014).

Discussion

There is a need to develop information access systems in cultural heritage that go beyond supporting search tasks to helping users with undertaking exploratory search activities, better support the interpretation of artefacts in digital collections and allow users to construct their own narratives (Van den Akker et al., 2013). In Information Retrieval research more generally there has been much work on supporting users with exploratory search tasks and cognitive processes, such as learning and decision-making (White and Roth, 2009; Marchionini, 2006). Recent developments in areas such as cultural heritage information dashboards and visualizations (Urban, Twidale and Adamczyk, 2010) are helping unlock rich cultural heritage collections, making them accessible to a wider range of end-users, including the general public. Allowing users to actively engage and interact with cultural heritage information is certainly in the minds of most providers of digital content. In the world of big data and open access, an increasing number of cultural heritage datasets are likely to emerge. Providing users with tools to help them navigate and make sense of this digital material will be increasingly important to prevent information overload.

Future information access systems must be able to support users with varying information needs and performing different tasks, such as fact-finding or more complex information gathering activities. As White et al. state, search systems should

> help users explore, overcome uncertainty, and learn. To accomplish this, researchers and practitioners must leverage their skills and experience to develop search systems that actively engage searchers using semantics, inherent structure, and meaningful categorization to organise intuitive visual interfaces.
>
> White, Kules and Drucker, 2007, 38

In the area of cultural heritage many have argued that keyword-based search is insufficient (e.g., Benjamins et al., 2004, 433). Techniques such as high-level overviews, the grouping and connection of related objects to create rich conceptual graphs, rapid previews of objects (e.g., 'dynamic query' interfaces) and visualizations ranging from ranked lists, clustered result displays, tag clouds and cluster map to data-specific designs such as timelines all help users to understand data structures and infer relationships. Future systems should also aim to support users with varying levels of domain knowledge with their broader 'information journey' and work/leisure tasks.

The collaboration of partners from different communities will be necessary to create more sophisticated systems that support users' activities. For example, the PATHS project has brought together people from cultural heritage, library and information science and computer science. The use of state-of-the-art NLP techniques has enabled us to create a user interface that is rich in features, supports novice and expert users alike and provides advanced features for exploring and using cultural heritage information. The design of the system has taken a user-centred approach, which is critical in providing systems with functionalities that effectively support users with their tasks and information seeking activities.

Summary

This chapter has discussed approaches for assisting users with exploring and making use of artefacts from digital cultural heritage collections. A case study based on the PATHS project has been used to exemplify the discussion and show what kinds of features can be developed to support users with accessing information in digital cultural heritage collections, and assist with their wider information-related activities, such as orientation, exploration, interpretation and information use. The PATHS system uses digital content from Europeana, an aggregator of the content available in European museums, libraries and archives, as a source of cultural heritage content. Work undertaken in the PATHS project has applied state-of-the-art natural language processing to enrich the content and enable rich user interface features that support a range of users in carrying out different tasks. Evaluation results to date indicate that the system fulfils its goals of supporting users with accessing cultural heritage content from Europeana and creating paths that can act as subject guides for other users. Further work on information access to digital cultural heritage information will probably take the form of projects, such as PATHS, to unlock the rich information contained within cultural heritage collection but often hidden from end-users, particularly novices. With increases in the availability of diverse sources of cultural heritage information then topics, including multilingualism, semantic enrichment, personalization, exploration and discovery, and collaboration and co-production, will probably come to the forefront of future information access developments.

Acknowledgements

The research leading to these results was carried out as part of the PATHS project (www.paths-project.eu) funded by the European Community's Seventh Framework Programme (FP7/2007-2013) under grant agreement no. 270082.

Notes

1   Europeana website: www.europeana.eu. [Accessed 7 November 2014.]
2   PATHS project website: www.paths-project.eu. [Accessed 7 November 2014.]

References

Agirre, E., Aletras, N., Clough, P., Fernando, S., Goodale, P., Hall, M., Soroa, A., and Stevenson, M. (2013a) PATHS: A System for Accessing Cultural Heritage Collections. In *Proceedings of 51st Annual Meeting of the Association for Computational Linguistics* (ACL '13), Sofia, Bulgaria, 4–9 August 2013, 151–6.

Agirre, E., Aletras, N., Gonzalez-Agirre, A., Rigau, G. and Stevenson, M. (2013b) UBCUOS-TYPED: Regression for Typed-similarity. In *Second Joint Conference on Lexical and Computational Semantics (*SEM), Volume 1: Proceedings of the Main Conference and the Shared Task: Semantic Textual Similarity*, Atlanta, GA, 132–7.

Van den Akker, C., Van Nuland, A., Van der Meij, L., Van Erp, M., Legêne, S., Aroyo, L. and Schreiber, G. (2013) From Information Delivery to Interpretation Support: evaluating cultural heritage access on the web. In *Proceedings of the 5th Annual ACM Web Science Conference* (WebSci '13), ACM, New York, NY, 431–40.

Aletras, N., Stevenson, M. and Clough, P. (2012) Computing Similarity Between Items in a Digital Library of Cultural Heritage, *Journal of Computing and Cultural Heritage*, **5** (4), Article 16.

Allen, B. A. (1996) *Information Tasks: towards a user-centred approach to information systems*, San Diego, CA, Academic Press.

Amin, A., Van Ossenbruggen, J., Hardman, L. and Van Nispen, A. (2008) Understanding Cultural Heritage Experts' Information Seeking Needs. In *Proceedings of the 8th ACM/IEEE-CS Joint Conference on Digital Libraries* (JCDL '08), Pittsburgh PA, 16–20 June 2008, 39–47.

Ardissono, L., Kufik, T. and Petrelli, D. (2012) Personalization in Cultural Heritage: the road travelled and the one ahead, *User Modeling and User-Adapted Interaction*, **22** (1–2), 73–99.

Audenaert, N. and Furuta, R. (2010) What Humanists Want: how scholars use source materials. In *Proceedings of the 10th Annual Joint Conference on Digital Libraries* (JCDL '10), 21–25 June 2010, Gold Coast, Australia, 283–92.

Benjamins, V. R., Contreras, J., Blazquez, M., Dodero, J. M., Garcia, A., Navas, E., Hernandez, F. and Wert, C. (2004) Cultural Heritage and the Semantic Web. In *Proceedings of 1st European Semantic Web Symposium*, 433–44.

Blandford, A. and Attfield, S. (2010) Interacting with Information, *Synthesis Lectures on Human-Centered Informatics*, Morgan Claypool Publishing, **3** (1), 1–99.

Borlund, P. (2003) The IIR Evaluation Model: a framework for evaluation of interactive information systems, *Information Research*, **8** (3).

Carmagnola, F., Cena, F., Cortassa, O., Gena, C. and Torre, I. (2007) Towards a

Tag-Based User Model: how can user model benefit from tags? In *Proceedings of the 11th International Conference on User Modeling*, Lecture Notes In Artificial Intelligence, vol. 4511, Berlin, Heidelberg, Springer, 445–9.

Clough, P., Stevenson, M. and Ford, N. (2011) Personalizing Access to Cultural Heritage Collections using Pathways. In *Proceedings of 3rd Workshop on Personalised Access to Cultural Heritage* (PATCH 2011), in conjunction with IUI2011 Conference, Stanford University 13 February 2011, 12–19.

Clough, P., Otegi, A., Agirre, E. and Hall, M. (2014) Implementing Recommendations in the PATHS System. In *Proceedings of 2nd Workshop on Supporting User's Exploration of Digital Libraries* (SUEDL 2013), 169–73.

Cramer, H., Evers, V., Ramlal, S., Van Someren, M., Rutledge, L., Stash, N., Aroyo, L. and Wielinga, B. (2008) The Effects of Transparency on Trust in and Acceptance of a Content-Based Art Recommender, *Journal of User Modeling and User-Adapted Interaction*, **18** (5), 455–96.

Darby, P. and Clough, P. (2013) Investigating the Information Seeking Behaviour of Genealogists and Family Historians, *Journal of Information Science*, **39** (1), 75–86.

Fernando, S., Hall, M., Agirre, E., Soroa, A., Clough, P. and Stevenson, M. (2012) Comparing Taxonomies for Organising Collections of Documents. In *Proceedings of the 24th International Conference on Computational Linguistics* (COLING 2012), 879–94.

Fernando, S. and Stevenson, M. (2012) Adapting Wikification to Cultural Heritage. In *Proceedings of the 6th Workshop on Language Technology for Cultural Heritage, Social Sciences, and Humanities* (LaTeCH 2012), 101–6.

Fernando, S., Goodale, P., Clough, Hall, M., Stevenson, M. and Agirre, E. (2013) Generating Paths through Cultural Heritage Collections. In *Proceedings of the 7th Workshop on Language Technology for Cultural Heritage, Social Sciences, and Humanities* (LaTeCH 2013), 8 August 2013, Sofia, Bulgaria, 1–10.

Fernie, K., Griffiths, J., Stevenson, M., Clough, P., Goodale, P., Hall, M., Archer, P., Chandrinos, K., Agirre, E., de Lacalle, O., de Polo, A. and Bergheim, R. (2012) PATHS: Personalising Access To cultural Heritage Spaces. In *Proceedings of 18th International Conference on Virtual Systems and Multimedia* (VSMM 2012), 469–74.

Goodale, P., Hall, M., Fernie, K. and Archer, P. (2011) *Paths Project D1.1 User Requirements Analysis*, www.paths-project.eu/eng/Resources.

Goodale, P., Clough, P., Ford, N., Hall, M., Stevenson, M., Fernando, S., Aletras, N., Fernie, K., Archer, P. and de Polo, A. (2012) User-Centred Design to Support Exploration and Path Creation in Cultural Heritage Collections. In *Proceedings of the 2nd European Workshop on Human Computer Interaction and Information Retrieval* (EuroHCIR 2012), 75–8.

Goodale, P., Clough, P., Hall, M. and Stevenson, M. (2013a) Supporting Information Access and Sensemaking in Digital Cultural Heritage Environments. In *Proceedings of 2nd Workshop on Supporting User's Exploration of Digital Libraries* (SUEDL 2013), 143–54.

Goodale, P., Clough, P., Hall, M., Stevenson, M, Fernie, K., Griffiths, J. and Agirre, E. (2013b) Pathways to Discovery: supporting exploration and information use in cultural heritage collections. In *Proceedings of Museums and the Web Asia 2013*, Hong Kong, 9–12 December 2013, http://mwa2013. museumsandtheweb.com/paper/pathways-to-discovery-supporting-exploration-and-information-use-in-cultural-heritage-collections.

Grieser, K., Baldwin, T., Bohnert, F. and Sonenberg, L. (2011) Using Ontological and Document Similarity to Estimate Museum Exhibit Relatedness, *Journal of Computing and Cultural Heritage*, **3** (3), 1–20.

Van Hage, W. R., Stash, N., Wang, Y. and Aroyo, L. M. (2010) Finding Your Way Through the Rijksmuseum with an Adaptive Mobile Museum Guide. In *Proceedings of ESWC 2010*, 46–59.

Hall, M. and Clough, P. (2013) Exploring Large Digital Library Collections using a Map-based Visualisation. In *Proceedings of the 17th International Conference on Theory and Practice of Digital Libraries* (TPDL 2013), 216–27.

Hampson, C., Lawless, S., Bailey, E., Yogev, S., Zwerdling, N., Carmel, D., Conlan, O., O'Connor, A. and Wade, V. (2012) CULTURA: a metadata-rich environment to support the enhanced interrogation of cultural collections. *In Metadata and Semantics Research – 6th Research Conference* (MTSR 2012), 227–38.

Hardman, L., Aroyo, L., Van Ossenbruggen, J. and Hyvönen, E. (2009) Using AI to Access and Experience Cultural Heritage, *IEEE Intelligent Systems*, **24** (2), 23–5.

Hearst, M. A. (2009) *Search User Interfaces*, Cambridge University Press.

Hein, G. E. (1998) *Learning in the Museum*, London, Routledge.

Inskip, C., Butterworth, R. and MacFarlane, A. (2006) A Study of the Information Needs of the Users of a Folk Music Library and the Implications for the Design of a Digital Library System, *Information Processing and Management*, **44** (2), 647–62.

Johnson, A. (2008) Users, Use and Context: supporting interaction between users and digital archives. In Craven, L. (ed.), *What are Archives? Cultural and Theoretical Perspectives: a reader*, Ashgate Publishing, 145–66.

Jörgensen, C. and Jörgensen, P. (2005) Image Querying by Image Professionals, *Journal of the American Society for Information Science and Technology*, **56** (12), 1346–59.

Kelly, D. (2009) Methods for Evaluating Interactive Information Retrieval Systems with Users, *Foundations and Trends in Information Retrieval*, **3** (1–2), 1–224.

Koolen, M., Kamps, J. and De Keijzer, V. (2009) Information Retrieval in Cultural Heritage, *Interdisciplinary Science Reviews*, **34**, 268–84.

Marchionini, G. (2006) Exploratory Search: from finding to understanding, *Communications of the ACM*, **49** (4), 41–9.

Patterson, E. S., Roth, E. M. and Woods, D. D. (2001) Predicting Vulnerabilities in Computer-Supported Inferential Analysis Under Data Overload, *Cognition, Technology & Work*, **3** (4), 224–37.

Ponzetto, S. and Strube, M. (2011) Taxonomy Induction Based on a Collaboratively Built Knowledge Repository, *Artificial Intelligence*, **175** (9–10), 1737–56.

Proctor, N. (2010) Digital: Museum as Platform, Curator as Champion, in the Age of Social Media, *Curator: the museum journal*, **53** (1), 35–43.

Rasmussen, K. and Petersen, G. (2012) Personas. In Dobreva, M., O'Dwyer, A. and Feliciati, P. (eds), *User Studies for Digital Library Development*, Facet Publishing, 105–14.

Ross, C. and Terras, M. (2011) Scholarly Information-Seeking Behaviour in the British Museum Online Collection. In *Proceedings of Museums and the Web 2011*, Philadelphia, PA.

Russell-Rose, T. and Tate, T. (2013) *Designing the Search Experience: the information architecture of discovery*, Morgan Kaufmann.

Shipman, F., Furuta, R., Brenner, D., Chung, C. and Hsieh, H. (2000) Guided Paths Through Web-Based Collections: design, experiences, and adaptations, *Journal of the American Society for Information Science*, **51** (3), 260–72.

Shneiderman, B. (2000) Creating Creativity: user interfaces for supporting innovation, *ACM Transactions on Computer-Human Interaction*, **7** (1), 114–38.

Skov, M. and Ingwersen, P. (2008) Exploring Information Seeking Behaviour in a Digital Museum Context. In *Proceedings of the 2nd International Symposium on Information Interaction in Context* (IIiX '08), ACM, New York, NY, 110–15.

Smith, J., Hall, M., Stevenson, M., Goodale, P. and Clough, P. (2014) PATHS in Context: user characteristics and the construction of cultural heritage narratives. In *Proceedings of iConference 2014*, 5-7 March 2014, Berlin.

Trant, J. (2009) Tagging, Folksonomies and Art Museums: early experiments and ongoing research, *Journal of Digital Information*, **10** (1).

Urban, R., Twidale, M. B. and Adamczyk, P. (2010) Designing and Developing a Collections Dashboard. In Trant, J. and Bearman, D. (eds), *Museums and the Web 2010: Proceedings*, Toronto, Archives & Museum Informatics, www.archimuse.com/mw2010/papers/urban/urban.html.

White, R. and Roth, R. A. (2009) *Exploratory Search: beyond the query-response paradigm*, Morgan and Claypool.

White, R. W., Kules, B. and Drucker, S. M. (2007) Supporting Exploratory Search, introduction, special issue, *Communications of the ACM*, **49** (4), 36–9.

Wilson, M. L., Kules B., Schraefel, M. C. and Shneiderman, B. (2010) From Keyword Search to Exploration: designing future search interfaces for the web, *Foundations and Trends in Web Science*, **2** (1), 1–97.

Yakel, E. (2004) Seeking Information, Seeking Connections, Seeking Meaning: genealogists and family historians, *Information Research*, **10**, paper 205.

CHAPTER 11

Cultural heritage information services: sustainability issues

Gobinda Chowdhury

Northumbria University, UK

Introduction

A number of cultural heritage information services have appeared over the past decade or so. Some of these services are offered as part of national library services, like the American Memory from the US Library of Congress, or as an initiative of several memory institutions and industries, such as the Europeana digital library. As discussed in Chapter 3, activities related to the development of such digital libraries of cultural heritage information are very resource-intensive – not only to begin with, for example because of the massive cost of digitization and processing of digital information, but also in the longer term, for preservation of digitized heritage content that is required to ensure future access. Therefore, cultural heritage information services require a continuous funding support, and so the economic sustainability of such services is a major issue. However, economic sustainability is not the only challenge for digital cultural heritage information services. There are a number of social and environmental sustainability challenges as well.

Social sustainability issues of digital cultural heritage information services may be associated with a number of factors, such as the users' accessibility to ICT and web, usability of information systems and services, and information behaviour and literacy of users. Other social sustainability issues include copyright and digital rights management regulations; international, national and local or institutional policies and practices with regard to information products and services; and some specific cultural issues, for example those that are associated with indigenous cultural heritage information. Some of these issues have been discussed in Chapter 3.

Cultural heritage information services make extensive use of ICT throughout their lifecycle – from digitization to indexing, management, access and preservation. Research (Baliga et al., 2009, 2011; Mell and Grance, 2011; Chowdhury 2014a, 2014b) shows that the use of ICT causes a significant amount of greenhouse gas emissions because of the energy required for manufacturing computing equipment and network infrastructure, and also the energy required for use of these devices for building and running various information systems and services. Hence, specific measures need to be taken for building green information systems and services that make more efficient use of ICT and thus are environmentally sustainable (Chowdhury, 2012a, 2012b, 2012c, 2013a, 2013b, 2014a, 2014b). This chapter discusses the economic, social and environmental sustainability of cultural heritage information systems and services.

Sustainability

Over the past few years a number of policies, guidelines and measures related to sustainability and sustainable development have appeared that have implications for the planning, management and future of every international organization, government, major business and institution in the world. A report published by the World Commission on Environment and Development in 1987, called *Our Common Future*, which is also known as the *Brundtland Report*, provided the 'classic' definition of sustainable development which reads as follows:

> development which meets the needs of the present without compromising the ability of future generations to meet their own needs.
>
> United Nations, 1987

According to the United States EPA (Environmental Protection Agency), sustainability creates and maintains the conditions under which humans and nature can exist in productive harmony, that permit fulfilling the social, economic and ecological requirements of present and future generations (EPA, 2010). It is generally accepted that sustainable development calls for a convergence between the three pillars of sustainability, viz. economic sustainability, social sustainability and environmental sustainability (Chowdhury, 2013a, 2013b, 2014a, 2014b; Drexhage and Murphy, 2010). These three dimensions of sustainability are interrelated and interdependent.

Thus, in order to achieve sustainable development in any sector – government, business, education, health, etc. – we need to build systems and services that are economically, environmentally and socially sustainable. Increasingly in most countries 'legislation requires public sector institutions and private businesses to comply with minimum social and environmental rules', and it is recognized that a sustainable business is the one that 'works towards minimizing environmental and social impacts while ensuring financial stability' (Dimireva, 2012). In order to build sustainable information systems and services, there is a need for an integrated approach to the three dimensions of sustainable development, viz. economic development, environmental protection and social development (Chowdhury, 2013b).

However, although this may sound rather simple, it may not always be easy to achieve all the three forms of sustainability at the same time; and sometimes measures taken to achieve one form of sustainability may affect or compromise the other form(s). For example, in order to achieve economic sustainability, one may try to do business – production, distribution, etc. – using cheap sources of energy, inefficient industries and technologies, cheap and unregulated labour markets, etc. Such an effort for achieving economic sustainability (by reducing costs) may compromise environmental sustainability and also in some way social sustainability by creating inequality in the labour market, standard of living, quality of health and well-being of the population. On the other hand, if one wants to use only clean energy and the most advanced industries and technologies, then the resulting businesses and products may be environmentally sustainable, but perhaps may be expensive, at least to begin with, and therefore may not be economically sustainable; and this may also create social inequality by compromising the affordability, well-being and quality of life of the population, and so on.

Many countries and international bodies have introduced specific measures that require businesses to comply with the sustainability requirements. Consequently businesses in every sector are taking the necessary measures to comply with the sustainability regulations and requirements that are causing several changes in the business workflow, products and services. However, in comparison with other businesses, the issue of sustainability has not been studied and practised well within the information science discipline or the information services sector (Chowdhury, 2010, 2012a, 2013a; Nathan, 2012; Nolin, 2010).

Sustainability of information systems and services

In order to study the sustainability of digital information services, it is necessary to identify the challenges that are associated with the design, delivery, access and use of digital information (Chowdhury, 2013a). Again, the issues of sustainability can be considered in the context of the major factors influencing the lifecycle of information, from creation to management, use/re-use, and disposal (when required: for example, disposal of analogue information resources and also disposal of computing infrastructure and equipment, etc.).

A generic model of sustainability of digital information services has been proposed by Chowdhury (2013a) (Figure 11.1). The model illustrates that in order to build sustainable digital information systems and services, one needs to take an integrated approach for achieving all the three forms of sustainability, as far as practicable. The model also points out some major issues and challenges that contribute to, or have impact on, each form of sustainability.

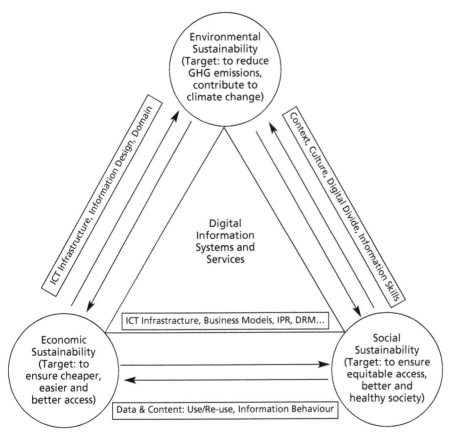

Figure 11.1 A model of sustainability of digital information systems and services (Chowdhury, 2013a)

Economic sustainability of digital information systems and services

Broadly speaking, economic sustainability means sustainable economic growth. Within a business context, economic sustainability may be defined as 'using the assorted assets of the company efficiently to allow it to continue functioning profitably over time' (BusinessDictionary.com, 2013). Spangenberg (2005) comments that 'in the economic debate, sustainable development is most often described as the need to maintain a permanent income for humankind, generated from non-declining capital stocks.' However, this may not be applicable for the service sector. In fact, measuring the economic sustainability of a service sector is a major challenge, because the outcome of a service cannot always be measured in terms of increase in direct profits or tangible assets that can be counted in pounds and pennies. The service sector produces 'intangible' goods, some of which are well known, such as government, health, education, etc., and some are quite new, such as modern communications, information and business services (World Bank, 2000). Nevertheless, they all help in building a better society. Thus one of the indirect measures for economic sustainability of service sectors can be the growth in human capital that is capable of engaging in sustainable development using fewer natural resources, alternative and innovative technologies and resources, and so on. By the same analogy, the economic success of an information service can be indirectly measured by its overall contribution to the development of human capital and an information society.

The target for the economic sustainability of digital information systems and services is to ensure cheaper, easier and better access to information. The economic success can be measured by reduction in direct costs, for example, by sharing resources for digitization and delivery of information services, and by reduction in indirect costs, for example, through better design of systems and services that can reduce user time and efforts required for information access and use.

There may be a number of other direct and indirect measures of contributions of digital information systems and services to the economy. The direct contributions of a digital information service may be measured through job creations; for example, through various digitization and management activities associated with digital information systems and services. Indirect contributions of digital information systems and services may be realized through:

- the provision of better information services to support various education and research-related activities;
- through the provision of better and value-added information services that can lead to a better, more efficient and more informed society, and so on.

Direct contributions of digital information systems and services may come from the commercial use/re-use of digitized information products and services, such as digital images, digital design, digital music and video, etc. Some examples of this in the context of digital cultural heritage information systems and services are discussed later in this chapter.

Social sustainability of digital information systems and services

By definition, information systems and services are social services, because they are designed to provide access to information as a shared resource that is required by a society or a community – be it a specific community group in an organization or institution like universities, hospitals, government and business houses, etc., or the general public. Thus the target for social sustainability of information systems and services should be to ensure easy and equitable access to information for every activity – education, research, health, leisure, etc. – that is required to build a better, well informed, efficient and healthy society. The success can be achieved by (a) improving the accessibility and usability of information products and services relevant to the user context, culture, etc., and (b) building tools and techniques for measuring and improving the impact of digital information services in every sphere of life and society (Chowdhury, 2013a). Ideally speaking, a socially sustainable digital information service should be ubiquitous, i.e., it should be embedded in the work and culture of people in such a way that they get access to the information that is relevant to their work or activities even without having to actively ask or search for it. Access is a rather broad term here that includes all the activities related to the discovery, access and use/re-use of information for day-to-day business, pleasure, well-being, knowledge and understanding, and so on.

Human information behaviour (HIB) and information seeking and retrieval (IS&R) have remained the two most widely researched areas of information science for the past few decades, giving rise to several models in information science in general (for details see Wilson, 2009; Ruthven and Kelly, 2011; Ingwersen and Järvelin, 2005, and in the context of digital libraries in particular Wilson and Maceviciute, 2012; Dobreva and O'Dwyer, 2012). These models discuss various personal, contextual, social, cultural and technological issues that influence access to, and use of, information, and thus the overall aim of the research that they report on has been to improve the social sustainability of information systems and services.

Like human information behaviour, information literacy has also remained a major area of research in information studies, and a huge volume of literature exists in this area (for a review of recent works see Hepworth and Walton, 2013). Like HIB and IS&R, the overall goal of this body of research is also to improve access and use of information and thus to improve the social sustainability of information systems and services. There are other related areas of research such as digital literacy, digital divide and social inclusion that also have implications for the social sustainability of information systems and services. Access to, and effective use of, digital libraries can be significantly affected by poor information literacy and digital literacy of people (Chowdhury and Chowdhury, 2011). In November 2012 BBC News reported that 16 million people in Britain, i.e., about one in four, or one in three in the adult British population, do not have basic internet skills (BBC News, 2012). It may be safely assumed that this is not an isolated case and many countries in the world have comparable, or even worse, information and digital literacy skills, causing social exclusion. Access to, and effective use of, digital information systems and services can be significantly affected by digital divide that is often manifested by:

- the social divide, which is characterized by the difference in access between diverse social groups
- the global divide, which is characterized by the difference in terms of access to internet technologies
- the democratic divide, which is characterized by the different applications and uses of digital information in order to engage and participate in social life

Chowdhury and Chowdhury, 2011

In the context of digital cultural heritage information services, social exclusion may be caused by a number of factors, ranging from the lack of adequate access to ICT infrastructure and services to the lack of digital and information skills that are the prerequisites for successful access to, and use of, digital information services. Furthermore, work culture as well as various customs, practices and lifestyles of users may also have implications for the social sustainability of digital information systems and services.

Environmental sustainability of digital information systems and services

ICT has a profound impact on the environment causing about 2% of global greenhouse gas (GHG) emissions (Chowdhury, 2012a, 2012b, 2012c). GHGs comprise carbon dioxide (CO_2), methane (CH_4), nitrous oxide (N_2O), hydrofluorocarbons (HFCs), perfluorocarbons (PFCs) and sulphur hexafluoride (SF_6) but GHG is generally expressed through a common metric of CO_2-equivalent emission (CO_2e) (IPCC, 2007). Digital information systems and services are based on a variety of ICT infrastructures and equipment that are used to build and use information systems and services. Thus the target for the environmental sustainability of digital information services is to ensure reductions in the environmental impact of digital information; this can be measured by reduction in the greenhouse gas emissions throughout the lifecycle of digital information services. As of this date, we do not have any data related to the environmental impact of digital libraries and information services. However, the following data may give us an indication of the level of GHG emissions from digital information systems and services.

According to some estimates, Google emits 1.5 million tonnes of CO_2e, which is slightly higher than the annual consumption of the country of Laos in south-east Asia and equivalent to the UN's operational footprint (Clark, 2011). According to the company's own figures, Google emitted 1.67 million tonnes of CO_2e in 2011 compared to 1.46 million tonnes in 2010; and the company's 'carbon footprint per million dollars of revenue – a measure of carbon intensity commonly used to track corporate sustainability – has decreased by an average of 10% each year since 2009' (Woody, 2012). So, according to this (Google's own) estimate, in 2011 Google's GHG emissions were equivalent to the annual emissions from nearly 14 typical power stations in Britain (estimates are based on the CARMA (2013) statistics). It may be argued that a large part of this emission, but not all, was for the search-related operations of Google.

It is reported that the typical Google user creates 1.46kg of CO_2e by consuming its various services, which is the equivalent of filling a deep bath or buying an imported bottle of wine (Clark, 2011). According to the same report, it is claimed by Google that producing and shipping a single DVD uses as much energy as watching YouTube non-stop for three days. The company further claims that each 10 minutes of viewing on YouTube generates 1g of CO_2e and a typical Gmail user generates 1.2kg of CO_2e per year (Clark, 2011). With over 6 billion hours of video being watched each month on YouTube, and over 425 million Gmail users worldwide, the carbon footprint of YouTube and Gmail users will be quite significant. However, the emission figures reported here do not include the client-side ICT and energy usage figures. The total carbon footprint of a Dell Latitude E6400 is approximately 320–370 kg CO_2e, depending on the energy source used (Dell, 2010). With a typical replacement period of four years and assuming that a laptop is used for 10 hours a day, i.e., 3650 hours a year, for a typical 10-minute use of a laptop while watching video on YouTube, the client-side carbon footprint would be about 4g. So, at this rate, the carbon footprint for watching YouTube video will be 30g ((1+4)x 6)) per hour, and the total carbon footprint (for 6 billion hours) will be 180,000 tonnes CO_2e per month or 2.16 million tonnes per year (equivalent to the annual emissions from 21.6 typical UK power stations (according to the CARMA, 2013 statistics).

It is estimated that the internet consumes between 170 and 307 GW (Gigawatts) of electricity, which is equivalent to 1.1–1.9% of the total energy usage of humanity (Raghavan and Ma, 2011). The higher education institutions (HEIs) in the USA produce 121 million tonnes of CO_2 in a year, which is equivalent to nearly 2% of total annual GHG emissions in the USA, or about a quarter of the entire State of California's annual emissions (Sinha et al., 2010). It is estimated that in 2008–9, HEIs in the UK alone used nearly 1,470,000 computers, 250,000 printers and 240,000 servers; and it is estimated that there would be 500,000 tonnes of CO_2 emissions from this electricity use (James and Hopkinson, 2009).

Some data related to the environmental impact of information services based on print and digital content is provided by Chowdhury (2012c). Studies also show that use of modern technologies, such as sharing of computing infrastructure through cloud computing and better cooling systems in data centres, can reduce both the economic and environmental impact of digital information (Baliga et al., 2011; Mell and Grance, 2011).

Economic sustainability of cultural heritage information services

As discussed in the other chapters, and also earlier in this chapter, cultural heritage information services can make significant contributions to the economy. The World Intellectual Property Organization points out that:

> Manifestations of traditional culture and cultural heritage are therefore often a source of creativity for indigenous, local and other cultural communities. The unalloyed re-creation and replication of past traditions is not necessarily the best way of preserving identity and improving the economic situation of indigenous, local and cultural communities. In recognizing this, the link between cultural heritage, culture and economic development is now being more appreciated. International and regional financial institutions, such as the World Bank, have begun to support cultural development projects that treat culture as an economic resource that is able to contribute to poverty alleviation, local job creation and foreign exchange earning.
>
> WIPO, 2003

WIPO also recognizes that alternative forms or manifestations of cultural heritage are also a source of inspiration and creativity for the cultural industries, acting as powerful engines of economic growth. Digital manifestations of various cultural heritage objects, such as handicrafts and designs, music, herbs and plants, art and architecture, and dance and other forms of performing arts, make them more widely and easily accessible to the public and with appropriate technologies and transaction mechanisms it is possible for industries to make commercial use of these resources either in their original or in some new, hybrid or value-added, forms. Digital cultural heritage information can also lead to some new and unprecedented use and this may boost the economy. A recent report (De Jager, 2014) shows how new electronic games are now being inspired by cultural heritage; for example, the game *Monument Valley* has been based on the 'impossible reality' lithographs of the Dutch artist M. C. Escher, and the developer of the game, the British digital creative studio ustwo, is bringing other cultural masterpieces, such as *Staircase*, *Tower of Babel* and *Belvedere*, to a new audience of gamers.

As discussed earlier, in order to be economically sustainable cultural heritage information services should have a steady stream of funding support on a long-term basis. Furthermore, it cannot be expected that such funding should always come from the public exchequer. In fact, as discussed in Chapter 3, most policy guidelines recommend a public-private partnership for covering the huge costs of digitization and digital preservation activities. Nevertheless, in order to secure a steady flow of funding support, such digital information services should prove evidence of value for money.

As discussed by Terras in Chapter 4, the Enumerate project noted that on average 15 staff are involved in the digitization process in national libraries, whilst other types of institutions have a team of around 5.5 staff; and the costs of digitization are in the range of €20,000 to €40,000 per full-time member of staff, unless the project involves audiovisual digitization, in which case the costs rise to €103,000 per full-time member of staff. These figures provide some indications of the costs involved in digitization alone. Quoting the same study, Terras further notes that funding for digitization is sourced from internal budgets in 87% of the institutions, although 40% mention some form of public grant or subsidy, 5% say they raised finances via private investment, and 4% indicate that they had some commercial sponsorship. These figures clearly point out that the economic sustainability of cultural heritage information services is a major concern. However, very few of the earlier digital library evaluation studies focused primarily on the economic sustainability of digital library and information services *per se*.

It is generally agreed that measuring the impact of information services in general, and digital libraries in particular, is difficult because it is not easy to convert the benefits of information services to dollar figures (Chowdhury, McMenemy and Poulter, 2008). Of late, however, some studies have attempted to measure the impact of digital libraries on the economy as a whole. For example, the *Europeana Case for Funding* (Europeana, 2013) document points out that over the past five years initial EU investment of €150 million has resulted in €70 million of co-funding from ministries in 21 countries. The document reports that these investments have facilitated massive digitization in different EU member countries and as a result 27 million digital objects are now available through Europeana. It is also reported that as of 2013 '770 businesses, entrepreneurs, educational and cultural organizations are exploring ways of including Europeana information in their offerings (websites, apps, games etc.) through our API' (Europeana, 2013). The document also points out that Europeana has helped in the creation of new jobs. For example, it reports that in Hungary, 'over 1,000 graduates are now involved in digitising heritage that will feed in to Europeana. Historypin in the UK predicts it will double in size with the availability of more open digital cultural heritage.' Such measures of the impact of digital libraries on the wider economy, job markets, etc., are very useful for justifying the case for funding, and thereby achieving the economic sustainability of digital libraries. However, it should be noted that activities related to the gathering of relevant and useful data for such measures are often very time-consuming and resource-intensive.

Social sustainability of digital cultural heritage information services

As discussed in different chapters in this book, for example by Sula in Chapter 2, by Chowdhury in Chapter 3, by Terras in Chapter 4, throughout Chapter 7 by Chowdhury, and by Stiller and Petras in Chapter 8, users should be at the centre of the design, in the context of user interactions, management and delivery of a cultural heritage information service. Consequently, understanding user needs and behaviours, as well as various constraints such as accessibility, usability and information skills, should be a basic requirement for achieving the social sustainability of cultural heritage information services. However, as discussed by Chowdhury (2013a, 2013b, 2014a, 2014b), although user studies has remained a major area of research in information science for several decades, social sustainability issues of digital libraries and information services have not been researched well. Social sustainability of digital information systems and services can be affected by a number of factors, and accessibility to ICT and the internet is one of them.

Although accessibility to the appropriate ICT and the internet is a major challenge for digital information service providers in the developing countries, as discussed by Phiri and Suleman in Chapter 6, digital divide is also present in the developed countries. For example, as of May 2013, 70% of American adults have broadband connection from home, but this percentage drops significantly for low educational attainment (only 37% for those with no high school diploma), low household income groups (54% for households with an income of less than US$30,000 per year), and higher age groups (65% for people aged 65 and above) (Zickuhr and Smith, 2013). Internet use statistics (penetration as percentage of population) in the EU vary significantly among the 27 EU countries. Some EU countries have internet access rate of 90% or more; for example, the Netherlands has 92.9% internet access, Sweden has 92.7% access, Luxembourg has 90.9% access and Denmark has 90% access, compared to 83.6% in the UK (www.internetworldstats.com/stats9.htm#eu). However, in some EU countries only about half the population have internet access; for example, Romania has 44.1% internet access, Bulgaria has 51% access, Greece has 53% access, Portugal has 55.2% access and Italy has 58.4% access (Internet World Stats, 2013). So, the vision of a cultural heritage information service like the Europeana digital library to provide digital information and culture to everyone in Europe cannot be fully utilized because a large proportion of people in many EU countries do not have access to the internet. The situation in the Third World countries is even worse.

In addition to the accessibility issues, there are many other factors that have implications for the social sustainability of cultural heritage information systems and services. Design and usability of digital information systems and services is one such issue. It is estimated that around 15% of the world's population, or an estimated 1 billion people, live with disabilities, and according to the United Nations 'they are the world's largest minority' (United Nations, 2013). In the third quarter of 2013, 43.8 million adults (86%) in the UK had used the internet, but there were 3.8 million disabled adults, as defined by the Disability Discrimination Act (DDA), who had never used the internet (ONS Statistics, 2013). Although persons with disabilities 'can equally participate in society and make substantial contributions to the economy if the appropriate internet tools are available', people in the broader community 'have limited understanding of how persons with disabilities use technology and of the significant benefits the internet can bring' (Internet Society, 2012).

According to the Internet Society, for persons with disabilities usability means being able to use a product or service as effectively as a person without a disability. In the context of cultural heritage information services, in some cases this may require universal design consideration for the information systems, products and services, and in others it may require the use of assistive technologies such as screen-reading software for users with visual impairment. Although specific international and national policies and guidelines exist for supporting access to internet services by disabled users, to date most cultural heritage information services are designed for mainstream users, and thus a significant proportion of the population is left out. More research and stringent measures are needed to make digital information services accessible and usable for disabled and marginalized users.

Usability of digital libraries and information services is often affected by the user needs and expectations that are set, often wrongly, by the search engines. In a usability study of the Europeana digital library it was noted that young users' information needs and search strategies and expectations were quite different from those of more mature users (Dobreva and Chowdhury, 2010). The study further noted that many younger users wanted to be able to download, annotate and share digital objects. The latter is a relatively new phenomenon which is caused by the recent proliferation of the easy-to-use search engine services that have created a different set of expectations, especially amongst the younger users.

Access to, and use of, digital information is often hindered by the inappropriate, and often stringent, intellectual property rights (IPR) and complex digital rights management (DRM) issues. This has been identified in several studies (see for example, Chowdhury, 2009; Chowdhury and Fraser, 2011; Hargreaves, 2011). Considering the various recommendations of the *Hargreaves Review* (Hargreaves, 2011), the UK Government commissioned a feasibility study that recommended the development of a Copyright Hub to serve a number of functions including:

- information and copyright education
- registries of rights
- a marketplace for rights-licensing solutions
- help with the orphan works problem.

Hooper and Lynch, 2012

The report concluded that a number of issues existed with copyright licensing laws making them unfit for the digital age (Hooper and Lynch, 2012). However, it will be interesting to see how the new IP laws influence the publishing industry and digital libraries.

Environmental sustainability of digital cultural heritage information services

Cultural heritage information services make extensive use of ICT throughout their lifecycle, ranging from the digitization of cultural heritage content to their processing, access, management and preservation. For each of these functions and the related activities one needs to consider two types of energy cost: the embodied energy costs and the socket energy costs. Embodied energy is the energy used to manufacture the myriads of computing and network devices that are used to build, run and use the cultural heritage information services, and socket energy is that used by the devices during a typical information search or use session.

Broadly speaking, in order to estimate the overall energy and environmental costs of a cultural heritage digital information service, one needs to estimate the energy costs of:

1 Digitization: embodied and socket energy costs of all the computing equipment and tools used for digitization of content, including any preparation costs, storage and transportation of heritage content, and so on. This can be classed as a server-side energy cost of a digital cultural heritage information service.

2 Processing costs: embodied and socket energy costs of all the equipment and tools used for processing of digital content, including the energy cost of software development, indexing and data management, etc. This can be classed as a server-side energy cost of a digital cultural heritage information service.

3 Access costs: embodied and socket energy costs of all the computing equipment and network resources used for access and use of cultural heritage information by the end users. This can be classed as the client-side energy cost of a digital cultural heritage information service.

4 Preservation costs: embodied and socket energy costs of all the computing equipment and tools used for preservation of digital content. This can be classed as a server-side energy cost of a digital cultural heritage information service.

It may be noted that the server-side energy costs of a digital cultural heritage information service will depend on the servers, tools, networking resources and processes used for all the activities from digitization to processing and preservation. Out of these, the energy and environmental cost of digitization and digital preservation can be quite significant if the collection is big, and complex digitization and digital preservation processes are involved. As discussed earlier in the chapter, use of shared computing resources and/or cloud-based information services can improve the environmental sustainability of digital information systems and services. However, a number of social, cultural and user-related issues are also associated with cloud-based information services, e.g.: access and management issues related to sensitive data and content, information behaviour of users in relation to remote access to data and content; institutional and user culture and practices in relation to access and use of remote digital content and data, and so on. To date no research has addressed all of these issues together in relation to cultural heritage information services, and specific user communities and contexts.

While the success of a cultural heritage digital library or information service can be measured by how many people use the service, the efficiency of the service can be increased, and the resultant search time and the corresponding energy costs can be reduced, by introducing better design and usability features so that people need to spend less time on the service looking for the required information. The more energy-efficient the user computing device is, and the less time the user needs to spend on a digital library for finding and accessing the required information, the more energy-efficient the service will be. Fortunately, research shows that the use of thin client technology such as mobile phones and tablets for accessing digital libraries is increasing. Nicholas et al. (2013) note that 'Over the 12 months from August 2010 to July 2011, page views from mobile devices grew at a rate four times greater than from fixed devices.'

Summary

As discussed in Chapters 2, 3 and 4 in this book, cultural heritage institutions as well as various governments and research funding bodies have made a significant amount of investment and effort in digitizing as well as providing access to digital heritage information. However, although sustainability has become a major agenda for every government, business and research and development activity, to date very little research has taken place on the sustainability of digital information systems and services *per se*.

As discussed by Chowdhury in Chapter 3, and Terras in Chapter 4, activities surrounding the design, development and management of cultural heritage information systems and services are very resource-intensive and they require a continuous flow of funding support. Digitization and digital preservation of cultural heritage content are the two major heads of expenditure in this context. Given the large amount of investment required for this, many reports and policy documents have recommended public–private partnership for raising funds for such activities, and some evidences of this have been noted in recent studies (as discussed in Chapter 4 by Terras). However, the investments in digitization of cultural heritage information can also see some returns, and it may come in several direct and indirect ways. Some digital cultural heritage information has significant commercial values. Therefore, with the introduction of appropriate systems and legal frameworks, it is possible to generate revenues from the commercial use of digital cultural heritage information. Indirect economic benefits may come from the use of cultural heritage information in various context, for example in education, research, creative activities and leisure. However, more research is needed to develop appropriate frameworks and benchmarks to measure such benefits.

While ensuring the economic sustainability, appropriate measures should also be taken to promote the social sustainability of cultural heritage information systems and services. This can be achieved by building more usable, user-centred and value-added information services. However, social sustainability can also be improved by promoting better access to ICT and internet services, better ICT and information skills education, and by building the appropriate legal and regulatory frameworks for protecting values embedded in some cultural heritage information resources. More research is also needed to promote the environmental sustainability of cultural heritage information systems and services by sharing of ICT and network resources throughout the lifecycle of information services, and also by building more efficient systems and services that can reduce the user's access time and thus the client-side energy costs of information services.

While the economic and environmental sustainability issues pose some major challenges, recent research and development activities in the areas of crowdsourcing and user-generated content (see for example, Jett, Senseney and Palmer, 2013; Liew, 2013, 2014), and big data/linked data (see for example, Fischer, 2013; France and Toth, 2013) can significantly boost the access and use, and thus the overall social sustainability, of digital cultural heritage information services. It is evident that more research and concerted efforts are needed to build and manage cultural heritage information systems and services that are economically, socially and environmentally sustainable.

References

Baliga, J., Ayre, R. W. A., Hinton, K. and Tucker, R. S. (2011) Green Cloud Computing: balancing energy in processing, storage, and transport, *Proceedings of the IEEE*, **99** (1), http://ieeexplore.ieee.org/stamp/stamp.jsp?arnumber=05559320&tag=1.

Baliga, J., Hinton, K., Ayre, R. and Tucker, R. S. (2009) Carbon Footprint of the Internet, *Telecommunication Journal of Australia*, **59** (1), 1–14.

BBC News (2012) Millions in UK 'Lack Basic Online Skills', www.bbc.co.uk/news/technology-20236708.

BusinessDictionary.com (2013) Economic Sustainability, www.businessdictionary.com/definition/economic-sustainability. html#ixzz2OdJ61yXN.

CARMA (2013) Carbon Monitoring for Action. United Kingdom, http://carma.org/region/detail/2635167.

Chowdhury, G. G. (2009) Towards the Conceptual Model of a Content Service Network. In *Globalizing Academic Libraries Vision 2020, Proceedings of the International Conference on Academic Libraries*, Delhi, 5–8 October 2009,

Delhi Mittal Publications, 215–20.

Chowdhury, G. G. (2010) Carbon Footprint of the Knowledge Sector: what's the future?, *Journal of Documentation*, **66** (6), 934–46.

Chowdhury, G. G. (2012a) Building Sustainable Information Services: a Green IS research agenda, *Journal of the American Society for Information Science and Technology*, **63** (4), 633–47.

Chowdhury, G. G. (2012b) An Agenda for Green Information Retrieval Research, *Information Processing and Management*, **48** (6), 1067–77.

Chowdhury, G. G. (2012c) How Digital Information Services Can Reduce Greenhouse Gas Emissions, *Online Information Review*, **36** (4), 489–506.

Chowdhury, G. G. (2013a) Sustainability of Digital Information Services, *Journal of Documentation*, **69** (5), 602–22.

Chowdhury, G. G. (2013b) Social Sustainability of Digital Libraries: a research framework. In Urs, S. R., Na, J-C. and Buchanan, G., (eds), *Digital Libraries: social media and community networks*, Springer, 25–34.

Chowdhury, G. G. (2014a) Sustainability of Digital Libraries: a conceptual model and a research framework, *International Journal of Digital Libraries*, **14** (3–4), 181–95, http://link.springer.com/article/10.1007/s00799-014-0116-0.

Chowdhury, G. G. (2014b) *Sustainability of Scholarly Information*, London, Facet Publishing.

Chowdhury, G. G. and Chowdhury, S. (2011) *Information Users and Usability in the Digital Age*, London, Facet Publishing.

Chowdhury, G. G. and Fraser, M. (2011) Carbon Footprint of the Knowledge Industry and Ways to Reduce it, *World Digital Libraries*, **4** (1), 9–18.

Chowdhury, G. G., McMenemy, D. and Poulter, A. (2008) MEDLIS: model for evaluation of digital libraries and information services, *World Digital Libraries*, **1** (1), 35–46.

Clark, D. (2011) Google Discloses Carbon Footprint for the First Time, *The Guardian*, 8 September, www.guardian.co.uk/environment/2011/sep/08/google-carbon-footprint.

Dell (2010) *Carbon Footprint of a Typical Business Laptop From Dell*, http://i.dell.com/sites/content/corporate/corp-comm/en/Documents/dell-laptop-carbon-footprint-whitepaper.pdf.

Dimireva, I. (2012) Doing Business in the UK: sustainability, *Eubusiness*, 20 February, www.eubusiness.com/europe/uk/sustainable-business.

Dobreva, M. and Chowdhury, S. (2010) A User-Centric Evaluation of the Europeana Digital Library. In *The Role of Digital Libraries in a Time of Global Change, Proceedings of the 12th International Conference on Asia-Pacific Digital Libraries*, ICADL 2010, Gold Coast, Australia, 21–25 June 2010, Lecture Notes in Computer Science Series 6102, Springer, 148–57.

Dobreva, M. and O'Dwyer, A. (eds) (2012) *User Studies for Digital Library Development*, London, Facet Publishing.

Drexhage, J. and Deborah Murphy, D. (2010) *Sustainable Development: from Brundtland to Rio 2012*, Background paper prepared for consideration by the High Level Panel on Global Sustainability at its first meeting, 19 September 2010, International Institute for Sustainable Development (IISD), www.un.org/wcm/webdav/site/climatechange/shared/gsp/docs/GSP1-6_Background%20on%20Sustainable%20Devt.pdf.

EPA (US Environment Protection Agency) (2010) *Inventory of U.S. Greenhouse Gas Emissions and Sinks: 1990–2008*, Executive summary, www.epa.gov./climatechange/Downloads/ghgemissions/508_Complete_GHG_1990_2008.pdf.

Europeana (2013) *Europeana: the case for funding*, www.eblida.org/News/Europeana%20-%20The%20Case%20for%20Funding.pdf.

Fischer, C. S. (2013) Digital Humanities, Big Data, and Ngrams, *Boston Review*, 20 June, www.bostonreview.net/blog/digital-humanities-big-data-and-ngrams.

France, F. G. and Toth, M.B. (2013) Access and Preservation: addressing challenges of linking cultural heritage datasets. In *10th IS&T Archiving Conference, National Archives & Records*, Washington, DC, 2–5 April 2013, 204–9, www.ingentaconnect.com/content/ist/ac/2013/00002013/00000001/art00044.

Hargreaves, I. (2011) *Digital Opportunity: a review of intellectual property and growth. An independent report*, https://www.gov.uk/government/publications/digital-opportunity-review-of-intellectual-property-and-growth.

Hepworth, M. and Walton, G. (eds) (2013) *Developing People's Information Capabilities*, Library and Information Science, vol. 8, Emerald Group Publishing.

Hooper, R. and Lynch, R. (2012) *Copyright Works: streaming copyright licensing for the digital age*, UK Intellectual Property Office, www.ipo.gov.uk/dce-report-phase2.pdf.

Ingwersen, P. and Järvelin, K. (2005) *The Turn: integration of information seeking and retrieval in context*, Dordrecht, Springer.

IPCC (2007) *Climate Change 2007: synthesis report*, Contribution of Working Groups I, II and III to the Fourth Assessment Report of the Intergovernmental Panel on Climate Change, www.ipcc.ch/publications_and_data/publications_ipcc_fourth_assessment_report_synthesis_report.htm.

Internet Society (2012) www.internetsociety.org.

Internet World Stats (2013) www.internetworldstats.com/stats9.htm#eu.

De Jager, W. (2014) *How Cultural Heritage Inspires Creative Studios to Create Best-selling Games*, http://blog.europeana.eu/2014/04/how-cultural-heritage-inspires-creative-studios-to-create-best-selling-games.

James, P. and Hopkinson, L. (2009) *Green ICT: managing sustainable ICT in education and research*, www.jisc.ac.uk/publications/programmerelated/2009/sustainableictfinalreport.aspx. [Accessed 23 September 2013.]

Jett, J., Senseney, M. and Palmer, C. L. (2013) A Model for Providing Web 2.0 Services to Cultural Heritage Institutions: the IMLS DCC Flickr Feasibility Study, *D-Lib Magazine*, **19** (5/6), www.dlib.org/dlib/may13/jett/05jett.html.

Liew, C. L. (2013) Digital Cultural Heritage 2.0: a meta-design consideration, *Information Research*, **18** (3), www.informationr.net/ir/18-3/colis/paperS03.html.

Liew, C. L. (2014) Participatory Cultural Heritage: a tale of two institutions' use of social media, *D-Lib Magazine*, **20** (3/4), www.dlib.org/dlib/march14/liew/03liew.html.

Mell, P. and Grance, T. (2011) *The NIST Definition of Cloud Computing: recommendations of the National Institute of Standards and Technology*, NIST Special Publication 800-145, http://csrc.nist.gov/publications/nistpubs/800-145/SP800-145.pdf.

Nathan, L. P. (2012) Sustainable Information Practice: an ethnographic investigation, *Journal of the American Society for Information Science and Technology*, **63** (11), 2254–68.

Nicholas, D., Clark, D., Rowlands, I. and Jamali, H. R. (2013) Information on the Go: a case study of Europeana mobile users, *Journal of the American Society for Information Science and Technology*, **64** (7), 1311–22.

Nolin, J. (2010) Sustainable Information and Information Science, *Information Research*, **15** (2), http://informationr.net/ir/15-2/paper431.html.

ONS Statistics (2013) www.ons.gov.uk/ons/rel/rdit2/internet-access-quarterly-update/q3-2013/stb-ia-q3-2013.html#tab-Disability.

Raghavan, B. and Ma, J. (2011) The Energy and Emergy of the Internet. In *Proceedings of the ACM workshop on Hot Topics in Networks (Hotnets)*, Cambridge, MA, November 2011, http://conferences.sigcomm.org/hotnets/2011/papers/hotnetsX-final.pdf.

Ruthven, I. and Kelly, D. (eds) (2011) *Interactive Information Seeking, Behaviour and Retrieval*, London, Facet Publishing.

Sinha, P., Schew, W. A., Sawant A., Kolwaite, K. J. and Strode, S. A. (2010) Greenhouse Gas Emissions from US Institutions of Higher Education, *Journal of Air & Waste Management Association*, **60** (5), 568–73.

Spangenberg, J. H. (2005) Economic Sustainability of the Economy: concepts and indicators, *International Journal of Sustainable Development*, **8** (1/2), www.environmental-expert.com/Files/6471/articles/6328/f211108463951127.pdf.

United Nations (1987) General Assembly, 96th plenary meeting, 1 December 1987, www.un.org/documents/ga/res/42/ares42-187.htm.

United Nations (2013) *Factsheet on Persons with Disabilities*, www.un.org/disabilities/default.asp?id=18.

Wilson, T. (2009) On User Studies and Information Needs, *Journal of Documentation*, special publication, 174–86.

Wilson, T. D. and Macevičiūtė, E. (2012) Users' Interactions with Digital Libraries. In Chowdhury, G .G. and Foo, S. (eds), *Digital Libraries and Information Access: research perspectives*, London, Facet Publishing, 113–28.

WIPO (World Intellectual Property Organization)(2003) *Consolidated Analysis of the Legal Protections of Traditional Cultural Expressions/Expressions of Folklore*, www.wipo.int/export/sites/www/freepublications/en/tk/785/wipo_pub_785.pdf.

Woody, T. (2012) Google's Business Is Booming, Its Carbon Emissions Are

Not, *Forbes*, 12 December, www.forbes.com/sites/toddwoody/2012/09/12/googles-business-is-booming-its-carbon-emissions-are-not.

World Bank (2000) *Beyond Economic Growth: meeting the challenges of global development*, Chapter IX, Growth of the Services Sector, www.worldbank.org/depweb/beyond/beyondco/beg_09.pdf.

Zickuhr, K. and Smith, A. (2013) *Home Broadband 2013*, PewResearch internet project, www.pewinternet.org/2013/08/26/home-broadband-2013.

Index

3D models
    digitization 66, 70, 74
    E-Curator project 66
    GLAM (Galleries, Libraries, Archives and Museums)
        66
    University College London (UCL) 74

AAT *see* Getty Art and Architecture Thesaurus
access modes, information *see* information access modes
access to digitized content 48–50
    see also PATHS (Personalised Access To cultural
        Heritage Spaces) project; social sustainability
    Australian National Library 48
    British Library Digitization Strategy 38, 44, 49
    Digital Copyright Hub 236
    digital rights management (DRM) 236
    disabilities usability 235
    European Commission 49
    future directions 213–14
    information access modes 156–8
    information search behaviour 199–200
    intellectual property rights (IPR) 236
    internet access, national statistics 234–5
    Library of Congress 48
aggregators, cultural heritage *see* cultural heritage
        aggregators
American Memory collection, Library of Congress 3
architectural design 113–31
    Bleek and Lloyd collection 127–8
    case studies 126–30
    design constraints and patterns 116–19
    digital library systems (DLSs) 113–15
    flexibility 121
    integration 120–1
    minimalist design 121
    motivation 119
    organization of information 122
    platform independence 117, 120
    portable architectures 118–19
    preservation process 122
    principles 119–22
    repository design overview 122–6
    resource requirements 115–16
    resource-constrained 122
    standards 121
archives, digitization in 72–6
archives, digital *see* digital archives
Archives Portal Europe, cultural heritage aggregator 166
Art Museum
    digitization 74–5
    University College London (UCL) 74–5

ArtBabble, cultural heritage aggregator 166
artefacts, digitization 63–84
ARTstor Digital Library, information search behaviour 187
Atiz Book Drive Pro, digital cameras 70
Australian National Library
    access to digitized content 48
    digitization policies and guidelines 43

Bentham, Jeremy, Transcribe Bentham project 66–7
Beowulf manuscript
    British Library (BL) 65
    digitization 65
BL *see* British Library
Blackwell Companion to Digital Humanities 18
Bleek and Lloyd collection, architectural design 127–8
Blue Ribbon Task Force (BRTF) Report (2010), digitization
        policies and guidelines 40–1
British Library (BL), *Beowulf* manuscript 65
British Library Digitization Strategy 38, 44
    access to digitized content 49
British Museum, Research Space 67
Browse, information access mode 157, 161–4
BRTF *see* Blue Ribbon Task Force Report (2010)

cameras, digital/SLR 69–70
case studies
    architectural design 126–30
    cultural heritage aggregators 167–74
    cultural heritage systems 126–30
    digital archives 107–9
    information search behaviour 187–92
    metadata 107–9
cloud-oriented layered model, digital archive 109
collaboration
    digital culture 146–7
    digital humanities characteristic 26
    digitization policies and guidelines 42
    digitization programmes 42
    managing resources for digitization 47–8
    users of cultural heritage information 146–7
collegiality and connectedness, digital humanities
        characteristic 26
CONA *see* Getty Cultural Objects Name Authority
Content interaction classes, cultural heritage aggregators
        168–9
Content interaction meta-class 159, 160
content service network (CSN), intellectual property (IP)
        rights 54
contents flow
    Functional Requirements for Bibliographic Records
        (FRBR) 92–4

metadata 92–7
controlled vocabularies
    cultural heritage digital libraries 181–3
    knowledge organization systems (KOS) 181–3
copyright
    Digital Copyright Exchange (DCE) 53–4
    digitization 66, 73
Copyright Hub
    access to digitized content 236
    cultural heritage information 46
    Hargreaves Review 52–5, 236
    intellectual property (IP) rights 46, 52–5
Council of the European Union, digitization policies and
    guidelines 42
crowdsourcing, users of cultural heritage information
    146–7
CSN *see* content service network
CT *see* Getty Conservation Thesaurus
cultural environment, digitization 76–8
cultural heritage
    categories 1–2
    content 1–3
    defining 180
    digitization priority of institutions 27–8
    diversity 180–1
    forms 1–2
    future directions 25–9
    humanities 21–5
    information resources 38–9
    tangible/intangible 1–2
    user-centred approach 21–5
cultural heritage aggregators 166–74
    Archives Portal Europe 166
    ArtBabble 166
    case studies 167–74
    Content interaction classes 168–9
    Curation interaction classes 169
    DPLA 166
    Europeana digital library 166–7, 170–4
    evaluating 166–74
    Gallica 166
    Google Art Project 166, 169
    HathiTrust 166
    Project Gutenberg 166
    Smithsonian Collections Search Center 166
    Support interaction classes 170
    World Digital Library 166
    Your Paintings 166, 167
cultural heritage digital libraries
    controlled vocabularies 181–3
    metadata standards 180–3
cultural heritage information
    access to digitized content 48–50
    Digital Copyright Hub 46
    goals 154
    guidelines 46–52
    indigenous 55–8
    intellectual property (IP) rights 50–5
    legal issues 50–5
    managing resources for digitization 47–8
    science vs humanities users 138–9
    users 135–48
cultural heritage information services
    economic sustainability 231–3

environmental sustainability 237–8
    social sustainability 234–6
cultural heritage institutions, digital humanities (DH) 27–9
Cultural Heritage Online and Digital Library, Meiji Era 103
cultural heritage systems
    see also digital library systems (DLSs)
    Bleek and Lloyd collection 126–30
    case studies 126–30
    core principles 117
    design 140–4
    design constraints and patterns 116–19
    digital obsolescence 117
    Europeana project 118
    federated architectures 117–18
    flexibility 121
    vs generic information systems 153–4
    integration 120–1
    interactions 153–75
    minimalist design 121
    motivation 119
    Open Archives Initiative Protocol for Metadata
        Harvesting (OAI-PMH) 118
    organization of information 122
    platform independence 117, 120
    portable architectures 118–19
    preservation 117
    preservation process 122
    principles 119–22
    Project Gutenberg 117
    repository design overview 122–6
    resource requirements 115–16
    resource-constrained 122
    routine maintenance 115
    scalability 116–17
    Spatial Archaeology Research Unit (SARU) 129–30
    standards 121
    technical expertise 115
    technological resources 116
    usability 140–4
    user-centred design 140–4
cultural works, defining 180
Culture24, impact of digitization 80
Curation interaction classes, cultural heritage aggregators
    169
Curation interaction meta-class 159, 160

Dao-Fa Hui-Yuan
    digital archive 107
    metadata 107
DCE *see* Digital Copyright Exchange
DCMI metadata registry 109–10
Department of Media, Culture and Sport
    digitization benefits 45
    digitization goals 45
design
    see also architectural design
    cultural heritage systems 140–4
    user-centred 140–4
DH *see* digital humanities
DIALOG databases, information search behaviour 185
Digital Agenda for Europe initiative, digitization policies and
    guidelines 42

Digital Agenda recommendation, European Commission
    49
digital archives 102–10
    Archives Portal Europe 166
    case studies 107–9
    cloud-oriented layered model 109
    for communities 103–4
    Dao-Fa Hui-Yuan 107
    Dublin Core Metadata Schema Registry 106–7
    Europeana digital library 103
    Great East Japan Earthquake 104–5
    Library of Congress 106
    Meiji Era, Cultural Heritage Online and Digital Library
        103
    Ministry of Internal Affairs and Communication
        (MIC) 104
    museums, libraries, and archives (MLAs) 102–3
    National Diet Library 106
    task-centric model 108–9
    Toppan Virtual Reality 103
    World Wide Web Consortium (W3C) 105–6
digital cameras, SLR cameras 69–70
Digital Copyright Exchange (DCE), intellectual property
        (IP) rights 53–4
Digital Copyright Hub
    access to digitized content 236
    cultural heritage information 46
    Hargreaves Review 52–5, 236
    intellectual property (IP) rights 46, 52–5
digital cultural heritage information
    access challenges 3–6
    content 1–3
    examples 3–4
    management challenges 3–6
digital culture, collaboration 146–7
digital divide, users of cultural heritage information 142–3
digital humanities (DH) 13–30
    alt[ernate-]histories 14–21
    Blackwell Companion to Digital Humanities 18
    collaboration 26
    collegiality and connectedness 26
    cultural heritage institutions 27–9
    defining 25–7
    Digital Humanities Start-Up Grants 15
    digitization priority 27–8
    diversity 26–7
    experimentation 27
    funding cuts 27
    future directions 25–9
    historical content 18–19
    history, alt[ernate-]histories 14–21
    interdisciplinary nature 13–14
    knowledge organization 24
    National Endowment for the Humanities (NEH) 15
    openness 26
    origin 13
Digital Humanities Start-Up Grants, National Endowment
        for the Humanities (NEH) 15
digital library systems (DLSs)
    see also cultural heritage systems
    architectural design 113–15
digital literacy, information literacy 81–2
digital obsolescence, cultural heritage systems 117

digital rights management (DRM), access to digitized
        content 236
digitization
    3D models 66, 70, 74
    advantages 68, 72–3
    Art Museum 74–5
    artefacts 63–84
    copyright 66, 73
    costs 77–8
    cultural environment 76–8
    defining 64
    European Commission 75–8
    expectation 78–81
    impact 78–81
    infrastructure 71
    institutional contexts 73–6
    Internet Library of Early Journals (ILEJ) 65
    Jisc, funding 65
    museums, libraries, and archives (MLAs) 72–6
    Optical Digital Image Storage System (ODISS) 64
    problems 73
    project management 71
    Research Space 67
    social media 66–7
    TIDSR (Toolkit for the Impact of Digitized Scholarly
        Resources) 79
    Transcribe Bentham project 66–7
    University College London (UCL) 74–6
    values 78–81
digitization benefits 45–6
    Comité des Sages 45–6
    Department of Media, Culture and Sport 45
    European Commission's Recommendations 45–6
digitization goals 45–6
    Comité des Sages 45–6
    Department of Media, Culture and Sport 45
    European Commission's Recommendations 45–6
digitization policies and guidelines 37–8, 39–46, 71–2
    Australian National Library 43
    Blue Ribbon Task Force (BRTF) Report (2010) 40–1
    British Library Digitization Strategy 38, 44, 49
    collaboration 42
    Council of the European Union 42
    Digital Agenda for Europe initiative 42
    European Commission's Recommendations 43–4
    Europeana digital library 43
    Federal Agencies Digitization Guidelines Initiative
        (FADGI) 38, 41
    Jisc Digital Media service 70, 72
    Jisc Digitization Workflow Guidelines 38
    Library of Congress guidelines 39
    *Library of Congress Technical Standards for Digital
        Conversion of Text and Graphic Materials* 72
    National Library of Australia 42–3
digitization priority, cultural heritage institutions 27–8
digitization process 67–72
digitization programmes 37–8
    collaboration 42
    European eContentplus programme 38
    Jisc Content Digitization programme 38
    public-private partnerships 41–2
digitization technologies 69–71
    OCR (optical character recognition) 69
    SLR cameras 69–70

disabilities usability, access to digitized content 235
diversity
    digital humanities characteristic 26–7
    users of cultural heritage information 137–8, 141–3
DLSs *see* digital library systems
documentation, digital resources 143–4
DPLA, cultural heritage aggregator 166
DRM *see* digital rights management
Dublin Core metadata format, Europeana project 118
Dublin Core Metadata Schema Registry, digital archives
    106–7
Dublin Core-based view, interoperable metadata 94–7

economic sustainability
    cultural heritage information services 231–3
    digital information systems/services 225–7
    Enumerate project 232
    Europeana digital library 233
    World Intellectual Property Organization (WIPO)
        231–2
eContentplus Programme, European Commission 75–6
E-Curator project
    3D models 66
    GLAM (Galleries, Libraries, Archives and Museums)
        sector 66
Engage, information access mode 158, 161–4
Enumerate project
    economic sustainability 232
    European Commission 76–8
environment, cultural *see* cultural environment
Environmental Protection Agency (EPA), sustainable
    development, defining 223
environmental sustainability
    cultural heritage information services 237–8
    digital information systems/services 229–31
EPA *see* Environmental Protection Agency
ethical issues, user-generated content 147
European citizens, users of cultural heritage information
    141–2
European Commission
    access to digitized content 49
    Digital Agenda recommendation 49
    digitization 75–8
    eContentplus Programme 75–6
    Enumerate project 76–8
    intellectual property (IP) rights 51–2
    *Survey Report on Digitization in European Cultural Heritage
        Institutions* 76–7
European Commission's Recommendations
    digitization benefits 45–6
    digitization goals 45–6
    digitization policies and guidelines 43–4
European eContentplus programme 38
The European Library *see* Europeana digital library
Europeana digital library
    cultural heritage aggregator 166–7, 170–4
    digitization policies and guidelines 43
    economic sustainability 233
    Europeana Case for Funding 233
    evaluating 170–4
    interactions 171–2
    museums, libraries, and archives (MLAs) 103

PATHS (Personalised Access To cultural Heritage
    Spaces) project 197, 201, 205–6
Europeana project
    cultural heritage system 118
    Dublin Core format 118
Europeana Travel, University College London (UCL) 75–6
expectation of digitization 78–81
experimentation, digital humanities characteristic 27

Federal Agencies Digitization Guidelines Initiative
    (FADGI) 38, 41
federated architectures, cultural heritage systems 117–18
Functional Requirements for Bibliographic Records
    (FRBR)
    contents flow 92–4
    Manga Metadata Framework (MMF) 99, 101
    metadata 91, 92–4, 97, 99, 101
funding cuts, digital humanities (DH) 27
future directions
    access to digitized content 213–14
    cultural heritage 25–9
    digital humanities (DH) 25–9
    PATHS (Personalised Access To cultural Heritage
        Spaces) project 213–14

Gallica, cultural heritage aggregator 166
generic information systems, vs cultural heritage systems
    153–4
Getty Art and Architecture Thesaurus (AAT), controlled
    vocabulary 181–2
Getty Conservation Thesaurus (CT), controlled vocabulary
    181–2
Getty Cultural Objects Name Authority (CONA),
    controlled vocabulary 181–2
Getty Museum, J. Paul, information search behaviour 187,
    190–1
Getty Research Institute, controlled vocabularies 183
Getty Thesaurus of Geographic Names (TGN), controlled
    vocabulary 181–2
Getty Union List of Artist Names (ULAN), controlled
    vocabulary 181–2
GLAM (Galleries, Libraries, Archives and Museums) sector
    3D models 66
    E-Curator project 66
Google, environmental sustainability 229–30
Google Art Project, cultural heritage aggregator 166, 169
Great East Japan Earthquake, digital archives 104–5
GTAA (Gemeenschappelijke Thesaurus Audiovisuele
    Archieven), controlled vocabulary 182–3

Hargreaves Review
    see also legal issues
    Digital Copyright Hub 52–5, 236
    intellectual property (IP) rights 52–5
HathiTrust, cultural heritage aggregator 166
HEREIN (the European information network on cultural
    heritage policies) 182
HIB *see* human information behaviour
High Level Thesaurus (HILT), controlled vocabulary 182
historical content, digital humanities (DH) 18–19
human information behaviour (HIB), sustainability 227–8
humanists
    research methods/materials 22–3

shelf-browsing/serendipitous interaction 22
technology use 23–4
working alone 22
humanities
cultural heritage 21–5
humanists' working methods 22–4
humanities vs science users, cultural heritage information 138–9

IconClass, controlled vocabulary 181–2
ILEJ *see* Internet Library of Early Journals
ILO *see* International Labour Organization
impact of digitization 78–81
Culture24 80
TIDSR (Toolkit for the Impact of Digitized Scholarly Resources) 79
indigenous cultural heritage information 55–8
World Intellectual Property Organization (WIPO) 56–7
information access modes 156–8, 161–4
Browse 157, 161–4
Engage 158, 161–4
evaluating interactions 163–5
Search 157, 161–4
information literacy
digital literacy 81–2
sustainability 228–9
information resources, cultural heritage 38–9
information search behaviour
access to digitized content 199–200
ARTstor Digital Library 187
case studies 187–92
DIALOG databases 185
evaluation framework 188–9
J. Paul Getty Museum 187, 190–1
knowledge organization systems (KOS) 184–7, 191–2
users of cultural heritage information 138–9, 184–7
Victoria and Albert Museum (V&A) 187, 191
information seeking and retrieval (IS&R), sustainability 227–8
infrastructure, digitization 71
institutional contexts, digitization 73–6
intellectual property (IP) rights
content service network (CSN) 54
cultural heritage information 50–5
Digital Copyright Exchange (DCE) 53–4
Digital Copyright Hub 46, 52–5
European Commission 51–2
Hargreaves Review 52–5
World Intellectual Property Organization (WIPO) 51
intellectual property rights (IPR), access to digitized content 236
interactions, cultural heritage systems 153–75
access modes, information 156–8
categorizing interactions 159–61
complexity of interactions 161–4
Content Interaction meta-class 159, 160
Curation Interaction meta-class 159, 160
defining 155–8
degree of interactions 161–4
information system model 156
Support interaction meta-class 160–1

International Labour Organization (ILO), indigenous cultural heritage information 57
internet access, national statistics 234–5
Internet Library of Early Journals (ILEJ), digitization 65
interoperable metadata 94–7, 107
IPR *see* intellectual property rights
IS&R *see* information seeking and retrieval

J. Paul Getty Museum, information search behaviour 187, 190–1
Jisc, digitization funding 65
Jisc Content Digitization programme 38
Jisc Digital Media service, digitization policies and guidelines 70, 72
Jisc Digitization Workflow Guidelines 38

KMM *see* Kyoto International Manga Museum
knowledge organization, digital humanities (DH) 24
knowledge organization systems (KOS) 177–8
application in cultural heritage digital libraries 179
context 178–9
controlled vocabularies 181–3
information search behaviour 184–7, 191–2
metadata standards 180–3
user interaction 184–7
Kyoto International Manga Museum (KMM), Manga Metadata Framework (MMF) 101

LCSH *see* Library of Congress Subject Headings
LCSH/TGM *see* Library of Congress Thesaurus for Graphic Materials
legal issues
see also Hargreaves Review
cultural heritage information 50–5
intellectual property (IP) rights 50–5
user-generated content 147
libraries, digitization in 72–6
Library of Congress
access to digitized content 48
American Memory collection 3
controlled vocabularies 183
digital archives 106
guidelines, digitization programmes 39
Library of Congress Technical Standards for Digital Conversion of Text and Graphic Materials 72
Library of Congress Authorities, controlled vocabulary 181–2
Library of Congress Subject Headings (LCSH), controlled vocabulary 181–2
Library of Congress Thesaurus for Graphic Materials (LCSH/TGM), controlled vocabulary 181–2
licensing, digitized content 73

managing resources for digitization 47–8
collaboration 47–8
public-private partnerships 47–8
Manga Metadata Framework (MMF)
Functional Requirements for Bibliographic Records (FRBR) 99, 101
Kyoto International Manga Museum (KMM) 101
metadata 98–102
usage scenarios 100
Meiji Era, Cultural Heritage Online and Digital Library 103

memory institutions *see* museums, libraries, and archives
(MLAs)
MetaBridge 109–10
metadata 89–111
    case studies 107–9
    contents flow 92–7
    cultural heritage digital libraries 180–3
    Dao-Fa Hui-Yuan 107
    DCMI metadata registry 109–10
    digital archives 102–10
    Dublin Core format 118
    Dublin Core Metadata Schema Registry 106–7
    Dublin Core-based view 94–7
    Functional Requirements for Bibliographic Records
        (FRBR) 91, 92–4, 97, 99, 101
    interoperable metadata 94–7, 107
    Manga Metadata Framework (MMF) 98–102
    meta-metadata 90–1, 105–7
    MetaBridge 109–10
    Open Archives Initiative Protocol for Metadata
        Harvesting (OAI-PMH) 118
    PREMIS (Preservation Metadata: Implementation
        Strategies) 91, 97
    publishing flow 92–7
    roles 89–91
    schema registry 105–7
    schema sharing 109–10
    schemas 92–7
    standards 91, 180–3
    task-centric model 108–9
    types 92
metadata standards 91
    cultural heritage digital libraries 180–3
    knowledge organization systems (KOS) 180–3
Ministry of Internal Affairs and Communication (MIC),
        digital archives 104
MLAs *see* museums, libraries, and archives
MMF *see* Manga Metadata Framework
mobile devices, trends 144–6
motivation
    architectural design 119
    cultural heritage systems 119
museums, libraries, and archives (MLAs)
    digital archives 102–3
    digitization in 72–6

NARA *see* National Archives and Records Administration
National Aboriginal and Torres Strait Islander arts policy,
        indigenous cultural heritage information 57
National Archives and Records Administration (NARA),
        Optical Digital Image Storage System (ODISS) 64
National Diet Library, digital archives 106
National Endowment for the Humanities (NEH), Digital
        Humanities Start-Up Grants 15
National Library of Australia, digitization policies and
        guidelines 42–3
NEH *see* National Endowment for the Humanities
Netherlands Institute for Sound and Vision, controlled
        vocabulary 182–3

OAI-PMH *see* Open Archives Initiative Protocol for
    Metadata Harvesting

OCR (optical character recognition), digitization
        technologies 69
ODISS *see* Optical Digital Image Storage System
Open Archives Initiative Protocol for Metadata Harvesting
        (OAI-PMH) 118
openness, digital humanities characteristic 26
Optical Digital Image Storage System (ODISS), National
        Archives and Records Administration (NARA) 64

PATHS (Personalised Access To cultural Heritage Spaces)
        project 197–215
    access to digitized content 198–200
    collaboration 214
    conceptual model 201–5
    content enrichment 206–7
    Europeana digital library 197, 201, 205–6
    vs existing models 201–5
    future directions 213–14
    key activities 202
    languages 205
    map-based visualization 208–11
    semantic enrichment 205–7
    user interaction 207–13
    user interface 201–5, 207–13
    user needs 201–5
    Wikipedia links 206–7
platform independence
    architectural design 117, 120
    cultural heritage systems 117, 120
policies, digitization *see* digitization policies and guidelines
PREMIS (Preservation Metadata: Implementation
        Strategies), metadata 91, 97
preservation process
    architectural design 122
    cultural heritage systems 122
Project Gutenberg
    core principles 117
    cultural heritage aggregator 166
project management, digitization 71
public-private partnerships
    digitization programmes 41–2
    managing resources for digitization 47–8
publishing flow, metadata 92–7

repository design overview
    architectural design 122–6
    cultural heritage systems 122–6
Research Space, British Museum 67
resource requirements
    architectural design 115–16
    cultural heritage systems 115–16
    RLG/OCLC Working Group on Digital Archive
        Attributes, 2002: 115, 120
resource-constrained architectural design/cultural heritage
        systems 122
resources for digitization, managing 47–8
RLG/OCLC Working Group on Digital Archive
        Attributes, 2002:, resource requirements 115, 120

SARU *see* Spatial Archaeology Research Unit
science vs humanities users, cultural heritage information
        138–9
Search, information access mode 157, 161–4

search behaviour *see* information search behaviour
search engine referrals, trends 144–6
Simple Knowledge Organization System (SKOS) 183
SLR cameras 69–70
Smithsonian Collections Search Center, cultural heritage
       aggregator 166
social media 146–7
       digitization 66–7
social sustainability
       see also access to digitized content
       cultural heritage information services 234–6
       digital information systems/services 227–9
       internet access, national statistics 234–5
Spatial Archaeology Research Unit (SARU), architectural
       design 129–30
standards
       architectural design 121
       cultural heritage systems 121
       digitization policies and guidelines 72
       *Library of Congress Technical Standards for Digital
       Conversion of Text and Graphic Materials* 72
       metadata 91, 180–3
Support interaction classes, cultural heritage aggregators
       170
Support interaction meta-class 160–1
*Survey Report on Digitization in European Cultural Heritage
       Institutions,* European Commission 76–7
sustainability 221–40
       digital information systems/services 224–31
       economic sustainability 225–7, 231–3
       Environmental Protection Agency (EPA) 223
       environmental sustainability 229–31
       human information behaviour (HIB) 227–8
       information literacy 228–9
       information seeking and retrieval (IS&R) 227–8
       integrated approach 223–4
       social sustainability 227–9
       sustainable development, defining 222–3
       United Nations 222
       World Intellectual Property Organization (WIPO)
       231–2
SVCN (Stichting Volkenkundige Collectie Nederland),
       controlled vocabulary 183

*Technical Guidelines for Digitizing Archival Materials for Electronic
       Access: creation of production master files – raster images,*
       US National Archives 72
technologies, digitization *see* digitization technologies
TGN *see* Getty Thesaurus of Geographic Names
TIDSR (Toolkit for the Impact of Digitized Scholarly
       Resources), digitization 79
Toppan Virtual Reality digital archive 103
Transcribe Bentham project, digitization 66–7
trends
       mobile devices 144–6
       search engine referrals 144–6
       users of cultural heritage information 144–6
TRIPS Agreement (the Agreement on Trade-Related
       Aspects of Intellectual Property Rights),
       indigenous cultural heritage information 57

UCL *see* University College London
ULAN *see* Getty Union List of Artist Names

UNESCO *see* United Nations Educational, Scientific and
       Cultural Organization
United Nations, sustainable development, defining 222
United Nations Educational, Scientific and Cultural
       Organization (UNESCO), indigenous cultural
       heritage information 57
University College London (UCL)
       3D models 74
       Art Museum 74–5
       digitization 74–6
       Europeana Travel 75–6
US National Archives, *Technical Guidelines for Digitizing
       Archival Materials for Electronic Access: creation of
       production master files – raster images* 72
usability, cultural heritage systems 140–4
usability studies 135–7
user-centred approach, cultural heritage 21–5
user-centred design, cultural heritage systems 140–4
user-generated content
       ethical issues 147
       legal issues 147
       users of cultural heritage information 146–7
user interaction, knowledge organization systems (KOS)
       184–7
users of cultural heritage information 135–48
       collaboration 146–7
       crowdsourcing 146–7
       digital divide 142–3
       diversity 137–8, 141–3
       documentation, digital resources 143–4
       European citizens 141–2
       information search behaviour 138–9, 184–7
       mobile devices 144–6
       science vs humanities 138–9
       search engine referrals 144–6
       trends 144–6
       user studies 135–7
       user-generated content 146–7

V&A *see* Victoria and Albert Museum
values, digitization 78–81
VIAF *see* Virtual International Authority File
Victoria and Albert Museum (V&A), information search
       behaviour 187, 191
Virtual International Authority File (VIAF), controlled
       vocabulary 181–2

W3C *see* World Wide Web Consortium
Wikipedia links, PATHS (Personalised Access To cultural
       Heritage Spaces) project 206–7
WIPO *see* World Intellectual Property Organization
World Digital Library, cultural heritage aggregator 166
World Intellectual Property Organization (WIPO)
       economic sustainability 231–2
       indigenous cultural heritage information 56–7
       intellectual property (IP) rights 51
World Wide Web Consortium (W3C), digital archives
       105–6

Your Paintings, cultural heritage aggregator 166, 167